D1759657

Regoverning Markets

Regoverning Markets

A Place for Small-Scale Producers in Modern Agrifood Chains?

Edited by

BILL VORLEY, ANDREW FEARNE and DEREK RAY

iied

International
Institute for
Environment and
Development

GOWER

Published by
Gower Publishing Limited
Gower House
Croft Road
Aldershot
Hampshire
GU11 3HR
England

Gower Publishing Company
Suite 420
101 Cherry Street
Burlington
VT 05401-4405
USA

Bill Vorley, Andrew Fearne and Derek Ray have asserted their moral right under the Copyright, Designs and Patents Act, 1988, to be identified as the editors of this work.

British Library Cataloguing in Publication Data
Regoverning markets: a place for small-scale producers in
   modern agrifood chains
   1. Produce trade – Case studies 2. Small business – Case
   studies 3. Produce trade 4. Small business
   I. Vorley, William II. Fearne, Andrew III. Ray, Derek
   381.4'1

   ISBN-13: 978-0-566-08730-1

Library of Congress Cataloging-in-Publication Data
Regoverning markets: a place for small-scale producers in modern agrifood chains / edited by Bill Vorley, Andrew Fearne and Derek Ray.
   p. cm.
   Includes bibliographical references and index.
   ISBN-13: 978-0-566-08730-1
   1. Grocery trade--Developing countries. 2. Supermarkets--Developing countries. 3. Agricultural industries--Developing countries. I. Vorley, William. II. Fearne, Andrew III. Ray, Derek.

   HF9329.D44R44 2007
   338.109172'4--dc22

                                                                              2006031458

Printed and bound in Great Britain by MPG Books Ltd, Bodmin, Cornwall.

Contents

List of Figures

List of Tables

Preface

Supermarkets and international food companies have become important economic, social and political agents in the twenty-first century. Their activities and consequences have been the subject of enquiry from government and regulatory agencies and lobby groups of various descriptions in recent years, resulting in the publication of numerous reports on their impact on a range of issues. These include economic growth, social cohesion, public health, the environment and fair trade to name but a few.

A key element in what is sometimes called the 'supermarket revolution' is 'supply chain management' (SCM). In the business literature, SCM is described principally from the downstream industry viewpoint. In other words, how a supermarket or food manufacturer finds, organizes and controls its suppliers. Very little space is given to SCM from a supplier's point of view, especially when those suppliers are small- or micro-scale, poorly capitalized, and have limited bargaining power, but are essential to a region's economy and employment.

The revolution that has swept through the agri-food system in industrialized countries, driven by modern retailing and SCM, is now moving into middle- and low-income countries with large rural populations. Changes that took 50 years in the USA or UK are happening in a decade.

In most low-income countries, small farms still predominate and much business activity is informal, in the hands of small- and medium-scale enterprises. Such farmers and businesses are facing domestic markets that increasingly make restrictive demands on suppliers and require new resources, improved internal organization and an enhanced managerial capacity.

Farmers, policy-makers and companies are struggling to keep up with or get ahead of the wave of new demands and, in the process, new questions arise. Can small farmers organize to meet the demands of corporate giants? Should governments liberalize Foreign Direct Investment (FDI) in the retail sector and expose numerous small shops to competition from multinationals? Can distribution systems be adapted to make markets work better for the poor?

The authors of this book are drawn from a score of countries. They analyze the access of small- and medium-sized farmers to supermarket and food company supply chains, based on case studies they have prepared within an international programme called 'Regoverning Markets'.

We hope that this book will provide food for thought for everyone interested in the global revolution in agri-food business, including students of business and of development, and commentators on 'corporate responsibility.' It is a contemporary look at what happens when modernization comes face to face with the livelihoods of rural and poor people.

Bill Vorley
IIED, London, April 2006

This book has been produced through a grant from the UK Department for International Development (DFID). DFID is the part of the UK Government that manages Britain's aid to poor countries and works to get rid of extreme poverty. DFID is committed to the Millenium Development Goals (MDGs) with the aim of halving world poverty by the year 2015. The MDGs include targets for a fairer trading and financial system.

About the Editors

Dr Bill Vorley has a background in ecology, and trained in the fields of southern England and SE Asia. After eight years working in agribusiness, he continued his research interest in the 'greening' of industry, spending three years at the Leopold Centre for Sustainable Agriculture in Iowa, after which he joined the Institute for Agriculture Trade and Policy in Minneapolis, Minnesota as director of the Environment and Agriculture Programme. He moved to London in 1999 to join the International Institute for Environment and Development, with a focus on policy and market research for sustainable agriculture and rural development. He has coordinated the Regoverning Markets programme since 2003. The findings of the Regoverning Markets Programme form the basis of this book.

Dr Andrew Fearne is Principal Research Fellow in Supply Chain Management at the Kent Business School (KBS), University of Kent. The son of a pig farmer in the south-east of England, Andrew graduated in French and Economics from Kingston University in 1983, after which he studied for his PhD at Newcastle University, where he subsequently spent six years as a lecturer in food marketing. In 1994, he moved to Imperial College London where he established the Centre for Food Chain Research. He joined KBS in February 2005. He has two specific research interests: supply chain management, and consumer behaviour, with particular expertise in the creation and management of value-added for sustainable competitive advantage in the food industry. He is the founding editor of the *International Journal of Supply Chain Management*, which addresses both practical and research issues concerned with the efficient and effective coordination of supply chains, from raw material supply to final consumption.

Derek Ray was a senior lecturer in agricultural economics in higher education before becoming a freelance writer and editor, specializing in distance learning for business. He has lived and worked in Edinburgh and Wye in the UK, and abroad in Malawi and the Sudan and on projects in countries such as Kenya, Uzbekistan, Russia and India.

Notes on Contributors

Parts 1 and 5

Estelle Biénabe is Senior Economist Researcher at CIRAD – French Agricultural Research Centre for International Development.

Dave Boselie is Manager of AgroFair Assistance & Development Foundation, based in the Netherlands.

Marie-Hélène Collion is Lead Agricultural Specialist in the World Bank's Middle East and North Africa Region.

Andrew Fearne is Director of the Centre for Supply Chain Research at the Kent Business School, University of Kent, UK.

Tom Fox works with the Growing Sustainable Business (GSB) initiative for UNDP and is based in Zambia. He was formerly with the International Institute for Environment and Development (IIED).

Derek Ray is a freelance writer and editor, formerly with Imperial College at Wye, UK.

Pierre Rondot is Senior Sector Economist in the World Bank's Middle East and North Africa Region.

Petra van de Kop is Senior Advisor Sustainable Economic Development at Royal Tropical Institute (KIT) in the Netherlands.

Bill Vorley is Head of the Sustainable Markets Group at the International Institute for Environment and Development IIED.

Parts 2–4

LATIN AMERICA
Julio A. Berdegué is President of Rimisp – Latin American Center for Rural Development. [Email: jberdegue@rimisp.cl]

Fernando Balsevich is a PhD student at Michigan State University, USA.

Luis Flores is an MSc student at Michigan State University, USA.

Pilar Jano is Research Associate at Rimisp – Latin American Center for Rural Development, Chile.

Thomas A. Reardon is Professor of Agricultural Economics at Michigan State University, USA.

Paul Schuetz is an Agricultural Economist at the International Livestock Research Institute (ILRI) in Nicaragua. [Email: aree@chiangmai.ac.th

ECUADOR

Miguel Zamora was an MSc student at Michigan State University, USA. He is currently working as Project Manager for TransFair US. [Email: miguel-zamora@sbcglobal.net]

THAILAND

Aree Wiboonponse is Associate Professor in the Department of Agricultural Economics at Chiang Mai University. [Email: aree@chiangmai.ac.th]

Songsak Sriboonchitta is Associate Dean in the Faculty of Economics at Chiang Mai University.

PHILIPPINES

Larry N. Digal is Dean in the School of Management, University of the Philippines in Mindanao. [Email: larryd927@yahoo.com]

Sylvia B. Concepcion is Professor in the School of Management, University of the Philippines in Mindanao.

SOUTH AFRICA

André Louw is Chair in Agribusiness Management in the Department of Agricultural Economics, Extension and Rural Development at the University of Pretoria. [Email: andre.louw@up.ac.za]

Hilton Madevu was a master's degree student in the Department of Agricultural Economics, Extension and Rural Development at the University of Pretoria.

Danie Jordaan is Research Fellow in the Department of Agricultural Economics, Extension and Rural Development at the University of Pretoria.

Hester Vermeulen is Research Fellow in the Department of Agricultural Economics, Extension and Rural Development at the University of Pretoria.

HUNGARY

Imre Fertő is Senior Research Fellow at the Institute of Economics, Hungarian Academy of Sciences, Budapest. [Email: ferto@econ.core.hu]

Csaba Forgács is Professor in the Department of Agricultural Economics and Rural Development at Corvinus University of Budapest. [Email: csaba.forgacs@uni-corvinus.hu]

Anikó Juhász is Senior Research Fellow at the Institute of Economics, Hungarian Academy of Sciences, Budapest.

Gyöngyi Kürthy is Senior Research Fellow at the Research and Information Institute for Agricultural Economics (AKII), Budapest.

POLAND

Jerzy Wilkin is Professor in the Department of Economics, Warsaw University. [Email: wilkin@wne.uw.edu.pl]

Malgorzata Juchniewicz is Professor in the Department of Economics, University of Warmia and Mazury in Olsztyn. [Email: malgorzata.juchniewicz@uwm.edu.pl]

Dominika Milczarek is Assistant Professor in the Department of Economics, Warsaw University. [Email: milczarek@wne.uw.edu.pl]

ROMANIA

Dinu Gavrilescu is Professor and Director of the Institute for Agricultural Economics, Romanian Academy, Bucharest.

Mariana Grodea is Senior Researcher, Institute of Agricultural Economics, Romanian Academy, Bucharest.

Camelia Serbanescu is Head of European Integration, International Agreements, Programs and Projects, Institute of Agricultural Economics, Romanian Academy, Bucharest. [Email: c.serbanescu@iea.org.ro]

Crina Turtoi is Director of the National Institute of Statistics in Bucharest.

CHINA

Xiang Bi is Senior Research Assistant at the Centre for Chinese Agricultural Policy, Chinese Academy of Sciences, in Beijing.

Xiaoxia Dong is PhD Candidate at the Centre for Chinese Agricultural Policy, Chinese Academy of Sciences, in Beijing.

Jikun Huang is Director and Professor, Centre for Chinese Agricultural Policy, Chinese Academy of Sciences, in Beijing. [Email: jkhuang.ccap@igsnrr.ac.cn]

Dinghuan Hu is Professor at the Institute of Agricultural Economics, Chinese Academy of Agriculture Sciences, Beijing.

Scott Rozelle is Professor and Chancellor's Fellow at the University of California, Davis.

VIETNAM
Phan Thi Giac Tam is Associate Dean in the Faculty of Economics, Nong Lam University in Vietnam. [Email: phantam@hcmuaf.edu.vn]

INDIA
K.K. Upadhyay is Programme Director at Development Alternatives in New Delhi. [Email: kkupadhyay@gmail.com]

Raghwesh Ranjan is Associate Programme Manager, Institutions Systems Branch at Development Alternatives in Jhansi, Uttar Pradesh, India.

PAKISTAN
Syed Qasim Ali Shah was at the Sustainable Development Policy Institute in Islamabad. He now works for ActionAid International. [Email: qasim.shah@actionaid.org]

Mosharraf Zaidi is Visiting Associate at the Sustainable Development Policy Institute in Islamabad.

Muhammad Ijaz Ahmed is Assistant Chief at the Agriculture Prices Commission in Islamabad.

Huma Nawaz Syal was Research Associate at the Sustainable Development Policy Institute in Islamabad.

BANGLADESH
Moinul I. Sharif is Fellow, Bangladesh Centre for Advanced Studies (BCAS), Dhaka. [Email: moinul.sharif@risoe.dk]

Khandaker Mainuddin is Fellow, BCAS, Dhaka. [Email: khandaker.mainuddin@bcas.net]

Mozaharul Alam is Research Fellow, BCAS, Dhaka.

Dwijendra lal Mallick is Research Fellow, BCAS, Dhaka.

KENYA
James K. Nyoro is Director of the Tegemeo Institute of Egerton University in Nairobi. [Email: jnyoro@tegemeo.org]

Joshua Ariga is Research Fellow of the Tegemeo Institute of Egerton University in Nairobi.

Isaac K. Ngugi is Research Fellow of the Tegemeo Institute of Egerton University in Nairobi.

ZAMBIA
Rosemary A. Emongor is a PhD Candidate at the Department of Agricultural Economics, Extension and Rural Development, University of Pretoria, South Africa. [Email: remongor@yahoo.co.uk]

Johann F. Kirsten is Professor at the Department of Agricultural Economics, Extension and Rural Development, University of Pretoria, South Africa.

UGANDA

Lucy Aliguma is Research Fellow, Uganda Agricultural Economics Association, Department of Agricultural Economics and Agribusiness, Makerere University, Kampala. [Email: lucyaliguma55@hotmail.com]

James K. Nyoro is Director of the Tegemeo Institute of Egerton University in Nairobi.

Acknowledgements

The editors would like to express their sincere thanks to the international team of experts who are behind this work: (a) the authors of the country studies; (b) the coordinators of the programme, especially Julio Berdegué and Petra Van de Kop; (c) the regional coordinators Jikun Huang, Nerlie Manalili, Csaba Csáki, James Nyoro, André Louw and Julio Berdegué; (d) the participants who took part in the e-conference; and (d) the Phase 1 programme advisors – Dave Boselie, Pierre Rondot, Estelle Biénabe and Tom Reardon.

Other people have also helped along the way. John Thompson was indispensable in getting the programme off the ground. Tom Fox prepared an important summary of Phase 1 results. Frances Reynolds gave valuable support.

We thank Jonathan Norman of Gower Publishing for his interest and patience. And last but by no means least, the UK Department for International Development (DFID) for financial support of the research and preparation of this manuscript, especially Lucy Ambridge who has been a stalwart supporter of this work.

The research projects behind the 'Latin America' chapter had the support of the US Agency for International Development via the RAISE/SPS Project of Development Alternatives, Inc. with Michigan State University, as well as DFID.

Bill Vorley
IIED, London, May 2006

1 *The Economic and Policy Context*

In this part, we describe the restructuring of food markets around the world and the research methodology used for the analysis of this restructuring in the specific countries involved in the Regoverning Markets project.

1 The Internationalization of Food Retailing: Opportunities and Threats for Small-scale Producers

Estelle Biénabe, Dave Boselie, Marie-Hélène Collion, Tom Fox, Pierre Rondot, Petra van de Kop and Bill Vorley

Agri-food systems in developing and transitional countries are experiencing unprecedented restructuring, partly as a result of the process of development and/or transition in which they are vigorously engaged and partly in response to the rising importance of supermarkets in the food retail sector.

For example, in Latin America, supermarkets buy 2.5 times more produce from local farmers than the region exports to the rest of the world (Reardon and Berdegué, 2002). In parts of Asia, supermarkets account for more than half of retail food sales (Hu et al., 2004; Zhang, 2001). In Central and Eastern Europe (Dries et al., 2004) there has been considerable investment (primarily foreign) in supermarkets in the wake of market liberalization and in anticipation of European Union (EU) enlargement. The supermarket format is even showing signs of growth in Africa (Neven and Reardon 2004; Weatherspoon and Reardon 2003), serving the rural poor as well as the urban rich.

The internationalization of food retailing is causing significant institutional changes that affect small producer agriculture and the livelihoods of rural communities the world over. Increasingly, domestic markets in liberalized economies have more in common with export markets, with product chains that have become buyer driven (Gereffi, 1994). In these chains, down-stream segments are determining the conditions such as scale and volume of procurement, higher quality and safety standards, packing and packaging requirements, and consistency of supply.

Buyer-driven chains are more regulated, and characterized by high levels of governance[1] and long-term vertical coordination between producers, supplier-integrators, processors and retailers. As a result, farmers require technology, financial capital, human capital and organization to avoid being excluded from this rapidly growing sector and take advantage of the opportunities for growth that clearly exist.

The high capital requirements for entering buyer-driven chains mean that the higher land and labour efficiency of small producer production may no longer be a comparative advantage. Nevertheless, there is growing evidence that small producers can participate in supply chains to supermarkets in a manner that enhances their livelihoods (Boselie et al., 2003). Yet the evidence to date suggests that small producer beneficiaries are the exception to a rule that

---

[1]   The basic 'rules of the game' that determine behavioural conduct and action – who sets the rules, when and how.

threatens to stifle the broader efforts of government and the private sector to speed up the development process in some of the world's poorest nations. Bearing in mind that 60–75 per cent of the world's poor live in rural areas (IFAD, 2001), depending directly or indirectly on agriculture for their livelihoods, it is clear that every effort should be made to ensure that the internationalization of retailing works for the benefit of the rural poor, who are in danger of being excluded, as well as for the urban consumers, who are in danger of becoming the sole beneficiaries of the rise of supermarkets.

The Regoverning Markets programme is part of this effort – to improve our understanding of the way supermarket expansion into developing and transitional economies is affecting the existing food production and distribution systems, to identify best practice in involving small-scale producers in supermarket supply chains, and to highlight the barriers to inclusion that need to be removed.

This chapter sets the global scene for the individual country case studies that make up the major part of the book. In it we attempt to explain the process of restructuring that is taking place in food systems as a result of global supermarket expansion and the implications, real and potential, for small-scale producers and rural poverty.

We begin by describing the globalization of food retailing, then focus on the implications for small-scale producers and the need for adaptation.

The internationalization of food retailing

Retailing has, in fact, been relatively slow to internationalize[2] in comparison with manufacturing and food processing. Wal-Mart only started expansion outside the USA in 1991, Carrefour from France in 1989, and Tesco from the UK in 1997. The biggest selling retailers are not always the most internationalized.

Market concentration outside Europe and North America is still quite low, with the top 30 retailers having a combined market share of modern grocery distribution in Asia and Oceania of just 19 per cent, and 29 per cent in Latin America, compared with 69 per cent in Europe. However, in the 1990s, there was a very rapid growth in supermarket internationalization, and by 2003, the top 30 food retailers had expanded into 85 different countries, up from 15 countries a decade earlier. From a global 'modern' food market valued at US$3.9 trillion, the top 30 global supermarket chains have captured around US$1.3 trillion.

The world's top supermarket chains are listed in Tables 1.1 and 1.2. With only around 5000 outlets, one company – Wal-Mart – has grown to become the world's largest retailer and largest grocer, with over US$ 280 billion in sales, 43 per cent of which is food.

Huge income disparities in many emerging economies, such as Brazil and China, mean that there may be no 'mass market'. Much of the country's spending power resides with a small percentage of the population. Markets are diverging into a dual economy, with most growth at both extremes of the pricing spectrum – the mass market and the premium market. Supermarkets have caught on to the benefits of rapid segmentation into different formats to deal with both ends of dualistic markets. For example, Carrefour has a 'three-banners-in-all-markets' strategy; its Dia discount store format and Champion supermarket chain were both launched in China to supplement its hypermarket presence.

2   Here, internationalization is defined as not just the establishment of branches overseas, but also the international expansion of procurement and the transfer of management expertise.

Table 1.1   The top 10 supermarkets, ranked by food sales (2005)

Company	Grocery Retail Banner Sales (US$ million)	Total Retail Banner Sales (US$ million)	Grocery percentage (%)
Wal-Mart	152 134	338 759	45
Carrefour	87 055	117 445	74
Ahold	67 953	80 165	85
Tesco	53 529	72 580	74
Seven & I	44 970	62 757	72
Rewe	43 704	57 359	76
Kroger	43 132	61 303	70
Edeka	42 658	49 948	85
Metro Group	40 854	86 008	47
Schwarz Group	40 843	49 517	82

Source: PlanetRetail (www.planetretail.net)

Table 1.2   Global presence of the top 10 global grocery retailers (2004)

Company	No. of stores	Countries of operation (end 2004)
Wal-Mart	5164	Argentina, Brazil, Canada, China, Germany, Japan, Mexico, Singapore, South Korea, UK, USA, Vietnam
Carrefour	10 704	Argentina, Belgium, Brazil, Chile, China, Colombia, Czech Republic, Dominican Republic, Egypt, France, Greece, Indonesia, Italy, Japan, Malaysia, Mexico, Oman, Poland, Portugal, Qatar, Romania, Singapore, Slovakia, South Korea, Spain, Switzerland, Taiwan, Thailand, Tunisia, Turkey, USA
Ahold	6841	Brazil, Costa Rica, Czech Republic, El Salvador, Estonia, Guatemala, Honduras, Latvia, Lithuania, Netherlands, Nicaragua, Norway, Poland, Portugal, Slovakia, Sweden, USA
Tesco	2294	Czech Republic, Hungary, Ireland, Malaysia, Poland, Slovakia, South Korea, Taiwan, Thailand, UK, USA
Kroger	3667	USA
Rewe	12 077	Austria, Bulgaria, Croatia, Czech Republic, France, Germany, Hungary, Italy, Poland, Romania, Slovakia, Spain
Aldi	6609	Australia, Austria, Belgium, Denmark, France, Germany, Ireland, Luxembourg, Netherlands, Spain, United Kingdom, USA
Ito-Yokado	14 448	Australia, China, Japan, Malaysia, Philippines, Singapore, South Korea, Taiwan, Thailand, Turkey
Metro Group	2370	Austria, Belgium, Bulgaria, China, Croatia, Czech Republic, Denmark, France, Germany, Greece, Hungary, India, Italy, Japan, Luxembourg, Morocco, Netherlands, Poland, Portugal, Romania, Russia, Slovakia, Spain, Switzerland, Turkey, UK, Ukraine, Vietnam
ITM (Intermarché)	10 753	Belgium, Bosnia and Herzegovina, France, Italy, Macedonia, Poland, Romania, Serbia and Montenegro, Spain

Source: PlanetRetail

There has also been a rapid penetration into the convenience sector with formats for central urban locations and smaller towns, driven in part by limited prime space and tough zoning regulations. For instance in Thailand, Tesco Lotus introduced a Value Store format aimed at serving smaller towns and Tesco Lotus Express mini-markets for service stations. These convenience stores are faster and easier to build and manage (Deloitte, 2004). As a result, existing franchised convenience chains such as 7-Eleven have had to shift their focus to ready-to-eat food products and develop new locations, such as service stations.

The success or failure of global expansion is built on sustaining an expansion, rather than entering new markets. This, in turn, is a reflection of the ability of a company to adapt its operations as a learning organization. AT Kearney (2003) divides strategies of the different global retailers into the 'early movers' such as Metro, an 'escalator' approach in which retailers alternate between periods of rapid growth and consolidation, typified by Wal-Mart, and a 'wait and see' approach as typified by Casino. Another way of categorizing a retailer's internationalization strategy is the level of centralized control. Others distinguish two different tactics: the 'intelligent federal', such as Ahold, which standardizes its back office operations but adapts its marketing to local conditions, versus the 'centralized' format as typified by Wal-Mart (Wrigley and Lowe, 2002). Metro's ability to grow even in the most difficult markets has been attributed to a combination of standardized store formats and ability to adapt to the local environment.

In the early 1990s, there were strong pulls for rapid retail globalization from markets in South-east Asia and Eastern Europe, in the form of rising levels of affluence, low levels of competition, low labour and land costs, and a favourable legislative climate (Wrigley and Lowe, 2002). Financial crises in Asia and South America made local companies cheap to acquire. Increased capitalization and buying power of the global chains was another factor, combined with shareholders and financial markets pushing for international expansion (GPN, 2003). All this gave rise to huge incentives for global retailers to leverage scale, distribution logistics and information technology (IT) systems for high returns on investment.

Global expansion of their operations also provided supermarket chains with an opportunity to 'leapfrog' from their domestic market niche as grocers into a preferred format of grocery plus general merchandise, allowing them to capture consumer spending from other sectors, such as department stores and financial services. At the same time, there was a strong 'push' in the form of market saturation and fierce price wars in home markets, combined with strict planning regulations and other policy restraints.

The rapid growth of supermarkets has not been without its problems. There have been many failures and something of a return to regionalization of retailing in recent years: Ahold has pulled back from Asia and Latin America; the Belgian global player Delhaize has disposed of its Thailand and Singapore assets; Sainsbury's sold its US business in 2004 following its withdrawal from Egypt in 2002, and Auchan exited the USA and Mexico in 2003, following exits from Thailand in 2001, to focus on Central and Eastern Europe (CEE), China and Taiwan. In most cases, the failures are the result of a lack of understanding of local markets – the local consumer, the local competition, and the local market conditions (Deloitte, 2004).

Often overlooked in the discussion about retail globalization is the growth of large and profitable national and regional players, who are themselves planning international expansion. Global retailers underestimate local players at their peril. Often learning from global players, for instance by expanding their fresh fruit and vegetable offers, local chains may well have better knowledge of domestic retail markets and intermediaries, which may be fiercely competitive. Local and regional players such as the Ramayana and Matahari chains in Indonesia and

Shoprite in southern Africa may also have more skills in working in risky environments with low-income consumer segments. Local players are likely also to be closer to local government and the possibility of preferential credit terms, cheaper rents and protective legislation.

A classic example of rationalization is the Central Retail Corporation (CRC), part of the Central Group, a family-controlled Thai conglomerate with an annual turnover of around US$ 700 million. CRC acquired TOPS and FoodLion stores from the departing Ahold and Delhaize multinationals in 2004. CRC now has 87 grocery outlets (2005) and has predicted annual sales from all its operations of US$1.8 billion. Moreover, its focus on supply chain improvements, which threatened to exclude many/most of the small-scale producers, resulted in institutional and organizational restructuring that directly benefited small-scale producers and enabled them to retain a stake in the rapidly growing retail sector in Thailand (see Box 1.1).

Box 1.1   Restructuring Fresh Produce Supply Chains – Serving the Urban Rich but Including Small-scale Producers

In recent years, a number of international retailers have established supermarkets especially to serve Thailand's urban conglomerates. In 1996, Royal Ahold established a joint venture with the Thai Central Retail Corporation and started to operate more than 30 TOPS supermarkets (most of which are located in Bangkok and Chiangmai). From the start, TOPS proliferated itself as the supermarket chain for quality fresh food.

In 1998, TOPS began a supply chain project aimed at providing Thai consumers with high-quality, safe, fresh produce with reliable availability at affordable prices. To achieve that goal, however, the supply chain faced a number of problems. For example, roughly 250 suppliers were delivering perishables directly to the back doors of 35 stores at least three times a week. This meant high handling costs, significant post-harvest and shrinkage losses and low service levels (meaning that produce was often out of stock).

TOPS enlisted public-sector assistance and embarked on a supply chain improvement project with four objectives: raising the level of service within the perishables supply chain; reducing lead times and post-harvest losses and shrinkage; improving quality and safety of produce by developing preferred supplier relationships and introducing good agricultural practices and a certification scheme; and raising the knowledge and awareness of employees and professionals in the local food industry through on-the-job training (for example, in Hazard Analysis Critical Control Point (HACCP)) and a mini-MBA program.

A number of noteworthy results were achieved:

- establishment of a fresh distribution centre in Bangkok
- reduction of the number of suppliers from 250 to 60, with 40 out of the 60 certified by the Department of Agriculture (DoA)
- provision of training to quality control managers at the TOPS distribution centre and in the stores, with the service level increasing to 98 per cent
- development of a 'road map' (or in other words, a practical blueprint) to achieve trusted third-party certification for food safety assurance in emerging fresh markets
- reduction of the time from farm-to-fork from 68 hours to less than 24 hours
- reduction of post-harvest and shrinkage losses
- standardization of crates, pallets and crate washing facilities.

In Indonesia, there are successful national chains that have honed a successful business model within a low-income consumer base. Ramayana operates 93 outlets (2003) – some supermarkets but mostly department stores that include supermarkets. The company's senior adviser for business development was quoted as saying: 'We sell to people earning $40 a month. Because of the [financial crisis] this space has become incredibly large. We have the best customers because they are poor. What they have, they have to spend' (Jacob, 2002).

In Latin America, the Chile-based chain Cencosud is now one of the biggest supermarket chains in South America. In 2004 alone, Cencosud acquired three of Chile's largest supermarket chains and, including the newly acquired Disco unit in Argentina, Cencosud has projected revenue of $4.7 billion in 2005.

Small producers were involved in the TOPS supplier network in two ways: first, via the network of contract farmers and buyers who became preferred suppliers because of their ability to exert backwards control on the supply chain and, second, via a new phenomenon of informal farmers' associations. In these associations, professional growers within a family or village joined forces and exchanged experiences and farming knowledge. These groups met all the pre-conditions for developing into full-fledged growers' associations and engaging in long-term direct business relationships with retailers. Although one of the goals of the preferred supplier program was to reduce the total number of suppliers, it did not specifically target small producers. On the contrary, those small producers who could deliver adequate volumes of consistent quality via contract farming schemes or new associations were included in the sourcing portfolio of the supermarket. Those producers/suppliers who could not meet minimum quality standards or develop value added activities were excluded, regardless of size.

In the Baltic region, the firm VP Market, based in Lithuania, has expanded very rapidly into Estonia, Latvia and Romania, and is looking for further growth in Bulgaria and Ukraine, as well as aiming to open 40 new stores a year. In Central Asia, Turkish retailer Migros Türk has 'first mover advantage' with stores in Azerbaijan, Bulgaria, Kazakhstan and Russia as well as its home market in Turkey, and is targeting other countries such as Ukraine, Macedonia, Serbia, Romania, and Iran. Sales in 2005 exceeded US$ 2.8 billion.

In India, a market that is still very fragmented, regional supermarket chains such as the Kerala-based Margin Free Market (MFM) cooperative, Hyderabad-based Trinethra and Tamil Nadu-based Subhiksha, have grown fast. By global standards, these are small players. The biggest player, MFM, has only 0.7 per cent of the national grocery market, but is using franchising to add 12 stores per month. Subhiksha's annual turnover of $48 million is equivalent to just half of one Carrefour hypermarket in France. But some have national ambitions and are aggressively expanding – Subhiksha aims to have 400 outlets and sales of $330 million over the next two years through organic growth and acquisition, moving into Bangalore, Mysore, Mumbai, Gujarat and Delhi.

Franchising is also part of the growth strategies of Shoprite and Pick 'n' Pay, the leading South African chains. Shoprite has developed a discount format – the Usave banner – for introduction into South Africa's poorer townships and residential areas and other countries in Africa. Since 2003, around 20 Usave stores have been opened in Namibia, Malawi, Angola, Tanzania and Ghana. Its franchised convenience 'OK' formats are expected to be the main growth format in the coming years on the domestic market.

Impact on 'traditional' markets and institutions

Small-scale retail, including small supermarkets, can be highly resilient in the face of hypermarket competition. In some countries that are considered quite mature in terms of modern supermarket growth, such as Mexico, traditional stores may retain a remarkably strong presence. They offer convenience, proximity and sometimes the availability of short-term credit. Informal (grey) markets may be an important part of the food economy – comprising 40 per cent of Russian retail – and also offer a refuge for small farmers who are insufficiently capitalized to deal with the demands of modern retail procurement. Market research (Booz-Allen Hamilton, 2003) confirms that for fresh produce, wetmarkets are still favoured by emerging consumers because of their high quality and variety of fresh fruits and vegetables (FFV) and meats at low prices, and the ability to buy the quantity desired. Problems of cheating on weight or quality, 'Can be mitigated through personal relationships' according to some. In these markets, large supermarkets are not considered as excelling in quality for fresh produce.

Innovation at the supermarket level can drive innovation in the independent retail level, for instance through the formation of purchasing groups to aggregate buyer power (with consequent impact on suppliers and primary producers). Locally owned stores have upgraded their premises with air conditioning, better lighting and display. And some 'traditional' retailers may be purchasing from global cash-and-carry outlets, or even supermarkets. It has been reported that Shoprite in Mozambique, for instance, makes a considerable amount of business by supplying small retailers in Maputo.

With the growth of supermarkets comes the establishment of centralized buying and distribution centres. The reasons are: (1) to reduce coordination costs; (2) to generate economies of scale by buying in larger volumes; (3) to work with fewer wholesalers and suppliers per unit merchandized; and (4) to have tighter control over product consistency in meeting standards (Dries et al., 2004). As a result, there have been significant shifts away from traditional brokers and towards new, specialized/dedicated wholesalers. These are generally more in tune with the quality, safety and consistency required by supermarkets than are traditional wholesalers. In the traditional system, a wholesaler aggregates products from many producers and there is little segregation according to quality.

Wholesalers are changing and some now redefine themselves. For instance, private sector investments such as the Thai Agro Exchange (Talaadthai) in Bangkok, create integrated centres for agricultural goods that meet high product standards. Also in Thailand, wholesalers try 'to mobilize the buying power of tens of thousands of wholesalers and small grocery stores nationwide in a bid to combat the growing dominance of modern discount stores and hypermarkets' (Siam Future Development, n.d.). The major oil companies have also had to evolve to meet the threat of supermarkets moving aggressively in gasoline sales, either by operating on lower gasoline retail margins or by providing other means of generating profits, such as on-site convenience stores.

While restructuring is invariably 'painful', as it usually involves institutional change and a reduction in the number of businesses able or required to serve a particular market channel, it also provides opportunities for improvement and growth for those most willing and able to embrace the challenges. This is exactly what happened in the Netherlands, over a decade ago. The country used to be famous for its auction system, similar to those found today in developing and transitional countries. However, people in the trade recognized the need to change and the auctions closed down. (Box 1.2).

Box 1.2   Adapting to the Business Environment: The Changing Face of Auction Markets

For more than 100 years, the auction was the dominant instrument for selling Dutch fresh produce such as fruits, vegetables and mushrooms (Bijman, 2002). The auction was an efficient way of selling perishable products supplied by a large number of growers and purchased by a large number of wholesalers, retailers and exporters. While it is still the main instrument for selling ornamentals, most Dutch fresh produce today is sold by way of contract mediation between retail and farmer associations.

During the early 1990s, growers with the potential to innovate and develop speciality products had an incentive to leave the auction cooperative and contract with wholesalers and retailers. The traditional auction system was failing to serve the interests of buyers and sellers, primarily because it was designed for the efficient allocation of large volumes of generic produce, from many sellers to many buyers. However, with retail concentration throughout Europe, the number of buyers shrank considerably and an increasing number of those who remained were seeking points of difference over their competitors, not high volumes of generic produce of variable quality. More importantly, retailers wanted to avoid relying on auctions because this confronted them with uncertain quality and unknown provenance.

Most fresh produce auctions in the Netherlands went through restructuring processes in the 1990s. The Greenery is by far the largest marketing cooperative for fresh produce, with an annual turnover of more than 1.5 billion euros. It sells about half of all vegetables produced in the Netherlands. It was established in 1996, with the merger of nine auction cooperatives. Since this merger, major changes have taken place in the functional and organizational characteristics of the company. First, only about one third of all members' products are now sold through the auction clock; the rest is sold through contract mediation. Second, the Greenery has become a major wholesale company, integrating its sales activities with the purchasing activities of two wholesale subsidiaries. Third, it has developed a customer-oriented strategy, seeking to become the preferred supplier of several large food retailers in Europe. Fourth, it has implemented an organizational division between the cooperative society on the one hand and the cooperative firm on the other, leaving growers with only indirect influence over the activities of the firm.

Although Dutch commercial growers have much bigger businesses than small producers in emerging economies, the same principals apply: the majority of them are too small to supply supermarkets or wholesalers individually, so some kind of clustering or collective organization is required in order to access these channels. In the case of the Netherlands, producers who left the cooperative system have established new producer organizations, some of which have also facilitated knowledge exchange among members, set up quality systems and developed marketing activities. Growers in developing countries also face demands that individually they cannot meet, but which they can accommodate collectively.

Organization is therefore a key component in the involvement of small-scale producers in supermarket supply chains and this role is generally taken on by producer associations, which standardize and aggregate production, ensure compliance with the requisite quality standards and deliver products on time and at a competitive price that enables producers to make a profit. Moreover, through their associations, small-scale producers can build trustworthy relationships with other supply chain stakeholders, secure credibility and realize mutually beneficial actions and investments (Stockbridge, 2003).

This kind of collective action is rarely spontaneous. In most cases, it is prompted by outside support to help small producers develop a strategy to challenge a specific market. Capacity building programmes in support of small-scale producers' collective action can help them to: (1) organize themselves to improve product quality, reduce production costs and participate in supply chain management; and (2) build a market intelligence capacity and design marketing strategies including strategic alliances with market entrepreneurs and/or consumer groups.

Small-scale producers: in and out of supermarket supply chains

For all the talk of 'global sourcing', global food retailing mostly relies on local merchandise and local purchasing, particularly for fresh food (fruit, vegetables, meat and dairy products). The performance of retailers depends primarily on the efficiency of national supply chains, and subsidiaries of global retailers usually purchase over 80 per cent of their merchandise from local suppliers (Deloitte, 2004).

On the positive side, supermarkets generally offer stable prices and a 'guarantee' to buy large quantities provided producers meet their quality standards. Thus, supermarkets can contribute to securing and stabilizing farmers' incomes. For example, in Nicaragua, the San Francisco de Axis Cooperative, which was selling fresh milk to agro-industrial firms and experiencing significant variability in prices and revenue from one season to the next, decided to diversify its products and sell cheese to supermarkets to stabilize its members' income (Mendoza Vidaurre 2003).

In addition, farmers sometimes receive targeted technical support from buyers, as part of a preferred supplier scheme, or from Government or non-governmental organizations (NGOs), to meet supermarket requirements. Under a preferred supplier scheme, the wholesaler may also provide various incentives to meet retailers' requirements such as implicit contracts, lower risk, a price premium and similar inducements. Selling to supermarkets may also give farmers access to credit, because it provides them with a contract and guaranteed payment, which serves to reduce the risk of default on loan payments.

For practical purposes, supermarkets deal with small producers only through intermediaries (wholesalers or producer organizations) that perform the following functions on their behalf:

- identify and characterize the supply
- communicate quality and quantity requirements to farmers
- provide technical support to producers to help them meet supermarket demand and ensure quality, quantity and adequate timing of supply
- assemble agricultural products

Without such an intermediary, it would be much more convenient and efficient for supermarkets to deal with large-scale producers, who have the capacity to deliver large volumes on a regular and timely basis and can more easily ensure food safety and quality standards. For example, in South Africa, specialized wholesalers deal primarily with fruit exporters to European supermarkets, who have thus demonstrated their ability to meet food safety standards for all products (Weatherspoon and Reardon, 2003).

Similarly, in some Eastern European countries, in the absence of large-scale producers, some supermarkets prefer to purchase their products from international markets instead of buying from small-scale local producers (Weatherspoon and Reardon, 2003). In Vietnam, supermarkets procure their pork solely from large-scale production enterprises and modern slaughterhouses, which have a greater ability to control quality than the traditional chains supplied by family agriculture and small-scale slaughterhouses (Moustier et al., 2003).

While the retailer sets the 'rules of the game' for participating in the chains, a key supplier may take responsibility for developing a product category's profile to give maximum returns, such as by devising new packaging strategies, or taking more responsibility for unsold produce. Within this concentrated chain structure, in which most power and leverage resides at the retail end of supply chains, benefits are passed to customers and shareholders. 'Insiders' in these chains may be able to prosper through investing in relationship marketing, product quality and brand reputation. But these 'insiders' may find themselves highly leveraged by their dependence on one buyer and the threat that a supermarket contract may be moved at any time. From a macro perspective, there is declining residual value to be shared between supermarkets and upstream actors in the chain.

The move to direct supplier relations is far from universal and other trends, such as supermarkets' use of highly competitive on-line auctions for procurement of own-label food and non-food products, have nothing to do with 'alliance capitalism.' For example, in Brazil, only Carrefour and the Brazilian retailer CBD have direct supplier relationships, and the wholesale market in São Paulo is still very strong. This is not surprising, as the process of supply chain rationalization and integration is slow and meets with varying degrees of resistance.

Traditionally, small producers in developing countries have operated outside the formal sector, selling largely their surplus produce to local spot markets. However the recent growing concentration in domestic agri-food systems and the reversal of food chains from being supply driven to demand driven, have led to significant institutional and organizational changes that are affecting small-scale producers.

Rise of standards

With the relatively recent rise of food exports from developing countries, the safety and phytosanitary standards applied by developed countries to exports from developing countries have increased considerably. In response to the demands of consumers, European retailers and their global suppliers have created and implemented a series of private standards such as EUREPGAP. This is a set of normative documents or a protocol, which farmers around the world can use to demonstrate due diligence and compliance with Good Agricultural Practices (www.eurep.org). In addition, there has been a consumer-driven demand for high quality FFV translated into supermarket quality standards.

Recently, there has been attention to the rise of standards in domestic markets in developing countries (Berdegué et al., 2005). According to these authors, the speed with which supermarkets develop these quality and safety standards depends on:

* demand-side factors (such as public education concerning health aspects of FFV consumption or enactment and enforcement of public health regulations with respect to produce)

- market factors (such as availability of laboratories and affordable service fees to test products for contamination; easier cross-border movement for produce to increase regionalization of products and further convergence of standards; and expansion and deepening of public-private initiatives)
- supply-side factors (such as investments in training and infrastructure at the farms, packing sheds and distribution centres as well as affordable private laboratories to audit farms; public extension services that deliver adequate services to upgrade production and post-harvest practices to meet supermarket's needs; and availability of year-round production)

These factors, particularly the supply-side constraints mentioned above can lead to the exclusion of small producers (Berdegué et al., 2005). Small and medium farmers' assets are far too meagre to meet the volume, consistency and year-round availability needs of supermarkets, and to deal with long payment terms.

To meet the new economies of scale, increased quality and safety standards, and to deal with the transaction costs, supermarket chains have in general shifted from a store-by-store procurement system, relying mainly on traditional wholesale markets and brokers, to centralized distribution centres and use of specialized, dedicated wholesalers (sometimes part of the chain itself), and increasingly the use of preferred supplier systems (Berdegué et al., 2005).

Coordination and cooperation

In order to deal with quality and safety parameters, as well as with quantity parameters and price premiums in restructured agri-food systems, there has been a rise of contractual exchange in the place of spot markets. Contracts exist with a range of modalities: from 'verbal contracts' to contracts with weekly price negotiations and volume agreements per cropping cycle (Boselie et al., 2003). Basically, there exists a continuum of coordination with on one end the spot market and on the other end vertical integration (Orden et al., 2004). Between the two are hybrid forms, which can be divided into specification contracts, relation-based alliances and equity-based alliances with different coordination characteristics of direction and control with regard to interdependence, information sharing and duration of the relationship (Peterson et al., 2001).

To meet the product and transaction conditions of retailers and processors, farmers require technology, financial capital, human capital and organization. The capacity of small producers to implement these changes is determined in large part by their assets (natural, physical, financial, human and social capitals). The high capital requirements for entering buyer-driven chains mean that the higher land and labour efficiency of small producer production is no longer a comparative advantage: increasingly supermarket buyers in both industrialized and developing countries are sourcing from large commercial growers who can meet the changed requirements of buyer-driven chains. Due to these changes, small producers are facing declining returns and increased risks for agricultural commodity production.

However, although this is leading to a push from small producer agriculture to wage labour in some cases, there is growing evidence that small producers can participate in supply chains to supermarkets and concentrated processing sectors in a manner that enhances their livelihoods (Boselie et al., 2003).

Converting traditional production systems to comply with the broad array of requirements from supermarkets and processing industries requires a combination of technological and organizational adjustments. For most small producers in developing countries, the concept of more formal 'contracts', or at least a commitment to supply an agreed quantity of a product at an agreed time, that meets pre-specified quality requirements, is novel (Boselie et al., 2003). This is particularly an issue where producers are geographically scattered and have little access to market information.

Where significant changes to production practices and/or development of infrastructure are required, the costs of achieving these standards, which is born even before supply, can be prohibitive for small producers with small amounts of land and limited or no access to credit. Where producers are widely scattered, transport costs from producers and processors to centralized collection facilities can be considerable, particularly where supermarkets or processors require chilled distribution. In Thailand, TOPS started a preferred supplier program and built a distribution centre to introduce this. Once fully operational the cooling tasks were gradually transferred to the preferred suppliers themselves. Furthermore, the coordination costs of supply chains that include numerous small producers can be prohibitive, particularly where monitoring and/or traceability requirements are in place. The Dutch cooperative auction system is an example where the bundling of fresh produce supplies has improved the efficiency of the supply chain and at the same time strengthened the bargaining position of individual farmers.

Furthermore, the risks to small producers of producing to strict quality requirements can be considerable. Dorward et al. (2004) distinguish four types of risks that may inhibit productive investments necessary to promote economic growth and wealth creation in poor rural areas: risks of natural shocks; price risks; economic coordination risks;[3] and risks of opportunism.[4] They argue that economic coordination risks and associated risks of opportunism are particularly bad in poor rural areas because of the low level of economic activity, poor transport facilities and thin markets.

Thin markets are of particular concern. In contrast to well-developed economies with rich competitive markets where players can generally be confident that the market will provide coordination, poor rural areas with thin markets need non-market coordination mechanisms to reduce these risks. For instance, to return to the Thailand example again, wholesale traders who were able to control the supply chain backwards, for example through contract farming schemes, were able to classify themselves as preferred suppliers for TOPS.

Comparative advantages of small-scale producers

Despite the challenges associated with buyer-driven chains, there is evidence that in some countries and in some sectors, small-scale producers continue to be involved in these chains. In the case of TOPS, this reflects the comparative advantage that the better small producers have over large commercial growers in some cases when organized into specialized associations for certain crops, but also the effort by TOPS and its suppliers to implement strategies that facilitate the continued involvement of small producers. This includes close cooperation between TOPS and Syngenta (an international life science company) to provide suppliers who

---

3   Economic coordination risk: risk that another actor will not make necessary complementary actions.
4   Risks of opportunism: risk that an actor who could make complementary actions has an effective monopoly and is able to capture an undue share of the revenue in the supply chain

manage out-grower schemes with high quality seeds, improved crop protection methods and agricultural extension services.

To a large extent the comparative advantage of small producers relates to the production characteristics of the crops concerned, production technologies and associated labour requirements. Experience from Hortico in Zimbabwe shows that small producers supplying a vegetable exporter managed to achieve lower rejection rates for certain non-traditional vegetables (for example, baby corn) than large scale growers because of their high commitment to the crop and labour-intensive production techniques (Boselie et al., 2003).

Given that many of the production techniques required for growing crops demanded by supermarkets and/or to meet quality requirements cannot be mechanized, there may be very limited economies of scale in production. Indeed, small producers may have lower costs of production because they achieve higher yields and/or are less capitalized. These can at least partially offset the higher management costs typically associated with procurement from small producers.

In certain cases, the traditional agronomic and production practices employed by small producers are more amenable to the requirements of supermarkets than the capital intensive methods typically used by large growers. A clear example is the production of organic fruit and vegetables. In Thailand, the domestic supermarket chain TOPS has found that small producers are able to adapt to organic production methods because practices such as crop rotation and selection of resistant varieties are long-established elements of their traditional production systems. Another example is the supply of chemical-free vegetables in Vietnam.

A geographically dispersed base of small producers can be an effective risk-spreading strategy for supermarket suppliers and/or can afford flexibility in the procurement of relatively small quantities of product that meet specific and exacting standards.

For small producers, a benefit of new supply chain management is that it provides them with information on new products. Other benefits include better access to inputs, credit and extension services, and marketing services. These can ease the resource constraints farmers face otherwise, and reduce production and marketing risks for farmers. Some services, such as information and extension services, that private supermarket supply chains may provide to farmers can also save scarce public resources. Because of supermarkets, agents such as traditional vendors based in villages and sub-districts, and wholesalers based in districts and big cities, are usually bypassed in the modern procurement system, reducing the transaction costs small producers will normally bear (see also Orden et al., 2004).

Furthermore, the role of strong social networks appears to be important. Strong social networks (or social capital) create trust and facilitate cooperation, reducing risks and transaction costs (Ashley and Carney, 1999). Trust is an important factor in shaping effective and efficient supply chains. Networks need to be strengthened both vertically (for example, from producers to retailers), as well as horizontally (for example, strengthen producer organizations) in order to increase people's trust and ability to cooperate, and expand access to markets.

It is increasingly clear that institutional infrastructure is critically important for small producers to maintain their competitiveness in restructuring domestic and regional markets. According to Gabre-Madhin (2004), institutions play five potential roles in strengthening markets for agricultural products produced, bought and sold by small producers: reducing coordination costs; reducing risk; enforcing contracts; enabling collective action; and building human capital. Increasingly, strategies aimed at including small producers in supermarket supply chains involve partnerships between public and private sector stakeholders. Frequently, these have been supported by donors and involve academic and/or research institutions from industrialized countries partnered with domestic institutions.

References

Ashley, C. and Carney, D., 1999. *Sustainable Livelihoods: Lessons from Early Experience*. London: UK Department For International Development.

AT Kearney, 2003. *Emerging market priorities for global retailers: The 2003 Global Retail Development Index*. Available: www.atkearney.com.

Berdegué, J.F., Balsevich, J.F., Flores, L., and Reardon, T., 2005. Central American supermarkets' private standards of quality and safety in procurement of fresh fruits and vegetables. *Food Policy* 30(3), 254–69.

Bijman, J., 2002. *Essays on Agricultural Cooperative: Governance Structures in Fruit and Vegetable Chains*. The Hague: LEI/ERIM.

Booz-Allen Hamilton, 2003. *Breaking myths about emerging consumers – learning from small scale retailers*. Exploratory study conducted for the Coca-Cola Retail Research Centre, Latin America.

Boselie, D., Henson, S., and Weatherspoon, D., 2003. Supermarket procurement practices in developing countries: The roles of the public and private sectors. *American Agricultural Economics Association* 85(5), 1155–61.

Deloitte, 2004. *Global powers of retailing*. Deloitte Touche Tohmatsu.

Dobson, P.W., 2002. *Retailer buyer power in European markets: Lessons from grocery supply*. Loughborough University Business School Research Series Paper.

Dorward, A., Kydd, J., Morrison, J. and Urey, I., 2004. A policy agenda for pro-poor agricultural growth. *World Development* 32(1), 73–89.

Dries, L., Reardon, T. and Swinnen, J.F., 2004. The rapid rise of supermarkets in Central and Eastern Europe: Implications for the Agri-food sector and rural development. *Development Policy Review* 22(5), 525–56.

Gabre-Madhin, E.Z., 2004. *Getting markets right: A new agenda beyond reform*. World Bank Presentation, May 2004, Washington, DC.

Gereffi, G., 1994. *The organization of buyer-driven global commodity chains: How US retailers shape overseas production networks*. In G. Gereffi and M. Korzeniewicz, eds, *Commodity Chains and Global Capitalism*, Westport, CT: Praeger, pp. 95–122.

GPN, 2003. *The internationalization/globalization of retailing: Towards a geographical research agenda?* Global Production Networks, University of Manchester School of Environment and Development Working Paper No. 8, July 2003.

Hu, D., Reardon, T., Rozelle, S., Timmer, P. and Wang, H., 2004. The emergence of supermarkets with Chinese characteristics: Challenges and opportunities for China's agricultural development. *Development Policy Review* 2(4), 557–86.

IFAD, 2001. *Rural Poverty Report 2001: The Challenge of Ending Rural Poverty*. Rome: International Fund for Agricultural Development.

Jacob, Rahul, 2002. A no-frills chain sells to the poor. *Financial Times*, 25 March.

Mendoza Vidaurre, R., 2003. *Productos derivados de la leche. La inserción de la Cooperativa San Francisco de Asís en los supermercados de Nicaragua*. Contribution to International E-Mail Conference on 'Participacion de organizaciones economicas ruralesen el circuito supermercadista en America Latina y el Caribe' by RIMISP Michigan State University, FIDAMERICA and PROMER. February–April, 2003.

Moustier, P., Dao The Anh, and Figuie, M., eds, 2003. *Food Markets and Agricultural Development in Vietnam*. Hanoi: MALICA.

Neven, D. and Reardon, T., 2004. The rise of Kenyan supermarkets and evolution of their horticulture product procurement systems. *Development Policy Review* 22(6), 669–99.

Orden, D., Torero, M. and Gulati, A., 2004. *Agricultural markets and the rural poor*. Draft Background Paper for the workshop of the Poverty Reduction Network (POVNET), 5 March 2004. Markets, Trade and Institutions Division, International Food Policy Research Institute, Washington, DC.

Peterson, H.C., Wysocki, A. and Harsh, S.B., 2001. Strategic choice along the vertical coordination continuum. *International Food and Agribusiness Management Review* 4: 149–66.

Reardon, T. and Berdegué, J., 2002. The rapid rise of supermarkets in Latin America: Challenges and opportunities for development. *Development Policy Review* 20(4), 371–88.

Siam Future Development, n.d. Available: www.siamfuture.com.

Stockbridge, M., 2003. *Farmer organization for market access: Learning from success*. Literature review, London, Mimeo Wye college.

Weatherspoon, D.D. and Reardon, T., 2003. The rise of supermarkets in Africa: Implications for agri-food systems and the rural poor. *Development Policy Review* 21(3), 333–55.

Wrigley, N. and Lowe, M. (2002). *Reading Retail: A Geographical Perspective on Retailing and Consumption Space*. London: Arnold.

Zhang, X., 2001. *Shanghai Consumer Studies, with Attention to Livestock, Dairy and Horticultural Products*. The Hague: LEI.

2 Country Studies:
Countries with Consolidating and Expanding Supermarkets and their Supply Chains

In this first set of country studies, chapters cover selected parts of the developing world where markets have begun to consolidate, supermarkets have taken significant market share, and suppliers are facing technical, commercial and organizational challenges. These are Central America, Ecuador, Thailand, the Philippines and South Africa. The Central America chapter has the added benefit of case studies of market linkages between small producers and these dynamic market sectors. Unlike the sudden changes ushered in by rapid opening and liberalization of centrally planned economies (Part 3), these countries represent a more gradual evolution, with traditional markets in the informal sector often very resilient in the face of the supermarket challenge.

2 *Central America*

Fernando Balsevich, Julio A. Berdegué, Louis Flores , Pilar Jano, Thomas A. Reardon and Paul Schuetz

Introduction

Most if not all of the countries of Central America are characterized by rapidly expanding modern food systems. Supermarkets now dominate retailing in the region and we look at an interesting example of inter-regional trade in this chapter that has extended vegetable supply chains. Our case studies are drawn from Nicaragua, Guatemala and Costa Rica.

A case study methodology was designed to address four key questions:

1. Does selling to the supermarket-market channel have different technological, managerial, organizational and financial requirements from selling to other channels, including traditional retail channels (in which retailers other than local/regional supermarkets are the final interface with the consumer) and extra-regional export channels?
2. Does selling to the supermarket-market channel pay better or worse (controlling for cost) than the other channels?
3. Can small and medium producers meet the requirements to access and to operate sustainably in the supermarket-market channel, and under what conditions?
4. Are rural communities better or worse off as a result of supermarkets gaining a greater share of the retail food sector?

In the first case study, we explain how Hortifruti, a specialist wholesaler and a subsidiary of a major regional supermarket chain, operates in the fresh fruits and vegetables (FFV) sector. Hortifruti illustrates the role companies can play in being proactive in seeking out small-scale suppliers. We see that things don't always go right in the second case study. The third case is an example of a processor supplied mainly by small-scale producers. The fourth case illustrates how small-scale producers can access a supply chain without being very noticeable. Finally, the fifth case study considers the experience of a producer group in the supply of tomatoes to a processor.

Three of the case studies are about tomatoes and four types of tomatoes are distinguished by our writers. Roma (the most common type, found in traditional markets, shops and supermarkets), salad (sold mainly by supermarkets), manzano (tomatoes produced under plastic with irrigation) and industrial tomatoes (mostly hybrids).

The other two case studies are about cattle ranching and beef supply.

REGIONAL RETAIL MARKET

Supermarkets are now dominant players in most of the agri-food economy of Latin America, having moved from around 10–20 per cent in 1990 to 50-60 per cent of the retail sector in 2000 (Berdegué et al., 2004). As supermarkets have increased in number, so they have in size. As a result, both small supermarkets and small shops have gone out of business. Between 1994 and 2002, small and independent supermarkets grew in number by 74 per cent but their market share diminished from 40 per cent to 36 per cent. Also, 64,000 small shops went out of business in Argentina between 1984 and 1993, a pattern found in other Latin American countries.

KEY DATA

	Guatemala	Nicaragua	Costa Rica
	2004	2004	2004
Population (millions)	12.7	5.5	4.02
Per capita GDP (US$)	2011	2300	9600
Urbanization (%) (2001)	40	57	60
Agriculture as % GDP	22.7	20.7	8.5
Per capita total food retail sales (US$)	544		
Per capita modern food retail sales (US$)	242		1500
Modern food retail sales as % total	44	27	50

Exchange rates (1 January 2006):
1 US$ = 15.688 Nicaraguan Córdoba Oro
1 US$ = 495.8 Costa Rican Colón
1 US$ = 7.615 Guatemalan Quetzal

TOP CHAINS, 2004

Country	Company	Ownership	Number of stores	Retail banner sales 2004 (US$ millions)	Market share (%)
Costa Rica	Wal-Mart	Joint venture	99	646	29.2
	Megasuper	Local	62	196	8.9
	Perimercados	Local	19	110	5.0
	Auto Mercado	Local	8	95	4.3
	PriceSmart	USA	3	84	3.8
	Other			1081	48.9
Guatemala	Wal-Mart	Joint venture	104	586	14.7
	PriceSmart	USA	2	65	1.6
	Other			3349	83.7
Nicaragua	Wal-Mart	Joint venture	20	83	21.0
	PriceSmart	Joint venture	1	22	5.6
	Other			290	73.5

Source: PlanetRetail (www.planetretail.net) and Berdegué et al., 2004

MARKET STRUCTURE

The traditional market sector is made up of open-air markets, traditional markets and numerous small 'mom & pop' stores (known as *pulperias*). Small shop numbers are in decline, squeezed out by expanding supermarket chains.

Supermarkets in the region initially served upper-income groups in large cities. During the 1970s and 1980s, supermarkets spread to middle- and working-class areas and into medium-sized cities and towns and to poorer countries in Central America.

Across Central America, Wal-Mart is now the undisputed market leader through its partnership with Costa Rican-based retailer Corporación de Supermercados Unidos S.A. (CSU) and Guatemala-based La Fragua (owned by the Paiz family). All their operations in the region are part of the Central American Retail Holding Company (CARHCO) joint venture, which has more than 253 stores in Central America.

La Fragua established a joint venture with Ahold in 1999. Then CSU (the dominant retailer in Costa Rica and already a regional multinational in Nicaragua, Honduras and El Salvador) merged with La Fragua and Ahold in January 2002 into the three-way CARHCO, a huge move in the retail sector in less than four years. And then in September 2005, Wal-Mart became the dominant player in Central America, when it acquired the 33.33 per cent stake that Ahold owned in CARHCO.

The aim of the joint venture is to create synergies in logistics, administration, purchasing and management. CARHCO is Central America's largest retailer, with 363 supermarkets and other stores in Guatemala, El Salvador, Honduras, Nicaragua, and Costa Rica, and sales during 2004 of approximately US$2.0 billion. These include hypermarket, supermarket and discount formats.

The other international player in the region is the US Warehouse club PriceSmart. Between them CSU (Wal-Mart's partner) and PriceSmart account for about half of supermarket sales in Nicaragua.

Local supermarket companies include Unisuper in Guatemala (local company, formed through 2001 merger of La Torre and Econosuper), La Colonia in Nicaragua, and in Costa Rica Megasuper, Perimercados and Auto Mercado. These chains have a combined share of 20 per cent of supermarket sales.

CONSOLIDATION AND 'MULTINATIONALIZATION' IN LATIN AMERICA

Two crucial changes occurred in Latin America's supermarket sector as it grew in the 1990s. First, there was rapid consolidation. Second, there was the growth of multinational retail chains. As a rule of thumb in Latin America, one or two of the top five retail chains in a country are multinationals (Chile is the exception). The entry and growth of multinationals has been the result of mergers and acquisitions (M&A), although these are gradually giving way to new store development. As a result of their expansion about 10 per cent of supermarket sales are accounted for by four multinationals in Latin America.

The first wave of M&A came in the late 1980s, before the multinationals arrived. Most of this consolidation was by large, locally owned chains buying local independents and small, provincial chains. This type of M&A continued into the 1990s.

The second, much larger, wave of M&A started in the early to mid-1990s. US and European supermarket firms were pushed by saturated home markets and pulled by underdeveloped retail markets abroad offering higher profit margins. The foreign companies bought many of the large domestic chains (already 'fattened' by their acquisitions of smaller chains) as well as joining the domestic chains in taking over smaller chains and independents. The case of CARHCO illustrates this (see above) and also shows how it led to the formation of inter-country chains.

Case study 1: Specialist wholesaler Hortifruti

The second pillar of the supermarket system (Reardon et al., 2003) involves a switch from using wholesale markets to using a specialist wholesaler. This company then takes over the job of ensuring growers are aware of a supermarket's standards, providing advice and other help where appropriate, obtaining the supplies and rejecting those that are below standard. The wholesale company then delivers the product to either the supermarket depot or individual stores. This is how companies like Hortifruti operate.

As we explain above, the main player in the Central American food business is the Central American Retail Holding Company (CARHCO). CSU has a subsidiary company called Hortifruti which supplies CSU stores in Nicaragua, Honduras, Guatemala and Costa Rica (where it has its headquarters) with FFV. Hortifruti buys in all four countries as well as elsewhere. Our case studies focus on Nicaragua.

Tomatoes are an important vegetable in Nicaragua; the monthly volume sold by CSU Nicaragua amounts to around 25,000 pounds of salad tomatoes and 75,000 pounds of roma tomatoes. Hortifruti's main function is to supply all the 22 CSU Nicaragua stores with produce (La Unión supermarkets for high- and middle-income customers and Pali supermarkets for lower-income customers). In other words, Hortifruti is the 'category manager'. It estimates future CSU requirements and plans its deliveries. These provide the basis for orders that are transmitted to growers. Hortifruti has made investments in two distribution centres, one in the capital city and one in the northern city of Sebaco. Additionally, Hortifruti owns a truck fleet that picks up from individual growers and grower associations and delivers to the distribution centres.

FFV are distributed to the two distribution centres as well as to some individual stores. Most suppliers are required to deliver the products to each store, although there are mixed strategies. Roma tomatoes are delivered to the centres and then the main store is in charge of delivering it to other stores. On average, the chain purchases approximately 70 per cent of the total value of produce on a centralized basis, which accounts for 30 per cent of the volume of FFV (currently, a total of 200 products). The rest is bought directly by each store from Hortifruti.

Until quite recently, tomatoes sold in Nicaraguan supermarkets were imported from Costa Rica or other countries. Now, local production has expanded in Nicaragua so that 40 per cent of Hortifruti's Nicaraguan requirements are locally sourced. Salad tomatoes require a higher level of management than roma tomatoes so it is harder to find local growers.

Specifically for tomatoes, Hortifruti Nicaragua has a list of 43 preferred suppliers (producers) who supply all roma tomatoes. Hortifruti also has a list of 29 growers from a grower's association (recently developed with the help of NGOs) that supply 40 per cent of salad tomatoes. The remaining salad tomatoes (60 per cent) are imported from Costa Rica. Of the 43 growers providing Hortifruti with roma tomato, 13 work individually and 30 are organized in two associations. Consequently, Hortifruti operates with a total of 16 supply units (organizations are accounted as one supply unit).

Hortifruti works directly with the growers and associations in terms of training and enforcement of quality standards, and crop planning (scheduling of required volumes). The company also provides recommendations and technical assistance, if required and/or needed by the grower. Hortifruti has stockpiling facilities in strategically located areas to centralize and facilitate the collection of FFV from growers in distant areas. Growers are selected according to their proximity to these assembly points.

Hortifruti also establishes partnerships with other institutions such as NGOs (for instance, Save the Children, ADRA and Technoserve) in areas where they do not have physical facilities operating. These partnerships provide growers with the required technical support to meet Hortifruti's tomato supply requirements.

Roma tomatoes are now all sourced by Hortifruti directly from growers rather than through wholesalers. This is estimated to have reduced the price paid by Hortifruti by 60 per cent. On the other hand, the change has required major investments in distribution facilities and transportation.

ALTERNATIVE MARKETING CHANNELS TO HORTIFRUTI IN NICARAGUA

To date, no other Nicaraguan retailer has set up their own version of Hortifruti. Instead, they rely on wholesalers. For instance, the second largest supermarket chain in Nicaragua is La Colonia. This has a monthly requirement for 22,000 pounds of salad tomatoes and approximately 80,000 pounds of roma tomatoes. This supermarket chain does not have an exclusive relation with any one wholesaler and has not got any assembly points or physical distribution centres.

La Colonia supermarket relies entirely on imports of salad tomatoes and local supplies of roma tomatoes. All roma tomatoes are bought under agreements with dedicated wholesalers who operate at or in coordination with wholesalers at the Managua wholesale market. La Colonia relies on four dedicated wholesalers and these provide the retailer with a high level of services. The dedicated wholesalers supplying La Colonia purchase their roma tomatoes from a total of 27 growers.

The supermarket chain has little capacity to enforce, control and monitor quality standards and a very limited capacity to influence the practices of growers. The supermarket mainly relies on rejection as a mechanism to control quality standards. This chain however has been recently shifting from a decentralized supply to a centralized supply, although without making the required investments in infrastructure.

Finally, the traditional procurement systems are very fragmented. Growers sell mainly to wholesale markets, to open air markets and on-farm sales (through the middlemen that buy at the farms and sell to open air markets, wholesaler markets). All these producers sell to the best bidder and it is precisely this lack of continuity that characterizes, to a large extent, the traditional marketing channels as compared to growers who access supermarket chains.

THE NET MARGIN FOR GROWERS

An analysis of the costs and returns of growing roma tomatoes in Nicaragua shows how net margins differ between selling to Hortifruti and selling to traditional wholesalers. Producers selling roma tomatoes to supermarkets generate 50 per cent more profits per unit of land than those selling roma tomatoes to traditional markets; and also generated 80 per cent more employment (labour days). This lends support to the conclusion that higher profits and employment generation are associated with the supermarket channel.

Nonetheless, competitiveness may not be a determinant for accessing this market. Production costs per unit of land for growing tomatoes destined for supermarkets are 38 per cent higher than for producing tomatoes for other markets. Further, there are only small gains in tomato production yield. Net revenue is higher when selling to supermarkets but working capital requirements are also higher, in part a reflection of a bigger wage bill.

Precise figures for the costs and revenue received from salad tomatoes are not available but estimates suggest that salad tomatoes are much more profitable and need much more labour and capital than other tomatoes. Growers selling salad tomatoes probably generate five times more profit per unit of land than those selling roma tomatoes and employ over three times more labour.

In the case of roma tomatoes, supermarkets pay a price premium of about 15 per cent for first-quality tomatoes over market prices and reject second quality tomatoes. For mixed quality, the price received by supermarket growers is 8 to 10 per cent higher than the price received from traditional markets. Producers selling to supermarket channels sell about 50 per cent of their tomatoes to supermarkets and the rest through traditional channels.

Neither farm size nor the scale of production of tomato crops are significant factors in determining access to supermarket chains. This appears to be an encouraging finding because it suggests that the supermarket channel is not biased towards large commercial farms. However, NGO support for producers is also a factor in helping small-scale growers access supermarkets, through Hortifruti or through other wholesalers. Growers in an association supplying a supermarket need much more credit and technical advice than is available to them on their own and here NGOs can help a lot. Supermarkets do not provide these aids.

The usual problems of running producer associations are also reflected in the extra costs of supplying supermarkets. These include free riding in the organization (such as not being able to trace quality levels to individual producers and hence dividing equally the losses of quality rejections among organization members) and longer payment periods (for example, organizational administrative cheque clearing takes longer than getting the cheque from the buyer, which in turn increases the incentives to avoid selling through the organization).

STANDARDS

Supermarkets impose strict tomato standards that reflect the quality demanded by consumers (Berdegué et al., 2005). Hortifruti introduced quality standards when it started buying directly from growers and associations in 1998 and these standards have gradually risen. For example, damage tolerance for tomatoes went down from 20 per cent to 10 per cent; critical damage tolerance fell from 3 to 1 per cent, and has now fallen to zero. That said, supermarkets are careful to impose these standards in the light of supply and demand in the tomato market.

The standards and tolerance levels are communicated to Hortifruti's buyers and quality auditors (agricultural engineers). Tomatoes delivered to Hortifruti's Sebaco processing plant are also checked for quality. Growers only send top-quality products to Sebaco and the rest are forwarded to other markets. In the case of independent growers, tomato quality standards are enforced at the point of origin rather than destination.

Hortifruti's technical standards and regulation system go beyond a simple quality standard control. For instance, Hortifruti's agronomists visit the farms to control field crop availability and also make recommendations to help reduce costs in the supply chain and/or to improve product quality. As a result, specific tomato varieties have been recommended to some growers to extend the shelf life of tomatoes. This has created some problems with growers because an optimal variety for shelf life is rarely an optimal variety for production; other varieties are usually more resistant to white fly and other pests and other viruses.

For other products, such as lettuce, produce is washed using chlorine at the distribution centres in order to reduce the effects of pathogens. Tomatoes cannot be washed and must be delivered in clean, plastic boxes. Agronomists recommend the use of chemicals to ensure the tomatoes are protected. Some standards and procedures have been implemented to improve the sanitary conditions in the handling of products throughout the chain; nevertheless, Hortifruti is planning to develop a risk management system already implemented in Costa Rica that involves the use of good agricultural practices (GAP) and good manufacturing practices (GMP).

Case study 2: Cross-border tomato sales

Salad tomatoes are imported into Nicaragua, mainly from Costa Rica. A group of growers in Guatemala entered this market and sold salad tomatoes of the manzano variety to Hortifruti Nicaragua. This case study looks at their experience. It is an example (probably rare) of a cross-border partnership between small-scale producers and supermarkets in another low-income country. Such partnerships are attractive to policy-makers: they help regional development and avoid the waste of long distance 'air miles' to northern markets. In short, this was a worthy attempt to group together small-scale producers and use the resources of government to upgrade them into potential supply chain partners.

However, the arrangement in this case proved impractical and lasted only a few years. Failure is instructive and we are grateful to those who couldn't make it work for being so frank about their experience. Failure will be commonplace when policy-makers try to bring together small-scale producers and a modern food system, and this story has many useful lessons for others to learn. The case relates to the period 1999–2002.

The producer organization in question was the Association of Small-Sized Irrigation Users of Palencia (ASUMPAL) of Guatemala. The manzano salad tomatoes were sold to Hortifruti Nicaragua. Growers were responsible for transporting the tomatoes to the northern depot of Hortifruti in Nicaragua (see above). A specialist wholesaler, López Foods, also bought manzano tomatoes, on behalf of McDonald's restaurants.

This story illustrates well the difficulties faced by an organization of small-scale growers. Some of the worst headaches revolved around compliance with the precise yet changing requirements imposed by supermarkets and restaurants (and, as they would add, imposed on them in turn by their customers). To overcome these problems in a future scheme there must first be capacity building and human and social capital strengthening. The first step is to create a strong and resilient producer organization, one able to operate in the demanding world of supermarket supply.

ASUMPAL

ASUMPAL was established following an initiative of the Ministry of Agriculture and Livestock (MAGA). The initiative gathered the members of four irrigation associations belonging to the Municipality of Palencia, Department of Guatemala, who produced güisquil (a type of chayote), miltomato (also known as 'small tomato' or 'green tomato', Physalisixocarpa), perulero (another type of chayote), carrots, potatoes, and Chinese long beans (called ejote). The products were sold directly and separately to wholesale middlemen trading at La Terminal, the wholesale market of the City of Guatemala. The irrigation groups had an interesting productive potential, being strategically located relative to the most important markets of the capital. All members are classified as small farmers (less than 1.4 hectares of cultivation).

ASUMPAL was legally established in 1997 and is now made up of 350 growers. However, being a member is not particularly onerous. Listings were collected of people equipped with irrigation systems in the region and they automatically became members of ASUMPAL. These people had little or no knowledge about ASUMPAL and some totally ignored it. This lack of motivation weakened the organization from the outset and it was unable to cope as the problems multiplied. Such a problem is common elsewhere; see for instance a study in Bolivia by Muñoz (2004).

There are several common interests among small-sized irrigation system users that favour creating an association like this. The most important is the need to manage water flow. In this case, growers have experienced the gradual reduction of their irrigation flow rates and seek access to more water sources. Another reason for an association is to build and manage joint irrigation systems, to access fertilizers then provided by the government to organized groups, and to build a common infrastructure such as the stockpiling centre and cold stores, both funded by the government. A further aspect of ASUMPAL was training farmers in irrigation techniques.

The initial government grant was only US$ 83 000, half for fixed investment and half for working capital. In fact, two-thirds was spent on fixed equipment. The grant set up an agricultural marketing centre as well. ASUMPAL was helped further with export business contacts channelled from another organization.

Initially, members showed little interest. The first milestone was a 'stockpiling centre', opened in 1999. Most growers ignored it for various reasons – not trusting the management, being too far away, disliking the delay in payment and the rejection of vegetables as low quality. In contrast, they could sell directly to wholesalers for cash from their farms and knew everything offered would be taken away to market, even if prices were lower. Less than 10 per cent of ASUMPAL members agreed to use the new centre. These 25 growers were the key to developing sufficient volume for the supermarket and restaurant trade. A failure to involve more growers was another weakness.

A HIGH-VALUE MARKET OPPORTUNITY

There was a delay in finding a good marketing objective that only further weakened the motivation of growers to become active members of the association. The export marketers eventually identified outlets in Central American countries that wanted to buy various vegetables, including manzano tomatoes produced intensively in irrigated greenhouses. Other vegetables were also produced but the manzano tomato was the one that seemed to offer the greatest profit to growers.

The response from growers was limited. Of the 350, around 25 were using the new stockpiling centre. Of these, only nine had irrigated greenhouses suitable for manzano tomatoes. These formed the sub-group that produced the tomatoes (one grower dropped out later, leaving eight). Other growers were situated too far from the centre, or could not accept the delayed payments (initially 15 days but soon a month in arrears). For others, the high rejection rate made it unprofitable. Additionally, there was no close and trusting relationship between ASUMPAL managers and growers.

POTENTIAL HIGH-VALUE BUYERS

In December 1999, a marketing relationship with Hortifruti Nicaragua began. It was followed by another agreement, this time with López Foods, suppliers of the local McDonalds's restaurant chain. Later, Hortifruti Costa Rica also bought some manzano tomatoes from the Guatemalan group. ASUMPAL sold other vegetables to these and other buyers. With hindsight, this can be seen to have been an over-ambitious marketing strategy, resting as it did on a few inexperienced growers with erratic technical and financial back-up. It led almost immediately to problems with quality, volume and sequencing.

Problems with quality

The technical requirements for this business are demanding, too demanding as it turned out. To grow manzano tomatoes, growers need greenhouses, a water source, a drip irrigation system, fertilizers, pesticides and good technical assistance. In addition, López Foods demanded the use of airtight greenhouses, improved sowing, proper use of chemicals, high water quality, product traceability and compliance with the standards of the Comprehensive Agricultural and Environmental Protection Programme (PIPAA),[1] for which purpose they conducted water analyses. Based on an irrigation water analysis, López Foods concluded that ASUMPAL did not comply with the PIPAA standards; even so, López Foods continued to buy its production from ASUMPAL members – thanks to the intercession of someone working for López who was from a government export development agency. Another factor was a reported shortage of manzano tomatoes in Guatemala.

According to López Foods, standards were not met because of a lack of investment, training and enthusiasm among ASUMPAL members. According to an ASUMPAL marketing official, the lack of enthusiasm probably stemmed from higher transport costs, higher rejection rate percentages and slower payment than that offered by independent wholesalers and exporters who pay for transport, take all the tomatoes and have no billing requirements. As a result of these high costs, even though López Foods paid higher prices, the profit was no better than from selling through independent export agents.

Sometimes there is a difference of opinion between an organization and individual growers and there seemed to be at least a difference of emphasis between ASUMPAL managers, from whose point of view manzano tomato exports were highly profitable, and individual growers, for whom the high price received was matched by high costs. If so, this suggests that the costs were not being shared equitably between the association and the growers.

For instance, ASUMPAL viewed the 7 per cent rejection rate by Hortifruti of manzano tomatoes as good compared with the rejection rates for ASUMPAL potatoes and broccoli. However, the tomato rejection rate for individual growers was much higher because ASUMPAL did a preliminary 'weeding out' of tomatoes before sending them to Hortifruti. That cost was entirely born by the grower. Thus ASUMPAL and growers understood two quite different things by the term 'rejection rate'.

Another source of frustration was that ASUMPAL could not identify which grower was responsible for tomatoes being rejected by Hortifruti since by then the individual origin of the tomatoes was lost. This meant that a grower delivering poor quality that got through the ASUMPAL net but was rejected by Hortfruti was never penalized. Instead, the cost of rejection

---

1   There is more information about the Comprehensive Agricultural and Environmental Protection Programme (PIPAA) at: www.ifpri.org/2020/focus/focus10/focus10_12.pdf.

was shared between all growers, good and bad alike. The result was opportunistic behaviour (free riding) by growers that in turn led the most accountable members to act outside the association.

The standards set by Hortifruti were exacting and much more complicated and onerous than those growers were used to. In addition to the written standards, Hortifruti provided ranking tables by tomato size. Rank 1 was the largest size, Rank 2 was the medium size, and Rank 3 the smallest size. Hortifruti only purchased Ranks 1 and 2, and only monitored the physical quality of the products. No health requirements were set. They also gave instructions on packing containers. Hortifruti provided a price that covered transport costs and value added taxes in Nicaragua, which ranged from 12 per cent to 15 per cent. However, the transport had to be arranged by ASUMPAL.

Payments were due within 15 days, but it was reported that in practice payments were not received by ASUMPAL for a month. According to ASUMPAL's accountant at that time (who was also a former President of the Association) a fixed US$0.48 per pound[2] price was established for tomatoes, which was considered relatively good.

At ASUMPAL's stockpiling centre, one person was in charge of verifying that the products complied with Hortifruti's quality standards. Nevertheless, according to ASUMPAL's former accountant, quality control was fairly flexible. Once at Hortifruti Nicaragua's plant, products were subject to a new quality control. Hortifruti agreed to pay for up to 2 per cent of rejection; if higher, Hortifruti did not pay for the rejected product (and as we note above the rejection rate at this stage averaged 7 per cent).

Regarding quality, Hortifruti Nicaragua's Sales Manager stated that imported tomatoes from ASUMPAL had problems with calibration (very small) and maturity (excessively matured). The latter aspect was also mentioned by Hortifruti Costa Rica. Both clients also stated that too many tomatoes arrived bruised. This may have been because the container was not full. Distance was also a factor with regard to excessive maturity.

The view from ASUMPAL was somewhat different. Managers argued that Hortifruti rejected much of their production (of all kinds of vegetables), which resulted in losses for ASUMPAL. In fact, they rejected far less manzano tomatoes than they did other products such as broccoli and potatoes.

Hortifruti responded that doing business with ASUMPAL involved a loss for them, because the rejects were thrown away and Hortifruti had to pay for the freight and taxes. Hortifruti Nicaragua's Sales Manager referred to the marketing of the tomato as a bad experience, even though the business relationship extended over several months.

López Foods' quality standards differed from Hortifruti's but were also stringent. They covered issues such as consistency, product cleanness, diameter, size, colour and evenness, lack of defects and maturity. Unlike supermarkets, in addition to quality standards regarding appearance, the company also monitored the production process through site visits. Further, to meet PIPAA standards (see above), they conducted water analyses.

There was no formal contract between López Foods and ASUMPAL regarding transaction conditions, only a verbal agreement. López Foods gave them a trial period, but no contract was signed in the end. A non-negotiable, fixed price of US$0.44 per pound was established, as reported by some members of ASUMPAL, who considered it a good price. However, in the first selection carried out at ASUMPAL's stockpiling centre, the ASUMPAL quality controllers rejected 80 per cent of tomatoes. Then, a second selection was made at López Foods' plant, with a further 1 to 5 per cent per cent rejection rate. When tomatoes were scarce, López Foods

---

2   1 kilo = 2.2 pounds.

became less demanding. However, the level of rejection was far too great for the eight growers to accept, so ASUMPAL stopped supplying López. According to López Foods' Manager, the final appearance of the product did not meet Mc Donald's requirements, as ASUMPAL growers began to have problems with plant disease.

The rejection rate had a devastating effect on the financial returns of growers. Each grower had to show ASUMPAL they had US$6300 in working capital before they could be accepted to grow manzano tomatoes. Further investments were also required to expand volume, keep effective control of pests and diseases, implement PIPAA standards, and comply with all the other requirements.

Problems with volume and sequencing

Sometimes, with a view to satisfying the volumes required by Hortifruti, ASUMPAL had to buy the missing production on the wholesale market. According to Hortifruti's Sales Manager, ASUMPAL had serious organization problems, failing to deliver the correct volume on several occasions. ASUMPAL also stopped selling to other outlets because of a lack of volume and increasing rejects, and because other outlets paid mostly in instalments.

Problems multiplied. Little information on market requirements, particularly what was happening at the Hortifruti arrivals depot, got back to growers. As a result there were unresolved discrepancies in weight between tomatoes shipped and those received by Hortifruti, problems in meeting the volumes scheduled and mounting rejections.

Yet more arguments erupted with other customers as the demands of the manzano tomato supply agreements with Hortifruti and López took their toll of the whole business. According to the President and some members of ASUMPAL, production was (until 2001) scheduled by the agronomist. This scheduling began because of the marketing process with Hortifruti Nicaragua. According to ASUMPAL, it has continued. However, a current customer says that there is no scheduling, and he reported that ASUMPAL fails to comply with deliveries from two to three times a year. This was confirmed by another current buyer who points out that there are no deliveries during four months of a year.

Discipline is necessary when growing according to specifications and fulfilling plans and this has been another problem for ASUMPAL. Poor monitoring along with ASUMPAL's organizational weakness have resulted in members not being penalized for their failure to comply with quality or volume commitments. Only once were two tomato growers, who delivered directly to customers, admonished for such an action, after which they decided to leave the association.

Regarding management, the compliance with volume and quality specifications required constant supervision and the implementation of strict control mechanisms. The association lacked an adequate accounting administration and carried out no ordered record keeping. Marketing information was only managed by the person in charge at a given time, and no regular meetings were held.

To improve control and address the worst problems, Hortifruti Nicaragua's Sales Manager visited ASUMPAL's plant twice. Some visits were also made by ASUMPAL's representatives to Hortifruti Nicaragua to verify the amounts of product rejected and the volumes received.

TECHNICAL ASSISTANCE

The loss of the Hortifruti and López contracts solved some problems but not others. Growers have been seriously affected by a pest or disease that has yet to be identified, presumably due to the lack of resources and professional advice. During the marketing relationship with Hortifruti, technical advice was available, though according to some disenchanted growers the pest already existed at that time. The pest has resulted in a gradual reduction in production volumes, with an impact on delivery consistency.

More generally, there is the problem that, within a partnership, 'technical assistance' seems more or less adequate according to your perspective. Hortifruti felt that the government-appointed agronomist provided ample technical assistance. ASUMPAL and the growers thought that there was no regular assistance, just an occasional visit. The agronomist himself objected that he was permanently there to help as required. This expert left in 2001 and with him went the main link between ASUMPAL and its customers. Some felt that the organization he worked for was too paternalistic towards growers. As a result, they never learned to 'stand on their own two feet' and technical problems multiplied when his services were withdrawn.

PROBLEMS IN ASUMPAL

Whilst the manzano tomato business was proving difficult for growers, ASUMPAL also had its troubles. First, they had to find money for more investment. To comply with volumes and quality and safety standards, the association invested in increasing the production area by setting up new greenhouses and identifying and controlling for pests and diseases. Investments were also required for training and the implementation of PIPAA standards (demanded by López Foods) covering traceability, water sanitation and the proper use of chemicals.

There were other problems such as a mismanagement of funds by two accountants hired by ASUMPAL. Also, a working capital shortage arose because of conflict on the border between Honduras and Nicaragua in 2000, when Honduras closed the border with Nicaragua and two containers were lost on their way to Hortifruti Nicaragua. This represented a loss of about US$8600, which, along with the mismanagement of resources, meant that ASUMPAL was unable to apply for a government marketing grant. According to a source, this 'de-capitalization' of ASUMPAL prevented it from continuing to provide advance payments to growers. This forced growers to reduce production and they were unable to reach the volumes required and lost the link with Hortifruti.

EPILOGUE

ASUMPAL became so weakened that both the President and some members were thinking of winding it up and merging with another grower's organization, AGROEXPASA. This is a looser association currently composed of about 20 growers who jointly plan annual production for export of a mixture of crops such as tomatoes, blackberries and carrots. Several members of ASUMPAL are already members of AGROEXPASA. However, for the moment ASUMPAL continues to sell manzano tomatoes, though now through independent wholesalers and export agents. Quality requirements and marketing conditions are more flexible, well below the standards required by Hortifruti and López Foods.

The unavoidable conclusion seems to be that ASUMPAL's eight small-scale growers failed to establish themselves in the Hortifruti/CSU supply chain as preferred suppliers because of their lack of technical proficiency and the difficulty of managing the business through an association. Instead, they found a less demanding market using traditional wholesale channels.

Case study 3: Tomatoes in Nicaragua

The case study focuses on the relationship between the Cooperativa de Producción y Comercialización R.L. (COOPROCOM) and Hortifruti in Nicaragua. As explained above, Hortifruti is a subsidiary of the CSU group, the main supermarket chain in Costa Rica and Nicaragua. Hortifruti is a specialized wholesaler responsible for supplying high-quality fruits and vegetables to the entire CSU chain in Central America.

This case study shows that an association of small- and medium-sized growers needs more than access to vibrant markets and compliance with complex and demanding requirements. To keep its market position, it must also sustain this compliance on a continuous and daily basis. The case study also shows that 'time must take its course': development programmes and agencies focused on helping small growers access markets as fast as possible should not circumvent initial efforts related with capacity building and human and social capital strengthening, which are preconditions for success after entering these demanding markets.

The COOPROCOM was established following the initiative of the Winrock international project funded by the US Agency for International Development (USAID). The project was aimed at providing small growers with market access. The area of Terrabona was selected because it was the poorest municipality of the Matagalpa Department and one of the poorest in Nicaragua. The cooperative was established to supply industrial tomatoes to Hortifruti. Before that, growers were unorganized and grew native onions and other products such as haricot beans, corn, chiltoma, and chili. These products were individually sold on the local market or through middle agents on the farm. The number of members increased with the transition from native onion to industrial tomato. Ten or 12 years ago they had grown tomatoes, but pest infestations made it uneconomic and they gave up.

The project provided organization, funds and technical assistance. It initially contacted Hortifruti to identify the product required by the supermarket. Notably, an agreement between USAID and Hortifruti established that the supermarket will purchase the products from all the projects funded by USAID. Both institutions are coordinated by Partnership for Food Industry Development (PFID), a joint university and food industry technical assistance programme funded by USAID.

The cooperative was established by 13 members of the Cuajiniquil Community. All the arrangements and costs were provided by Winrock (7500 cordobas = US$470), including the services of an attorney-at-law (drawing up of bylaws and registration of the cooperative) and 40 hours of training on cooperative issues. The cooperative's legal capacity was approved in September 2003 with 21 members. The Winrock project also provided 314 443.07 cordobas (US$ 20 028), which were used to cover the costs of a van, a motorcycle, a computer, a supply warehouse, tunnel-shaped greenhouses for seedlings, sowing trays and an irrigation system. Approximately 60 000 cordobas (US$3800) remaining from these expenses were used to create a revolving fund for the operation of the cooperative. COOPROCOM also received a PFID grant-in-aid towards establishing the Stockpiling Centre. The cooperative was established to develop business on a formal basis (that is, as a company) and to obtain funding from Winrock and others.

The first delivery to Hortifruti took place on 5 June 2003. The Winrock project ended in November 2003, after which the Technoserve NGO, together with PFID continued supporting the farmers (with technical assistance and marketing, respectively). In addition to providing technical assistance, Technoserve keeps accounting ledgers and monitors and supports growers in the resolution of disputes between COOPROCOM and Hortifruti. Therefore, the cooperative is somewhat dependent on the NGO.

Currently, COOPROCOM members only grow industrial tomatoes and their main marketing channels are to Hortifruti, for first quality production, and to the local market for second quality production.

The agreement with Hortifruti states that growers must sell first quality production to Hortifruti and all rejects on informal markets. There is an exclusivity agreement in place between Hortifruti and PFID for the delivery of first-quality tomatoes by the cooperative. As set forth by COOPROCOM's technicians, Hortifruti does not explicitly require exclusivity from growers; nevertheless, they state that they are 'wary' regarding sales to other customers.

According to Hortifruti's Sales Manager, a verbal agreement is established at the beginning, and then a written agreement is reached, providing a commitment to comply with the technical guidelines. Hortifruti has a very general written agreement with COOPROCOM that involves a sales agreement or alliance. According to growers, no agreement is in place between them and Hortifruti, but between Hortifruti and USAID. This suggests poor communications or information sharing between growers and Hortifruti.

Initially Winrock negotiated quantities and, to some extent, prices with Hortifruti. Presently, and as part of administrative reforms introduced by PFID and Technoserve aimed at promoting cooperative self-management, Hortifruti and the members of the cooperative negotiate prices.

According to the officials in Hortifruti's Sebaco plant, COOPROCOM is currently their most important tomato supplier. COOPROCOM accounts for a relatively large share (44 per cent) of the tomatoes delivered at the Hortifruti distribution centre in Sebaco. Average delivery (three deliveries per week) to Hortifruti by the cooperative amounts to 2578 kg (112 50-pound boxes). Based on data provided by Technoserve, of the total volume delivered by the Cooperative, 45 per cent goes to Hortifruti and 55 per cent to local markets (average volumes between December 2003 and May 2004).

Both price and quality are regulating mechanisms implemented by Hortifruti. Greater supply results in lower prices and/or higher quality standards. The contrary is true in case of poor supply. Due to occasional non-deliveries, Hortifruti has increased the prices paid to COOPROCOM (for example, by 100 per cent between March and May 2004). Some disputes have also arisen regarding Hortifruti's prices compared to the informal market.

It is interesting to compare the price paid by the wholesale market to other growers (outside the cooperative) with the price paid to COOPROCOM growers. This price can represent the cooperative's loss for selling only the rejects at the local market, assuming that other growers sell both top- and lower-quality production. The price difference is 15 per cent less for COOPROCOM growers. Another reason for this, in addition to the delivery of lower-quality tomatoes to the local market, may be the time of delivery. After delivering to Hortifruti between 16:00 and 17:00, the truck that carries COOPROCOM production takes the rejected tomatoes to the Sebaco market, probably arriving there much later than other growers. Considering total production and sale of tomatoes of both cooperative and non-cooperative growers, both prices paid for the production and profitability show no significant difference in all the destination markets.

Rejections vary according to the tomato crop season. This could give rise to problems, since once the product is on the truck to be carried to the supermarket it is impossible to trace its source. Therefore, a grower who delivers lower-quality tomatoes could be affecting other growers with higher-quality tomatoes. This could result in a lack of incentive for growers who provide better-quality products and promote free riding.

Cooperative management receives the cheque from the supermarket and then pays each grower after discounting outstanding credits. This means there is an incentive for growers to sell to 'coyotes' in order to avoid reimbursing the debt or credit amount to the cooperative. Defaulting growers still get additional credits and no penalties are applied, which further encourages non-payment behavior.

Hortifruti pays on an eight days basis. However, the cooperative collects payment every 15 days to reduce the transportation expenses involved in sending the collector to Managua to pick up the cheque. Once the cheque has been received, the technician in charge of accounting discounts the corresponding debts. This results in growers complaining about late payments and creates an incentive for them to sell the tomatoes outside the agreement with Hortifruti, additionally encouraged by the fact that informal markets pay on the same day.

Programmes and projects should not only provide small- and medium-sized growers with access to dynamic markets and grants. They also need to refocus part of their policies to issues such as capacity building and human and social capital strengthening within organizations. This can help guarantee success after the growers have accessed demanding markets and will further foster the groups' sustainability.

Several incentives can result in failures to comply with marketing agreements. One way to offset them is by implementing adequate control mechanisms based on premiums and penalties applied by the cooperative, all of which requires a strong organizational structure. Another way is through market diversification, which leads to an increased negotiation power of the cooperative provided production volumes are enough to supply such markets. A third way is to implement an effective dispute resolution system among growers and buyers.

In addition to market diversification, the cooperative should diversify its production, so as to reduce technical and financial risks. PFID is aware of this and plans to increase the number of products to five.

Another relevant issue deals with the cooperative's high production costs, which lead to similar net incomes to those of producers that use other marketing channels, in spite of its higher gross income. So, what is the actual benefit from selling in more demanding markets? One is family income (60 per cent more than non-cooperative growers). Another is market security, although this is contradicted by the claims of cooperative growers, most of whom (60 per cent) said that selling their production at the wholesale market in the town was more secure. So, the answer to the question above is not self-evident. What is clear, however, is the major benefit that Hortifruti gets from buying from heavily subsidized cooperatives, a combination of quality assurance, secure supply, freshness and reduced costs or purchasing price.

What is also notable is a dynamic buyer like Hortifruti is willing to work with NGOs and small growers and do business with growers who lack market experience. In addition, Hortifruti has remained a firm buyer, even when the growers' performance level has not satisfied the agreements. As mentioned above, growers have faced disputes and non-compliance, but this did not result in losing the market share allocated by Hortifruti. Basically, the strength of the cooperative relies on its more than 40 per cent share of the Hortifruti market. Importantly, due to its inexperience, the cooperative seems to be unable to envisage the huge opportunities involved in selling to a high-volume buyer.

Tomato production was promoted not only as an ideal product for the purchaser, but also as a high-value added optional addition to other subsistence produce grown by these growers, as reported by NGOs. Consequently, although these growers are not getting the most attractive profits in the industrial tomato market, they are getting average returns on a very dynamic market with great growth potential, not only for tomatoes, but also for other products. This supports the ultimate goal of the project: improving the living conditions of its beneficiaries and reducing poverty and subsistence crops. The cooperative's Vice President is a clear example of success in terms of better living conditions. Before joining COOPROCOM, he had to migrate to Costa Rica as a temporary worker.

Local employment opportunities created by the cooperative are valuable. The crops and production require temporary labour, but work is full time in the stockpiling centres, in hauling and in growing seedlings.

Case study 4: Small-scale beef producers in Costa Rica

This is an example of a cooperative of 2200 members, some of whom are classified as 'small scale', that has been successful in becoming a preferred supplier to the main supermarket chain in the country. The story gives an insight into how small-scale producers can find a way into supermarkets through joining an organization. The study is about the relationship between Cooperativa Matadero Nacional de Montecillos – (COOPEMONTECILLOS R.L.; www.montecillos.com) and the Supercompro retail chain, both of Costa Rica.

BACKGROUND TO COOPEMONTECILLOS (CM)

CM began operating in 1964 as a cooperative of cattle breeders after the government published a law supporting the establishment and operation of the National Slaughterhouse of Montecillos. The cooperative was established under the National Production Council (CNP), a state-owned standalone institute for cattle breeders to manage the slaughterhouse facilities and to improve health measures in the handling of meat for human consumption at rural slaughterhouses or wholesale meat markets (where some butchers did their own slaughtering).

In the 1970s, CM began exporting meat processed from the members' cattle. Additionally, it manufactured sausages and bought a meat packaging plant in the area of Barranca, Costa Rica. As this growth was not supported by its own capital resources and a sound management, in 1977 the cooperative faced a financial and administrative crisis that almost ended in its bankruptcy. This gave rise to an alliance between cattle breeders and CM's workers, who were granted a loan for 7 million colons (US$15 660) by Banco Nacional de Costa Rica. One of the bank's requirements was workers' participation within the company. A new joint management model was established for the first time in Latin America. Since then, workers and cattle breeders have shared the company's ownership (22 per cent for workers and 78 per cent for cattle breeders), management and surpluses.

After the crisis, CM continued to diversify by exploring the leather business (1978) and the production of industrial gelatine. In the 1980s, it entered the fish, shellfish and poultry processing businesses. In 1995, the Barranca Division – CM's export slaughterhouse that had recorded significant losses – was sold to Fomento Ganadero S.A. (FOGASA), a company partially owned by CM and two other enterprises that were almost bankrupt, to export meat. This merger went bankrupt in 1999, causing significant losses to CM, which are still being settled (US$2.4 million of debt). In the second half of the 1990s, CM decided to refocus on the original business: the processing and marketing of meat and its by-products.

The cooperative and its members have been negatively affected by inadequate management (fund misappropriation) and political intervention in management positions.

CM TODAY

CM operates as a private company organized in a pyramidal structure led by a board of directors chosen by the members. It is owned by cattle breeders (78 per cent) and the plant's workers (22 per cent). The general management is in charge of managing different business units (slaughterhouse, meat centre, sausage, leather, soap, and Styrofoam). No specific requirements are needed to be part of the board of directors; nevertheless, according to a former chairman, currently all five board members are medium-sized cattle breeders and all have university degrees. Three of them are devoted to their farms on a full-time basis, and the remaining two on a part-time basis.

CM has about 2200 cattle breeders registered throughout the country and 570 workers. Seventy-one per cent of members have farms of less than 100 hectares, which is considered small. There are about 600 active cattle breeders. Some members no longer work in the field, others have shifted to breeding, and others have been discouraged, mainly due to the developments described above. This has led to the reduction of the services provided by the cooperative to the members, the failure to distribute the members' capital, which was previously distributed on an annual basis (about ten years ago, according to a cattle breeding member) and which is currently earmarked for the recapitalization of CM. According to some members, 'the cooperative began to think more like an industry than like a cattle breeder company.'

CM's objective today is the processing and marketing of meat (beef and pork) and its by-products, so currently the business consists of the slaughtering and marketing of beef and pork. The processing and marketing of sausage, leather, soap and Styrofoam, and the direct sale of meat through CM's meat centres.

CM has the second largest slaughterhouse in Costa Rica, carrying out about 28 per cent of local cattle slaughtering in 2003. On average, it has slaughtered 22 per cent of the national herd in the past eight years, meaning about 80 870 head/year. Members' cattle account for 25 per cent to 30 per cent of CM's slaughtering volume.

CM's marketing channels with the applicable per cent of the slaughterhouse's sales are as follows:

- Exports: 35%
- Traditional butcheries: 38.5%
- Own butcheries: 10%
- Supermarkets: 8.5%
- Sausage unit: 8%

The slaughterhouse's sales manager pointed out that there has been a business relationship with supermarkets since the establishment of the cooperative.

This relationship between supermarkets and CM features four aspects of interest: the sale of packaged beef cuts, carcasses, and processed products; inbound processing or slaughtering of supermarket's or specialized wholesaler's animals; CM butcheries within the supermarket; and competition, due to the strategic location of the CM butcheries (meat centres).

For meat sales, CM has three important customers. The most important customer is Supercompro, a 22-store supermarket chain in the Guanacaste region. The second most important customer is PriceSmart, a three-store chain in the metropolitan area. Sales to Supercompro began six or seven years ago, sales to PriceSmart about three years ago. The third customer is less important than these two, Auto Mercado, an eight-store chain targeted at higher income customers. There are also sales to small supermarkets that buy packaged beef cuts and serve medium-to-high-income consumers. The most demanding supermarkets in terms of quality standards and marketing conditions are PriceSmart, Supercompro and Auto Mercado, according to the Sales Manager.

For inbound processing or slaughtering of the supermarket or specialized wholesaler animals, CSU is the main supermarket chain in Costa Rica, accounting for about 70 per cent of supermarket sales. We saw in Case Study 1 how CSU used Hortifruti to provide specialist wholesale services for FFV. In meat and meat products, the equivalent specialist is called Industrias Cárnicas Integradas S.A. (ICI), a specialized wholesale subsidiary of the CSU group and responsible for supplying high-quality meat to all of its stores. ICI has been integrated vertically, so it is supplied by its own breeders and only uses inbound processing services from CM. The volume of beef required from CM by the CSU amounts to 30 cattle per week, of which 30 per cent are delivered as beef cuts and the remaining 70 per cent as carcasses. CM also supplies hamburger patties and pork to supermarkets. In terms of total production, CSU is not a major customer; most meat is sold outside the supermarkets – CSU takes 2 to 4 per cent of CM meat production. Another important client is Auto Mercado.

Partnerships are being established with small supermarkets located in strategic sectors and which have important sales volumes, the butcheries of which are managed by CM.

Meat centres are stores that were traditional butcheries in the past, but now use a new approach under a system that reduces product handling, with an emphasis on issues such as quality, health conditions, appearance and homogeneity. These centres are the most profitable marketing channels for CM. At present, there are three stores of this kind, and efforts are being made to increase this number and develop a system of franchises.

Here we focus on the meat sales to local supermarkets, specifically the relationship between CM and Supercompro, the most important chain for CM in terms of supermarket sales volume, and also the most demanding chain in terms of quality requirements and marketing conditions.

CM AND SUPERCOMPRO

Carcass quality standards required by Supercompro mean that the supermarket only buys bulls, so the dressed carcasses must include the testicles, have a maximum weight of 300 kg, and be free of solid wastes and fat. Each beef cut must meet certain quality parameters, such as low fat quantity, cleanness (free of solid wastes) and due appearance. The Ministry of Agriculture and Livestock (MAG) Inspector working at CM issues a certificate regarding safety standards. Hauling should be under cold conditions, which is monitored by each supermarket. Proper clothing should be used to handle products. All these quality and safety parameters were established by a veterinary surgeon hired by the supermarket

There is a non-exclusive business agreement in place between CM and the supermarket. However, due to frequent cattle quality problems previously experienced with other private companies, Supercompro decided seven years ago to be 100 per cent supplied through CM.

Products are delivered daily, with shipments scheduled by telephone on the previous day. CM is responsible for the hauling and distribution of orders to each store, covering the corresponding costs. Quality is controlled at each sales point by the butchery's manager, who has been previously trained on the standards established by the supermarket. Payments are made by the supermarket within eight days.

Supercompro offers promotions based on certain purchase amounts or on the purchase of any product as decided by the supermarket and sponsored by CM. According to the supermarket's Business Director, there are five benefits from buying from CM: secure supply; MAG's quality certificate; the plant's health standards; negotiation facilities; and compliance with required quality standards.

According to the slaughterhouse's Sales Manager, sales to supermarkets are a safe business, because of continuous supply needs. Supermarkets are also identified as the most demanding clients in terms of volume and consistency.

In general, CM could do with more supplies of cattle. One way is to improve the productivity of CM cooperative members on their farms. The amount of technical advice and help available to members has declined over the years and led to a lack of motivation among cattle producers.

Supermarkets like PriceSmart and Auto Mercado are more demanding than Supercompro and only buy from plants approved for exporting. This means that the slaughterhouse must meet the safety standards included in the Hazard Analysis and Critical Control Points (HACCP) system. Supercompro still requires a certification from MAG for the meat received.

Summing up, the cooperative and CM slaughterhouse make a major contribution to the incomes of small- and medium-sized cattle producers in Costa Rica. At present only a small proportion of meat sales go to supermarkets, but for supermarkets, CM is a major supplier. Consequently as supermarkets expand in Costa Rica, we expect CM to be able to fulfil the growing demand, either by attracting new members, or improving productivity, or, if all else fails, by switching sales from traditional to supermarket buyers.

A cooperative like CM can establish different types of relationships with supermarkets, and even become an important competitor in the meat sector.

CM's product sales to supermarkets are an important means to showcase the Montecillos trademark. This could become a major factor for the success of the new development strategy, Meat Centres, CM's current and medium-term target.

Compensation for quality and implementation of a carcass rating system with price differentiation is encouraging breeders to improve cattle quality, and therefore, production and handling technology.

CM obtains cattle based on supply and demand, and member cattle breeders show no special commitment. Consequently, further support and service to members is required, for example by increasing the number of services provided by CM, so as to foster member ownership, and, therefore, the amount of cattle delivered. On-farm promotion – through more frequent visits and technical assistance to breeders – should be emphasized so that breeders feel further committed to the Cooperative. Payment terms should certainly be shortened as they are an important incentive for breeders to deliver cattle to other slaughterhouses that pay cash.

Conclusions

The first case study shows how important a specialist wholesaler can be. Hortifruti Nicaragua has clearly helped small-scale producers to access the CSU supermarket chain. The second case study shows another aspect: how difficult it can be from the grower's point of view. The Guatemalan farmers who supplied manzano salad tomatoes to Hortifruti Nicaragua found themselves mostly out of their depth. The provision of technical advice was insufficient and the costs spiralled. The third case study demonstrates that simply providing smaller-scale growers with access to dynamic markets and grants is not enough; issues of capacity building and human and social capital strengthening within organizations are equally important to guarantee success, as is flexibility by the buyer while growers build their market experience. The fourth case study is a much more successful venture and shows how a well-run association of small-scale producers can gain access to a processor and thus onto supermarket shelves.

References

Berdegué, J., Balsevich, F., Flores, L. and Reardon, T.A., 2005. Central American supermarkets; Private standards of quality and safety in procurement of fresh fruits and vegetables. *Food Policy* 30(3), 254–69.

Berdegué, J.A., Reardon, T.A., Balsevich, F. and Flores, L., 2004. *Supermarkets and agrifood systems in Latin America: An overview.* Report to Regoverning Markets Project, September 2004. Available as pdf file: www.regoverningmarkets.org.

Muñoz, D., 2004. *Small Farmers' Economic Organisations and Public Policies: A Comparative Study.* London: IIED.

Reardon, T., Timmer, C.P., Barrett, C.B. and Berdegué, J., 2003. The rise of supermarkets in Africa, Asia, and Latin America. *American Journal of Agricultural Economics* 85(5), 1140–46.

3 *Ecuador*

Miguel Zamora

Introduction

Supermarket chains in Ecuador have increased their retail market share in the last six years and almost doubled the number of outlets (from around 85 in mid-1998 to some 160 in August 2004). Almost 55 per cent of the outlets of the three largest supermarket chains are located in the country's two largest cities (compared to 70 per cent five years ago). Some sources estimate the retail food market share of supermarkets in Ecuador at 40 per cent for 2002 and 35 per cent for 1999 (Alarcón, 2003; Blanco, 1999), while other sources estimate market share at only 25 per cent in 2003 and 20 per cent in 2000 (PlanetRetail, 2004). This growth occurred while Ecuador was going through a deep economic crisis (1999–2001). Sales in the modern grocery distribution sector increased 66 per cent between 1999 and 2003. However, the largest supermarket chains, Supermercados La Favorita (SLF) and Importadora El Rosado (IER), increased their total sales by more than 200 per cent during the same period.

SLF is the largest supermarket chain and we describe how this chain procures FFV. Two case studies look at potatoes and dairy products. Both are areas where small-scale producers have had some success in accessing the supermarket chains.

KEY DATA

	2002	2003	2004
Population (millions)	12.81	13.01	13.20
Per capita GDP (US$)	1898	2066	2222
Urbanization (%)	63		
Agriculture as % GDP			8.7
Per capita total food retail sales (US$)	404	442	473
Per capita modern food retail sales (US$)	145	155	167
Modern food retail as % total			35

TOP CHAINS, 2003

Company	Total sales (US$ millions)		Total market share (%)		Food sales (US$ millions)		Food market share (%)		Number of stores	
	1999	2003	1999	2003	1999	2003	1999	2003	1999	2003
La Favorita (SLF)	173	570	12.3	24.2	144	351	11.9	17.4	28	50 (2004: 66)
El Rosado	92	293	6.5	12.4	54	179	4.5	8.9	23	30
TIA	60	93	4.3	3.9	54	78	4.5	3.9	28	44
Santa Maria	N/A	20	N/A	0.8	N/A	17	N/A	0.8	4	6
El Conquistador	N/A	2	N/A	0.1	N/A	2.5	N/A	0.1	3	5
Exxon-Mobil	2	3	0.1	0.1	2	2	0.2	0.1	7	13
Santa Isabel	2	3	0.1	0.1	2	3	0.2	0.1	2	1
Others	1,076	1,375	76.6	58.3	956	1,385	78.9	68.7		

Source: PlanetRetail (www.planetretail.net); Alarcón, 2003; Blanco, 1999; Superintendencia de Compañías del Ecuador, 2004; personal communications with Jorge Hernandez and Sandro Sgaravatti.

All the top players are local firms, as Ecuador is too small and poor to interest foreign investment yet. Grocery stores have experienced a greater growth rate in the past five years than the other two types of outlets.

SLF is the largest supermarket chain in the country, owning two hypermarkets, 24 supermarkets (named Supermaxi), 21 discount stores (named Super Tiendas AKI) located in lower-income neighbourhoods and small cities, and 13 toy stores. SLF has more than 3000 stockholders, which distinguishes it from the rest of the Ecuador supermarket chains that are primarily owned and run by family or business groups (Mi Comisariato, Santa María, TIA, Santa Isabel). SLF's major stockholder is the Wright family, founder of the supermarket chain in 1950. The SLF Group also has other companies that supply its supermarkets with a variety of food products (eggs, meat, and milk for instance), although most of their products are purchased from external suppliers.

SLF has traditionally catered for middle- and upper-class consumers, but this perception has changed in recent years as a result of the popularity of its new outlet format (AKI), the opening of new stores in lower-income neighbourhoods and lower prices. SLF is one of the largest companies in the country, the seventh largest in terms of tax revenue for 2002 and third in sales in 1999. SLF recorded sales near US$350 million in 2001 and US$478 million in 2002 (38 million in profits in 2002, or near 8 per cent of total sales), with total sales amounting to US$570 million in 2003 (a 6 per cent net profit margin). SLF is Ecuador's largest non-financial company in terms of sales and one of the two largest companies. SLF was listed in the América Economía magazine's top 500 most efficient companies in Latin America in 2003. An estimated 24 million customers annually shop at SLF stores, in a country with only 12 million inhabitants.

IER is the second largest supermarket chain with a mixed bag of 25 stores including hypermarkets, supermarkets (named Mi Comisariato), toy stores and hardware stores. Tiendas Industriales Asociadas (TIA) has sales totalling about a third of IER's. It operates around 50 stores, including superstores (Super Tia), supermarkets and neighbourhood stores (Tia) and discount stores (Multiahorro). The company is not much focused on fresh produce, such as fruit, vegetables and milk. TIA is oriented to middle- and lower-income groups. The company operates 50 stores in 34 towns and cities and 13 provinces of the country. About 40 000 customers shop at TIA daily in its three types of outlets. Other chains include Mega Santa Maria and El Conquistador.

Supermarket chains in Ecuador are expanding with outlets oriented to lower-income consumers and smaller cities. For example, SFL's greatest growth has been through its Tiendas AKI outlets targeting low-income consumers in various cities. TIA has continued to grow its presence throughout the country with seven stores opening in the past nine months, mostly in cities other than the two largest, Quito and Guayaquil.

SLF and IER offer discounts to customers who purchase supermarket membership cards (the yearly card price is US$ 44.80 for SLF and US$ 50 for IER). Discounts range from near 5 per cent at SLF to slightly over 7 per cent at IER (discounts vary according to the type of product purchased).

Besides the usual local distributors and manufacturers of food products there are a few foreign fast food restaurants such as Kentucky Fried Chicken and suppliers of fast food ingredients such as Frito Lay.

In the case of milk, processing plants supply supermarkets. Nestlé, Toni, Parmalat, Pasteurizadora Quito and Rey Leche are the major milk processing companies in the country and the ones with the greatest market share for milk in supermarkets. Their market share is estimated at 70 per cent of the total milk supplied to supermarkets.

Evolution of procurement: SLF and FFV

SLF had 2500 suppliers of FFV in 2002, but this had narrowed to only 240 FFV suppliers by the end of 2003. Nevertheless, SLF's FFV purchases increased from US$120 000, or 350 metric tons per day, to US$150 000, or 400 metric tons per day, during the same period – a 15 per cent volume increase and 25 per cent increase in value in one year. Since SLF is Ecuador's dominant supermarket chain, it is likely that the other chains will copy the changes SLF has made to its procurement system.

For more than 25 years, SLF has used a centralized procurement system, with its main warehouses located in Quito. This centralization has allowed SLF to obtain consistent quality and a standardized variety of products for all of its stores, invest in process automation and reduce storage costs (storage cost per square metre at warehouses is considerably lower than in stores, especially in malls). Suppliers also get benefits by delivering their products to a single site rather than to different stores in the country. Its new distribution centre is one of the most sophisticated in the Andean region, with 100 000 m² available for its various outlets.

Case study 1: Potato procurement

Middlemen obtain potatoes from small-scale farmers by purchasing produce directly from farms. A small percentage of farmers sell non-harvested potatoes to be harvested by these merchants. There are six or seven actors in the potato supply chain in Ecuador. The number of actors depends on the site where potatoes are produced and finally sold. In total there are an estimated 2000 potato traders in Ecuador and over 400 wholesalers.

Some wholesalers purchase potatoes from several middlemen and distribute the product to different markets throughout the country. There are other large wholesalers, especially in the wholesale market in Quito, who also gather great volumes of potatoes and distribute them to smaller wholesalers in open markets. The producers, or in some cases local traders who buy from small-scale producers, deliver their product on consignment to wholesalers. The wholesalers check the product, generally taking one to three sacks per vehicle. These potatoes have not been washed and price is established according to the above-mentioned quality standards. The samples of the different suppliers are laid on the floor at the beginning of the marketing period.

Medium- and large-scale producers arrive at Quito Wholesale Market with their truckloads of potatoes (trucks with some 240 100-pound sacks) where the greatest volumes of potatoes are sold in the country (around 50 per cent to 70 per cent of the total production is currently sold at this market, against 80 per cent five years ago, according to one source). There are about 90 traders registered at the Quito Wholesale Market who purchase potatoes (50 to 70 per cent of the total domestic production is traded there). However, retailers believe the volume of potatoes going through this market has decreased, due to the increased sales at the Ambato Wholesale Market and directly to Guayaquil. Once potatoes have been sold, the wholesaler takes a portion of the price, maybe a fixed amount (50 cents/quintal) or an amount relative to the selling price.

The free trade agreement and the Free Trade Area of the Americas (FTAA) will increase the volume of potatoes from Colombia, already entering Ecuador as contraband.

Supermarkets, potato chip producers and fast food chains have increased their share in the potato chain and have become the largest buyers of this product in the country. Nevertheless, their share in the total potato chain is still relatively small (less than 10 per cent). Supermarkets purchase potatoes from dedicated distributors and these in turn purchase their produce from small-, medium- and large-scale farmers and wholesale markets. Potato chip producers and fast food chains purchase their potatoes from large-scale farmers. Some of these farmers are selling their produce to SLF under direct contracts. These contracts usually include price conditions under which suppliers get profits once their production costs have been covered (that is, 30 per cent on costs).

The increased share of supermarkets, potato chip manufacturers and fast food chains in the potato retail sector can be seen as a shock to the system currently in place. This shock brings about institutional changes of various kinds – private, more demanding grades and standards, new formal or informal 'contracts' or agreements that entail specific volumes of a product with certain features at a specific time. There are also changes in logistics needed to switch from markets to depots. Finally, there is the distinction between being a 'preferred supplier' and not.

These changes create high barriers to entry that eliminate most small farmers from even applying to join the supermarket and fast food processing supply chains. In a few cases, local authorities are encouraging farmers to form groups and negotiate acceptance as a single preferred supplier. For instance, the government of the province of Tungurahua has been active in this way. A group of small-scale producers are negotiating with Frito-Lay to supply potatoes. The group is also negotiating with restaurants, and producers and processors of chicken broilers in the province, in an attempt to sell potatoes directly to them. Here the idea is to help provide the main ingredients (chicken and potatoes) for processed food products.

In the case of potatoes, potato chip and fast food chains also require certain specific varieties that are better for processing (some of these varieties are already grown in Ecuador on larger farms). In order to enter this market it is also necessary to manage crops differently, through the use of irrigation systems, technical assistance, changes in post-harvest management, and so on, and the use of certified seeds in many cases. Plainly this is a major challenge for small-scale producers.

Supermarkets purchase potatoes from wholesalers who are dedicated suppliers (with a certain degree of dedication). These firms in turn buy potatoes from small-, medium- and large-scale producers as well as wholesale markets. SLF is continuously trying to establish a potato procurement system made up of a limited number of specialized and dedicated suppliers. SLF buys about 15 500 kg of potatoes daily and is the largest individual buyer in Ecuador, although its purchases total only 2 per cent of the country's total potato production. Nevertheless, SLF has increased the volume of potatoes purchased (14 000 kg/day a year ago) and this amount is expected to grow further in the future as long as its share in the retail market continues to grow. SLF has implemented a *Feria de las Legumbres* (vegetable fair), where fresh vegetables are sold at a 20 per cent discount in all its Supermaxi stores on Wednesdays. Wednesday was the day when Supermaxi stores used to record the lowest total rate of sales, but they have picked up and Wednesday now records the highest rate of sales for this chain.

SLF has rigourous standards in terms of general appearance, shape, mechanical damage, phytosanitary features, texture, cleanliness, size, colour, ripeness degree, temperature and packaging. These grades and standards are verified when the product arrives at the distribution centre. Failure to comply leads to rejection and can result in an end to business relations with the supplier.

There are also standards for buyers on traditional wholesale markets in terms of variety, size, colour and damage to potatoes. Failure to meet these standards results in price reductions. In traditional markets, standards are not formal or very demanding, and depend largely on the buyer's opinion. Public potato grades have been in force since 1987, but nobody, including the authorities, takes much notice of them.

SLF is now moving to buying from suppliers who can meet even higher grades and standards, such as the use of certified seeds, irrigation systems, comprehensive farm management, farms with technical assistance and farmers in different geographic locations to grow potatoes. Designated suppliers will also be visited and inspected by SLF. This means that SLF will no longer purchase potatoes from all their current suppliers, but from large-scale farmers (over 50 hectares) who own land in different geographic areas and use their own technical groups. These suppliers sell most of their produce almost exclusively to fast food chains or supermarkets with a residual volume sold through wholesalers. Some of these large-scale growers have direct contracts with potato chip producers and fast food chains to produce specific volumes and varieties of potatoes in a given time and quality.

Clearly, a lack of organization is the main hurdle facing small-scale potato producers. We consider Ayllucunapac below, one of the few small-scale potato producer associations that sells to supermarkets and fast food chains. Some NGOs (for example, REDCAPAPA) have played a key role in helping these producers organize themselves.

REDCAPAPA

The Strategic Network for the Development of the Potato Food Chain (REDCAPAPA) is an NGO that tries to unite Ecuador's potato food chain stakeholders and ensure a fair and efficient potato supply chain. REDCAPAPA is sponsored by the First Zone Chamber of Agriculture, the International Potato Centre and the Andean Potato Project for the development of its operations. In this section, our sources are several interviews conducted by us with senior managers.

REDCAPAPA is primarily aimed at strengthening the potato food chain through the establishment of alliances, agreements and contracts that foster innovation, the creation of associations, improvement of services, quality of supplies and the development of agribusiness supporting systems. In particular, REDCAPAPA designs actions to promote and strengthen potato farmer associations, especially for small-scale producers.

REDCAPAPA has helped establish new food retailing circuits with producers in the communities of Licto and Pungalá in Chimborazo, and also with Frito-Lay. REDCAPAPA also works together with the Ayllucunapac group to gain access to other markets for their produce.

AYLLUCUNAPAC

Ayllucunapac is an indigenous association of some 500 small-scale farmers in the Guamote, Chimborazo region. Assisted by REDCAPAPA, they got together successfully, obtained a bar code, and contacted SLF, who agreed to buy 180 quintals (8 metric tons) of potatoes.

The group ran into problems, however, as the quality of their potatoes did not meet SLF standards (due to the spread of the potato white worm in the region). The group is now supplying potatoes to community groups in low-income urban sectors in Quito (almost 9 metric tons delivered to nearly 2500 families) that are purchasing their produce directly from wholesalers. The group is working on improving the overall quality of their produce in order to increase its added value (packaging) and sell to retail markets and industrial plants.

César Hurtado is a potato producer who has been in the industry for several years. He has sold his produce through direct contracts with Frito-Lay and Kentucky Fried Chicken, and will be soon selling to SLF. According to one source, the quality standards among these groups are quite similar, though SLF does not require specific features for frying potatoes as the industry does.

The number of potato sellers for these markets has fallen during the last decade, as many of them did not comply with the quality standards required. The number of Frito-Lay suppliers has dropped from 30 in 1995 to 10 in 2000, and is now about six, and 10 to 15 for Kentucky Fried Chicken.

Case study 2: Milk and cheese procurement

The scope for small-scale producers looks greater in milk than our conclusion as regards potatoes. Milk is important to small-scale producers in Ecuador. Around 46 per cent of the country's total milk production comes from small-scale dairy farms (smaller than 20 hectares in size), accounting for 76 per cent of cattle farms in Ecuador. Nearly 75 per cent of the total milk is produced in small- and middle-size dairy farms (less than 100 hectares in size), while the remaining 25 per cent comes from the 4 per cent of farms larger than 100 hectares in size.

Milk is utilized in several ways. A quarter is consumed on farms and 20 per cent is sold as liquid milk. Of the 55 per cent processed, 25 per cent is made into cheese in rural areas; the rest is processed in large factories.

A major problem for small-scale dairy farmers is their lack of cold storage. Group investment is an obvious strategy and small farmers should perhaps lobby government to help them achieve this. However, it is the country's large-scale dairy farmers who have joined associations with enough political power to demand policies that protect domestic production (in particular related to high tariffs). Such large farms plainly have no interest in lobbying for refrigeration plants to aid small-scale farmers.

Three agents in the milk supply chain are interesting examples of how small-scale farmers in Ecuador access processors and, either through them or directly, retail outlets. We look at each in turn. The piqueros offer a market but not a viable way of accessing supermarkets. Floralp shows how large farms have the advantage of organized milk marketing not open to small producers. Nestlé illustrates how a processor can help small farms.

PIQUEROS

Most small farmers sell to a wholesaler called a *piquero*, who transports milk to sell to processors. Naturally, prices paid to farmers by the piquero for milk are low. Smaller producers have very few options available for selling their milk. They are basically located in the inter-Andean region of Ecuador and in remote areas with limited access. They usually only have a couple of cows and the only money-making activity is milk production. Piqueros buy milk at low prices and try to sell it to processing plants or nearby depots. They have no cold storage facilities, but the region's natural climate helps conserve the products. When this milk is sold to processing plants, a price penalty is usually applied to lower-quality milk.

FLORALP

A main buyer of milk on behalf of processors is Floralp. This company pays farmers a price that reflects: (1) base price for basic quality parameters (e.g fat, protein, temperature and somatic cell count); (2) price paid for specific quality standards (the same features as for base price, but with more demanding standards); and (3) extra bonus for presence or absence of growth retardants.

Floralp does not purchase milk from piqueros but directly from producers who have previously refrigerated it. The company Floralp receives milk from 60 to 80 large, medium- and small-scale producers.

Floralp representatives regularly visit suppliers to settle any quality and farm management problems (reproduction, production, fodder, and so on). If milk quality problems persist among these suppliers in spite of the technical recommendations, they are given a three-month period to solve them, after which they are removed from Floralp's list of suppliers.

NESTLÉ

Nestlé is the largest milk processing company in Ecuador, estimated at 300 000 litres of milk processed per day. Other important milk processors are Parmalat, Pasteurizadora Quito, Indulac and Toni. Although there are milk processing plants in the country with larger installed capacity, they have a much lower scale of plant space occupancy. Several of the major dairy processing companies (Toni, Nestlé) have also increased their total sales to supermarkets. These companies demand higher quality milk from their suppliers than is sold at traditional markets.

Nestlé has made an effort to buy milk from small-scale farmers. The company has more than 2500 suppliers and 80 per cent of them deliver less than 100 litres/day. Nestlé collects the milk at distances of up to 400 km from their plants. It also has depots with cold storage tanks and several refrigerated trucks to collect the milk.

Nestlé suppliers must deliver a constant volume, no matter the amount (it purchases from as little as 5 litres). It also provides training programmes for dairy farmers who supply it with milk and offers credit to build stables, buy milking equipment, establish grazing areas, supplies, and so on. It has also funded the construction of local side roads in several rural areas in order to have better access to its suppliers. This is an example of how a group of small-scale producers can become part of a modern supply chain.

SALINAS CHEESE FACTORY

There are several other groups of small-scale farmers in Ecuador that supply dairy products to supermarkets. The Salinas Group, for example, is an association of farmers producing and selling processed cheese and other dairy products to supermarkets and other retail stores. Its sales to supermarkets are growing steadily.

The Salinas Group is an organization that has been operating for about 25 years, sponsored by an SDC (Swiss Agency for Cooperation and Development) project. It is currently made up of 60 peasant organizations (cooperatives or associations) in seven provinces in the Andean region. Each peasant organization has a small dairy processing plant, with cheese as the main product. They daily process near 30 000 litres of milk for the group (with the capacity to process an additional 20 000 litres, but this volume is sold externally) and produce almost 3000 kg of cheese per day (traditional and hard cheeses). This group not only sells dairy products but also other food products such as mushrooms and cold cuts of meat.

The group sells its products at points of sale and through a total of 15 agents in several cities throughout the country. However, most of the cheese produced (60 per cent) is sold at supermarkets and other smaller retail outlets. The volume sold at supermarkets is steadily growing.

SLF's purchases of Salinas Group products have grown, albeit reducing the variety of products requested (SLF focuses on products with the highest returns and turnover). As part of its stock restructuring plans for perishable dairy products, SLF has increased its purchases of certain types of Salinas Group cheeses and eliminated other products, with a decline from 16 products three years ago to eight now. The criterion used by SLF is the product turnover and return. The set of products sold to SLF is less varied but greater in volume than that sold to other supermarket chains such as IER and Santa María. Products are delivered to the main warehouses in the case of IER and SLF, whereas for Santa María they are delivered to each individual store. Payment is generally 30 days after delivery. The sales agreements with these chains are usually on a verbal basis. From time to time, SLF conducts laboratory tests on Salinas Group products, and visits their plants every six months.

Other developments also provide optimism for the place of small dairy farmers in modern supply chains in Ecuador. Farmer associations, such as the mountain and eastern region farmer association (AGSO), have milk processing plants and milk depots open also for small- and medium-scale producers. This association has a depot in Cayambe that receives milk from nearly 100 producers. The association is making efforts to have its small-scale farmer membership increased.

PRIVATE AND PUBLIC POLICIES

Supermarket chains in Ecuador use their lists of preferred suppliers as their first (or only) source of products. Groups of organized farmers, with assistance from NGOs, have reached agreements to supply chains like SLF. There are different features for products and processes that are currently in place or will soon be required by supermarkets in the procurement of products.

SLF and IER have lists of preferred, unique suppliers for the purchase of potatoes. Standards required are high, too high for small-scale farmers, and these standards are getting more restrictive. Smaller supermarket chains such as TIA, Santa María and Santa Isabel also have lists of suppliers, but they are less rigorous when it comes to purchases. To become a supplier of these large supermarket chains, suppliers must be registered at the taxation office and provide information on personal and business residency, on volumes of production/sales and on the source of the products sold. SLF has a short list of suppliers of perishable products.

Only 2 per cent of farms smaller than 5 hectares in size have any real access to funding from public sources. Moreover, the technical assistance offered by the Ministry of Agriculture has lately almost disappeared. The government has established high tariffs to protect the dairy and potato sectors, but inefficient control at borders facilitates smuggling. Some local governments are working with NGOs in an attempt to find alternatives for small-scale farmers.

Public standards are taken as minimum approval points for milk. The private sector in Ecuador is implementing – and effectively controlling – its own higher standards of quality, which benefits the final milk consumer. We note above that Floralp and Nestlé do this already. However, more generally, there is little government control of milk quality at processing plants since only annual, and not very strict, inspections are conducted in these companies, especially during election periods! There are suspicions of corruption, because inspections are usually ill-intentioned and easy to avoid.

Conclusions

Both potato and milk producers interviewed stated that the most important change to potato and milk sales in recent years has been due to the increased contraband from Colombia and Peru. Dollarization has increased production costs in Ecuador in comparison to neighbouring countries. This, together with the lax border controls, has meant that large amounts of potatoes and milk are entering the country, and this has closed off access to markets for Ecuadorian producers.

The likely signing of free trade agreements with the USA and other countries in the Andean region and the MERCOSUR countries is another matter of concern to these producers. Farmers, representatives of producers and experts interviewed are all concerned that milk and potatoes will not be excluded from these free trade agreements. They believe that given the sensitivity of these products (a large number of small-scale farms are solely dedicated to them and are also direct sources of employment for hundreds of thousands) and the high costs of production that the dollarization has caused, these products should be excluded from these agreements. There is concern, however, that the negotiating teams representing them in these negotiations do not have the necessary human capital to negotiate effectively and ensure that the agreements benefit these productive sectors.

The only way to ensure the inclusion of small-scale farmers in this growing supermarket sector is to work closely with retail chains. It is encouraging to see SLF's willingness to communicate and cooperate. The interest, knowledge, and contact with experts also contribute to this communication and the search for solutions. The work done by numerous NGOs, associations and groups of organized farmers in the form of the Salinas Group is an example of what can be accomplished.

The strengthening of human capital and organizational structures may well attract financial capital to invest in and supply the most demanding buyers. There seem to be a number of ways of achieving this.

AGSO is trying to implement a credit programme for its members to buy cold storage tanks. Almost 26 000 medium- or large-scale farmers are taking part in training or funding programmes. One aim is to create a network of depots and cold storage tanks to improve the quality of the product and the conditions for members to sell their products. A challenge is to allow groups of small farmers to access the network.

Finally, there is a push factor encouraging small-scale producers to join associations for potatoes and milk. Wholesale markets are in decline and no longer offer producers a satisfactory outlet. This push, along with the pull of the modern food system, provides an environment for small-scale producers to rise to the challenge.

References

Alarcón, A., 2003. *Ecuador retail food sector report 2003*. USDA Foreign Agricultural Service: Gain Report. Quito, Ecuador. Available: www.fas.usda.gov/GainFiles/200304/145885404.pdf.

Blanco, E., 1999. *Ecuador retail food sector 1999*. USDA Foreign Agricultural Service: Gain Report (edited by Susana Sánchez). Available: www.fas.usda.gov/GainFiles/199911/25546317.pdf.

PlanetRetail, 2004. *Ecuador's retailer profiles*. Available: www.planetretail.net.

Superintendencia de Compañías del Ecuador, 2004. *Las 100 compañías más grandes*. Available: www.supercias.gov.ec.

4 *Thailand*

Aree Wiboonponse and Songsak Sriboonchitta
with a contribution from Dave Boselie and Petra van de Kop

Introduction

Thailand has experienced rapid growth in hypermarkets and supermarkets in recent years. This rapid growth stems largely from government policy measures that relaxed controls on foreign direct investment after the economic crisis in 1997. With the low price of land that prevailed after the economic crisis, large businesses were able to expand their branches at lower investment cost.

As a result, there are many new opportunities and challenges for small-scale producers. We focus on this in the chapter in our review of several case studies of individual suppliers. Their stories offer insights into the diversity of factors that help small-scale producers succeed in becoming suppliers to modern food chains.

Thailand has a strong agricultural sector and a number of important agricultural exports, both commodities and processed products, and a wide range of food products can be sourced from small-scale producers. Tourism is also important, bringing with it new demands for food.

Two thirds of food continues to be marketed through traditional channels such as local wholesalers and transporters, small shops, wetmarkets, street hawkers and small restaurants. While important in the agri-food economy, we do not look at this sector in the chapter.

KEY DATA

	2002	2003	2004
Population (millions)	62.19	62.82	63.46
GDP per capita (US$)	2029	2214	2429
Urbanization (%)	31.6		
Agriculture as % GDP			9
Per capita total food retail sales (US$)	420	459	499
Per capita modern food retail sales (US$)	152	162	177
Modern food retail as % total			36

Exchange rate (1 January 2006): 1 US Dollar = 41.03 Thai baht

TOP CHAINS, 2004

Company	Ownership	Number of stores	Retail banner sales 2004 (US$ millions)	Market share (%)	Grocery sales 2004 (US$ millions)	Grocery market share (%)
Tesco	Joint venture	107	1864	8.5	1310	7.3
Central Group	Local	324	1831	8.3	597	3.3
CP Seven Eleven	Local	2,861	1380	6.3	739	4.1
Casino	Joint venture	44	1327	6.0	761	4.2
SHV Makro	Joint venture	29	1148	5.2	895	5.0
Carrefour	Foreign	20	555	3.9		
Other			14 408	65.6	13 644	76.0

Source: PlanetRetail (www.planetretail.net)

The share of food sold through the modern retail system amounts to about 35 per cent of the total food retail sales.

Hypermarkets have emerged as the major format in Thailand's retail sector. The number of these stores reached 100 in 2002, almost double the number in 2000. They are extremely competitive in terms of margins and prices when compared with smaller supermarkets. All companies have their own brands offered at cheaper prices. As an added strategy for customer retention, hypermarkets and supermarkets provide membership, loyalty and credit cards. Hypermarkets have been the format preferred by most of the foreign grocers that have entered the market over the last decade.

Tesco currently operates the largest network, having more than doubled its store numbers in the past five years. Tesco's closest competitor is the Casino-owned Big C chain. The other major hypermarket operator in Thailand is Carrefour, which is now planning to break out of Bangkok and establish stores elsewhere in the country. However, the majority of hypermarkets still tend to be concentrated in Bangkok and its vicinities. Because Thais treat shopping at a hypermarket as a sort of leisure activity, many hypermarkets, especially those housed within shopping centres, have provided built-in entertainment to encourage shoppers. All companies claim that they provide their customers with safe food products.

With the combined attraction of wide product ranges, low prices and impressive store environments, hypermarkets are increasingly inching out traditional wetmarkets, 'mom and pop' stores and smaller supermarkets.

The enduring popularity of wetmarkets lies in their strong fresh food offering, which many modern retail operators have attempted to replicate by providing the feel and product range of the wetmarkets in their stores.

Superstores are also popular and, like hypermarkets, are almost exclusively the domain of foreign retailers. Ahold's TOPS network has been the most significant, although the Dutch retailer sold the chain to its local partner, the Central Group in March 2004, completing the group's withdrawal from Asia. The other major superstore operator is Siam Jusco, a subsidiary of Japan's AEON. However, as a result of increasing competition from hypermarkets and the high investment involved in opening a new superstore, the company has reduced the number of stores to seven, from a peak of 14 superstores, and now plans to concentrate its resources on supermarket operations.

Supermarket development in Thailand has been hampered by the dominating influence of the hypermarkets and has seemingly reached a saturation point at a 500 store level. As a result, there are only a handful of supermarket chains, the most important of which has been the Delhaize's Food Lion network, with a focus on fresh produce with the aim of creating stores that resemble 'shopping at a wet market near home.' Delhaize withdrew from the market in September 2004, selling stores to Central Food Retail Company.

There are some Thai-owned supermarket chains that were able to carve out a presence in the foreign-dominated retail sector, namely the Bangkok-based Foodland, Villa Market, Home Fresh Mart and Tang Hua Seng.

Multinational chains have moved towards smaller types of stores such as convenience formats jointly with gasoline stations. The presence of discount stores in the market is not yet very noticeable. However, this may soon change with Casino's launching of the Leader Price soft discount format in March 2002. By the end of 2005, Casino is hoping to have a network of around 50 Leader Price stores in operation.

With competition among the hypermarkets intensifying, convenience stores are seen as an important growth format for the future. Almost all of the major operators have ambitious expansion plans that will see their chains proliferate in most of the major urban areas. There are approximately 3600 convenience stores in Thailand at present.

The 7-Eleven chain, operated by CP Seven Eleven under franchise from Ito-Yokado, is by far the largest and is geared towards rapid expansion. A relatively new entrant into the convenience store sector is Tesco, which is pushing ahead with a number of trial Express stores located at both Esso petrol forecourts and standalone stores in more crowded neighbourhoods across the country.

'Mom and pop' grocery stores have long been traditional features of Thai groceries. Compared with supermarkets, they operate at lower cost but without trained managers, leading to lower efficiency. While 'mom and pop' owners adopt a traditional management style, convenience stores like 7-Eleven use modern supply-chain management techniques. Because of a lack of efficient logistics management and poorer facilities, prices in 'mom and pop' stores have become uncompetitive. 'Mom and pop' stores acquire supplies from various sources – not only secondary and tertiary wholesalers, but also supermarkets such as Cash & Carry. Table 4.1 shows the results of a sample survey of 'mom and pop' stores (multiple answers were allowed).

Table 4.1   Sources of supply to 'mom and pop' stores

Sources of supply	Percentage of 'mom and pop' stores using this source
Wholesalers	77
Producers	49
Supermarket chains:	
Makro	43
Tesco Lotus	40
Big C	20
TOPS	11
Other supermarkets	4

Source: ABAC and Krungthep Thurakit, 2002

The extent of foreign domination of modern retailing and the impact of hypermarkets, supermarkets and especially convenience stores on the survival of 'mom and pop' stores became a controversial issue in 2000, which led to zoning regulations that took effect in 2003. The regulations, which apply to all provinces outside Bangkok, limit large stores, defined as having at least 1000 square meters of retail space, to locations at least 15 km from an urban centre. In addition, each store must be at least 500 metres away from an intersection. Operators must also reserve 30 per cent of their sites for green areas. Large retailers seeking to establish outlets require the approval of a 21-member provincial town planning sub-committee.

As a result Tesco, Casino and Carrefour rushed into all areas of Thailand, especially the north, in order to secure sites before the draft regulations became effective. These regulations also stimulated the diversification into convenience store formats such as Tesco Express.

In March 2005, the Commerce Minister stated that the government intends to revise its zoning policy for superstores, cutting the required distance from city centres to 5 km, down from 15 kilometres. PlanetRetail report that 'It is understood that the move may have resulted from lobbying by French chains such as Carrefour and Casino's Big C, who have said they were put at a disadvantage against other retailers, such as Tesco Lotus, that built outlets in municipal areas prior to zoning law changes' (PlanetRetail, n.d.).

The fact that the market share of modern trade is expected to increase at about 9 per cent per annum has alarmed local businesses and provincial Chambers of Commerce who want to prevent the opening of new branches of modern retailers in their provinces.

Some sources argue that the competition among modern trading chains has had a great impact on the traditional stores, reducing their profits and at the same time benefiting consumers. A survey conducted in nine provinces in 2002 revealed that 68 per cent of retail stores faced a decline in total sales while 49 per cent of local stores reported their clients switched to 7-eleven and Tesco Lotus, Casino's Big C and Carrefour. The Seven-Eleven chain was blamed for the collapse of a large number of local grocery stores. Half of the surveyed stores had adjusted their strategies to survive.

The most important customer-retention strategy is to improve the poor service provision (56 per cent), which is considered as the most undesirable factor and the one pushing customers away from traditional retailers in the past. Solutions identified include improvements to store layout, a better selection of goods to satisfy demand, clearer price labelling, product quality enhancement, lower prices and improved inventory management. Some stores have also introduced home delivery services.

To protect local retailing business, retailers suggested that the government support the sector by reducing taxes on small and medium-sized enterprises (SMEs), limiting the expansion of foreign joint venture retailing branches, providing loans to small businesses, setting price floors and limiting the opening hours of discount/hypermarkets. However, it seems to us that controlling foreign supermarket chain expansion will not help traditional stores. On the contrary, it will only increase the economic rent earned by existing supermarkets and their large-scale suppliers.

An initiative undertaken by the Ministry of Commerce to help traditional stores handle competition from modern chain stores (supermarkets and convenience) was the formation of Allied Retail Trade (ART) in 2002 with over 100 000 members. The company plans to create an ART house brand for small- and medium-scale enterprises' products and develop franchise member stores, currently numbering 14 000. One of the main mandates of ART is to support traditional grocery stores both at local and national level in the face of growing competition. The government has provided ART with a loan of 395 million baht. The company's plan is to become a private organization and repay the loan within three years. ART stores have the format and appearance of a modern convenience store.

PROBLEMS FOR SMALL-SCALE PRODUCERS

Consolidation of chains and increasing size of stores and depots favours large- rather than small-scale suppliers. This is likely to be a growing problem in Thailand for the small farmer and processor. As local chains get absorbed by bigger ones, so they may lose their supply chain partnerships unless they can increase the volume of sales and match rising quality standards. The introduction of the TOPS distribution centre has accelerated this process (we deal with TOPS in Case Study 5 below).

Although the modern chain is said to be accessible to new suppliers, a new vendor always finds it difficult to make an initial contract with modern stores, whether hypermarket, supermarket or discount stores. While a typical procedure set by any modern chain is a standard process, it is still more straightforward for a small-scale supplier to deal with Thai or local supermarkets. A standard process usually starts with a supplier approaching the headquarters with samples. When the headquarters finds that the products are in demand and conform with the company's specification, then the supplier is asked to submit sample products for quality inspection.

The third and fourth steps involve price negotiation. The supplier must make a price offer for the given quality and specification of products, which depends strongly on the cost of obtaining supply. However, price setting is competitive since there are other suppliers.

Usually, prices can be negotiated. Suppliers can ask to maintain the price offer when their goods are of relatively better quality and when they have incurred higher costs than their competitors. Discount stores like Big C, however, always search for the lowest price in order to secure their discount price policy. The contract will be signed when price agreements are reached. However, none of our interviewed vendors have a copy of their contracts. Only the stores hold the contract document. Local vendors who cannot supply large volumes for all branches of a given chain can contract via a local branch.

Once a vendor is contracted, their products are shipped to the buyers' distribution centre(s) for quality and specification inspection. The inspection is done randomly in most cases. The vendor is responsible for shipping back any rejected product. For the accepted products, the distribution centres distribute to various branches as planned and scheduled. The financial division takes over from here to prepare an invoice, of which payment will be done in 15–60 days. However, the terms of payment are also negotiable.

The basic criteria for selecting a vendor for any modern store are similar and are as follows: (1) be reliable in terms of time and frequency of deliveries; (2) offer a commercial volume of specified quality; (3) provide traceability of products; and (4) make a satisfactory offer price.

These criteria imply that vendors supplying to hypermarkets are medium- to large-scale. However, local vendors supplying to only a few branches are also accepted by all discount stores, hypermarkets and supermarkets. This is partly because of social pressure; foreign stores need to show their concern and demonstrate that they are pulling their weight as part of the local community. Thus, local taxes paid by Big C are publicized as a social benefit. Tesco Lotus displays its sensitivity through the promotion of local suppliers.

Two 'high-end' supermarkets have begun to procure directly from farmer groups (Paopongsakorn, 2004). However, the number of these farmers is small though increasing. In October 2004, TOPS announced a policy of direct procurement from small growers. In the north, the Royal Project foundation and large private firms are major local vendors for all modern trade chains for high-quality chemical residue-free (CRF) products.

One of the vendors revealed that all the modern retailers he contracts with carry out inspections of his produce, checking the appearance or external physical quality based on the experiences of experts. A fresh food department representative of one of the modern retailers said that his staff are skilled and able to judge the taste of a fruit from its appearance, although they still strictly adhere to the specification list for each product. Almost 95 per cent of products carried by TOPS are certified either by Public Health (Food and Drug certification) or by the Ministry of Agriculture.

Since new sources of supply usually carry inherent risks, modern retailers inspect products more carefully. Besides conformity to specifications, new and differentiated products are likely to receive higher scrutiny.

Modern retailers strictly adhere to the conditions and stipulations in the contract and enforce penalties when suppliers cannot deliver products accordingly. The details of contract terms and conditions are not disclosed. However, all store managers interviewed revealed that terms and conditions vary on a case-by-case basis depending on how much the buyers want the products. An example is good quality rice: retailers pay favourable terms for high volumes.

ENTRANCE FEES AND CAPITAL REQUIREMENTS

Some hypermarkets demand that vendors pay entrance fees, offer the buyer price reductions for special sales and events, pay advertising fees and special product display fees. The stores also sell their own brand products next to similar brand-name products from vendors. Both Tesco and Carrefour were found guilty in 2002 of breaching the 1999 Trade Competition Act, which forbids these practices. Some companies require vendors to pay additional fees per product when the chain opens a new branch, costing up to 10 000 baht per item per new branch. These fees are a big obstacle for small farmers wanting to participate directly in supplying produce to a supermarket.

The degree of flexibility in supplying Thai-owned stores varies from company to company and place to place, and a vendor needs to consider which is best suited to his scale of operation. Villa Market and Foodland Supermarkets, the Thai-owned supermarket chains, as well as the Thai–Japanese joint venture UFM Fuji Super in Bangkok offer premium quality product to high-income consumers. One of the new vendors found it difficult to supply fresh produce to these chain stores, as the produce accepted must be only of premium grade. Each of these chains presents its own problems for suppliers.

The Villa Market operates a consignment system, where the retail price is set at 100–150 per cent of the price paid to the vendor for mangoes. However, the store can reduce the price after each delivery if the store so decides and also vendors are expected to take part in promotion programmes to introduce their product. The vendor finds this risky and costly since the logistics costs in Bangkok are high and he has to bear the risk of the return of unsold products. On the other hand, the store serves a lot of customers, which can absorb a large-scale supplier's volume.

As for the Foodland Supermarket, superior quality is the store's comparative advantage. The company emphasizes quality, such that inspection is conducted carefully for both external physical specifications and internal factors such as sweetness. While some vendors may find that it is most difficult to meet the specifications of Foodland, this is offset by the added prestige of having products sold there.

Suppliers to UFM Fuji face a different problem. The firm offers good prices to vendors but, we were told, provides the most difficulty in collecting payment.

For Thai stores, personal contact and relationships are particularly important. There was a case where a foreign chain store accepted a particular product from a cooperative, partly because of the collaboration required of the store in response to the local government agency's request.

Rice and fresh vegetables are the selected commodities for this research, as both are produced by a large number of small farmers. Even though Thailand is the largest rice exporter in the world, over 60 per cent of production is still consumed domestically. The value of rice sold in the modern retail system is estimated to be 10 000 million baht. This makes the retail market for rice highly active and competitive with over 100 brands available in the market.

The shelf allotment for vegetables has been increasing rapidly in hypermarkets and supermarkets in recent years, although the value of sales has not been revealed.

Consumers are paying more attention to food safety in fresh fruit and vegetables than in rice. The reasons cited for this are health concerns and a realization of the environmental dangers of chemical use. Consumers place confidence in the store rather than quality certification from government agencies or brand names. TOPS and Foodland fully implemented strategies to gain consumer confidence with regard to 'safety and freshness'.

As more and more consumers are becoming health conscious, producers are moving towards CRF (also known as 'safe' or 'hygienic') vegetables (in which the products are supposed to contain pesticide residues lower than the maximum level set by Codex) and towards organic production practices. Apparently, the prices of safe vegetables are attractive in most retail outlets, with the price difference between safe and conventionally grown vegetables said to be more than three-fold, even for common vegetables such as cabbage or water spinach.

Case study 1: Vegetable supplier

Mr Thee, a professional vegetable supplier in Chiang Mai, is an assembler of CRF vegetables. He organizes 40 members in a district who grow temperate vegetables such as head lettuce, cos lettuce, Chinese cabbage, Japanese cucumber, and Japanese pumpkin. Mr Thee delivers his produce to three buyers in Bangkok, two of whom are companies and one an independent businessman. These buyers are all suppliers to TOPS and Tesco Lotus, while one of them also exports fresh produce.

In order to obtain CRF vegetables, Mr Thee conducts a residue test 20 days prior to harvesting. He has designed a sampling method for his growers to collect vegetables and bring them to the collection centre. If residues are found, the test will be repeated in the following week and the harvest is postponed. To prevent growers from delivering non-member's vegetables, Mr Thee must visit growers' plots before harvesting. This way he can estimate production and observe chemical applications. Mr Thee is responsible for quality inspection, grading, dressing and packaging.

The three buyers in Bangkok do not provide Mr Thee with exact product standards or grades except for head lettuce, which should weigh at least 300 grams per head. He grades vegetables by inspecting physical appearance based on his experience, which is well accepted by the buyers. After grading, vegetables are kept in cold storage owned by the Agricultural District Officer. The storage period is normally one day and not longer than three days.

The contract between Mr Thee and Bangkok suppliers is verbal, without the benefit of any document. They do business based on mutual trust. Payments are made seven to 15 days after delivery. Prior to delivery, Mr Thee must send information on quantity, price and quality of vegetables. His pricing is cost plus four to five baht per kilogram. The cost includes the local price of the vegetable and the handling cost. However, there are times when the purchase price is pushed down as a result of the prevailing market price.

A supplier like Mr Thee must be responsible to his grower members in terms of finance, production and price problems as well as late payments. He has to pay his members promptly. The upstream part of the supply chain is a modified form of contract farming. The process started with calling for members, providing technical training (supported by government agencies), planning production schedules, selecting and controlling chemical usage, and selecting vegetables and varieties to meet market demand. Mr Thee in turn is contracted by the three buyers in Bangkok. From past experience, he finds it advantageous to trade with these companies, as the market is assured and his revenue is reasonably certain.

Capital investment in this business is derived from three sources. The first is a long-term loan (five years) of 800 000 baht from the Bank of Agriculture and Agricultural Cooperatives (BAAC) at a low interest rate of 12 per cent per year. The second source is a small short-term credit from the Residue-Free Vegetable Fund. The third is his own investment in equipment and tools. Mr Thee provides his members with farm manure and has installed sprinklers. The costs of input supplies are deducted from gross revenue without charging for interest.

Case Study 2: Vegetable grower – supplier

Mr Nik is a vegetable grower and the chairman of In-Net-Vegetable Growers' group (INVG) at Sarapee District of Chiang Mai Province. Sarapee has long been known for year-round production of commercial vegetables such as kale, cabbage, beans and broccoli. Seventy-two members of the group from eight villages cultivate about 2 hectares and together produce 45 kg per day.

As the chairman, Mr Nik is responsible for production planning to meet expected market demand, as well as carrying out marketing tasks. The group members deliver vegetables to Mr Nik at the price of 3 baht per 300 g bag. In this regard, he actually acts as buyer for the members' produce.

The produce is delivered to two Rim Ping Supermarket stores (a local supermarket aiming for a high income and targeting expatriate customers) at the price of 10 baht per bag. The supermarket deducts 25 per cent from total sale value. In this supermarket, suppliers must take care of product shelving and display. The other outlets are shops in two wetmarkets and the MCC shop operated by the Faculty of Agriculture at Chiang Mai University, which opens daily to sell safe, or hygienic, products.

Vegetables are inspected and tested for residues. The Rim Ping Supermarket visits farmers' fields each year and the produce is checked for freshness and cleanliness. The purchasing manager of Rim Ping pays particular attention to the quality control of products from any new suppliers. The fruit is inspected piece by piece and this leads to high rates of rejection. To guarantee freshness, Rim Ping will discard unsold vegetables daily. Thus, a supplier like Mr Nik must carefully determine the right quantity to deliver each day to avoid losses.

There is no specification or product standard, only grading. The produce is dressed and packed in a clear plastic bag. The labels on the bags are granted by the Department of Agricultural

Extension (DAE) and a product can be traced through the written code of each member. The members must be responsible when produce is found to be contaminated with chemical residues. However, no penalty is imposed apart from a revenue reduction on the next delivery.

Mr Nik did supply produce to Makro but his contract was terminated because he could not deliver the pre-agreed quantity. Consequently, he was fined. He has been supplying to Rim Ping for more than 15 years now without any written contract.

Since the Rim Ping purchasing system is by consignment, Mr Nik must absorb the risk and therefore tries his best on the product display as well as the amount supplied each day. The two advantages of selling in the supermarkets are that the produce is in air-conditioned rooms and kept fresh for the whole day, and the certainty of a market because of the large number of customers that visit these stores.

Payment is made every 45 days, which is a very long period of time. Surprisingly, Mr Nik has charged the same price per bag for the last 15 years: 10 baht per bag. His profit then varies from season to season because of the amount of production and supply. The earnings in the hot and the cold seasons are 15 000 and 10 000 baht per month, respectively. As a vegetable grower, Mr Nik revealed that his production cost totals 10 830 baht.

Members of the INVG group pay no membership fee, but each pays 120 baht for a share. This is used as a start-up fund and operating capital for the group. The most important role of this fund is to provide loans for those who need credit for purchase of inputs. The group obtained a 70 000 baht loan from BAAC at an interest rate of 7 per cent – a rate lower than that charged to Mr Thee.

The group also received substantial financial aid from the Sub-district Administration Office with 500 000 baht. This money was allocated to members for constructing protective net houses to reduce pest pressure. Mr Nik took charge of the allocation of the fund. The INVG group members invested in water pumps and tube irrigation. In order to cultivate safe, or hygienic, produce, the growers employ net houses and yellow sticky traps to trap insects instead of using insecticide. The INVG group is one of the few farmers' groups that successfully employ farm record-keeping.

Case study 3: Vegetable grower – wholesaler

Mr Boon was a vegetable grower just like the rest of his family. In 2000, he found vegetable prices to be unfavourable and faced difficulty in marketing his own and his members' vegetables at a price higher than prevailing market prices, which were too low. He successfully approached the Auchan supermarket chain and supplied the hypermarket with plastic bag-packaged vegetables. The store inspected the quality and freshness of vegetables and specified the quantity (0.5 kg per bag). The bag had to have the label of the DoA. Later, Mr Boon used his own brand 'Sarapee Fresh Vegetables' instead.

Auchan withdrew from Thailand in 2001, selling its Chiang Mai superstore to Casino's Big C. Mr Boon has since discontinued his production and collection from the group's members, instead relying on vendors in Chiang Mai who buy vegetables from the wholesale markets. However, the vegetables must be good enough to meet Big C (formerly Auchan) requirements. The minimum amount delivered to the hypermarket is 40 kg per day of various kinds of common vegetables. Auchan and now Big C acquire products through a purchasing system rather than consignment. However, the store reserves the right to reject poor-quality supplies. There was no entrance fee charged but the store charges 1 per cent of sales value. The payment was made every seven days by Auchan and is made every 15 days by Big C. Mr Boon offers prices to Big C based on market price plus his desired profit margin.

Besides Big C, Mr Boon also consigns with Rim Ping supermarket. He conforms to Rim Ping's system in the same way as Mr Nik (see Case Study 2 above), but he is charged 28 per cent of the total sales value. He delivers the vegetables to Big C at 08:00 and to Rim Ping at 09:00. In cases where he has a large supply, the third outlet is a shop at a wetmarket near Chiang Mai University, one of the shops Mr Nik supplies as well. This particular shop charges 30 per cent of total sales value to all suppliers with the unsold produce returned to suppliers.

With regard to food safety, Mr Boon's supply is not tested for residues, as either it is not his concern or he has great confidence in his suppliers. However, it is commonly believed that vegetables from wholesale markets are not up to safety standards. The price the middle agents charge is usually market price plus 1–2 baht per kilogram.

Mr Boon terminated his business with TOPS. According to him, he received orders for 2 to 3 kg for each item, which is not cost-efficient to manage. However, as mentioned earlier, the TOPS branding strategy has focused on food safety as well as freshness, and Mr Boon's supply seems unable to meet the standards required.

In fact, another supplier of vegetables guaranteed as safe, or hygienic, also faces the same problem. As a full-time vendor, he also seeks to contract with Carrefour and Tesco Lotus. But he found the terms of contract (including the type of consignment system used by Carrefour) unattractive. As for Tesco, it is difficult for him to contact the headquarters in Bangkok. Obviously these reasons reflect obstacles for small farmers in dealing directly with foreign modern hypermarkets or discount stores.

Case study 4: Producer organization supplying rice

This case illustrates the possibility for a small miller of participating in a modern trading system. Marketing rice to hypermarkets or discount stores seems to be only for large millers and trading companies because of the bulk needed and the size of business. Most existing products are sold in modern stores under national brand names. Only one or two local brands are available in each of the large chain stores. However, there are exceptions and it is the policy of both Big C and Carrefour to support local producers and purchase local brands.

Mr Witt is the leader of the Thirteenth Farmers' Group of the San Kamphaeng Cooperative. The group includes 50 members who produce field crops, fruits and paddy rice. The leader also owned a small rice mill in 1966, which by 1994 had grown into a medium-sized business. He then stopped growing rice, and milling became his main business. The members of the Thirteenth Farmers' Group have their paddy milled there. During the period 1978–94, Mr Witt sold milled rice in sacks (100 kg) and by the litre for retailing, as commonly practised by all millers. In 1994, he observed that rice sold in small quantities (5 kg packages) was becoming popular. The national brands such as Maboon Krong rice were sold at the Agricultural Fair at Airport Plaza in Chiang Mai and later were made available in the supermarkets there.

Mr Witt and his group then supplied bagged rice to the supermarkets at Airport Plaza (currently a TOPS supermarket) for three years. The group quit because the store changed to bar coding and it would have entailed high costs to the group to comply. The second supermarket that the group marketing committee contracted was the Rim Ping supermarket. Rim Ping bought rice in bags from the group with payment 20 days later. The store's mark-up was 25 per cent of the price paid to the group. The group decided to terminate the sale to this store because of defaults on payment.

The Carrefour purchase manager contacted the group in 2001. Here, suppliers must pay 4000–5000 baht as entrance fees for each product line. The group sold two items to Carrefour: 5 per cent jasmine rice and white rice. The contract was later terminated because the stores lowered the price paid.

At Auchan and later on Big C, the Purchase Manager approached the group on the recommendation of the Chiang Mai Chamber of Commerce. The provincial agency assisted the group's entrance at the initial stage. When Big C took over business from Auchan, the group's contract was automatically transferred to Big C and no entrance fee was charged.

However, there are several fees a supplier has to conform with: (1) entrance fee of 5000 baht (in 2000) and 10 000 baht in 2003 for any new item; (2) an annual rebate at the rate of 3 per cent of total sales value; (3) an annual fee of 10 000 baht, and (4) 10 000 baht per item when the company opens a new branch (this is subject to the company's policy that a supplier should supply his products to all branches).

Currently, the group supplies Big C with all of its requirements of jasmine rice and jasmine brown rice plus 10 per cent of its white rice. The minimum quantity per delivery is 100 bags. The group is required to deliver any amount ordered directly to each of the other two branches in Chiang Rai and Lamphang provinces. This often becomes uneconomical and leads to losses for the group. The group also has to replace any bags found defective or infested with bugs. The products are inspected regularly.

Payment is made every 60 days. The price margins that the store sets differ from item to item depending on the rate of turnover and the prevailing prices both in Bangkok and the local (rice mill) markets.

According to Mr Witt, the group found that selling to hypermarkets is an effective way to promote the brand because there is no other local brand in Big C. It brings more customers to the group, particularly institutional ones such as hospitals and offices in the industrial estate in Lamphun. A disadvantage of selling to Big C is that the producer group makes a very small margin and sometimes incurs losses due to transportation costs and the new branch fee.

This finding is consistent with the finding that suppliers in general complain that their margins are extremely low, lower than other wholesaling alternatives (Paopongsakorn, 2004). But they still do business with hypermarkets for two reasons: (1) to maintain a high volume of business; and (2) hypermarkets always pay promptly.

The group expressed the view that it is difficult to enter TOPS and Tesco Lotus because these two stores have contracts with the large businesses such as CP Seven Eleven. The group finds it hard to compete with these businesses in terms of store space.

Case study 5: Supplying 'TOPS' supermarkets

This case describes how a leading international supermarket developed a domestic sourcing strategy for fresh produce through the creation of infrastructure (a value added distribution centre) and a preferred supplier programme. Although the programme was not specifically designed for small producers, the category was included through two types of organizational strategy: contract farming and newly informal grower associations.

In 1996, Royal Ahold established a joint venture with the Thai Central Retail Corporation and started to operate more than 30 TOPS supermarkets, most of which were located in

Bangkok and Chiangmai. From the start, TOPS positioned itself as the supermarket chain for quality fresh food.

In 1998, TOPS began a supply chain project aimed at providing Thai consumers with high-quality, safe, fresh produce with reliable availability at affordable prices. To achieve that goal, however, the supply chain faced a number of problems. For example, roughly 250 suppliers were delivering perishables directly to the back doors of 35 stores at least three times a week. This meant high handling costs, significant post-harvest and shrinkage losses and low service levels (meaning that produce was often out of stock).

TOPS enlisted public sector assistance and started the project with four objectives:

- raising the level of service within the perishables supply chain
- reducing lead times and post-harvest losses and shrinkage
- improving quality and safety of produce by developing preferred supplier relationships and introducing good agricultural practices and a certification scheme
- raising the knowledge and awareness of employees and professionals in the local food industry through on-the-job training (for example, in HACCP) and a mini-MBA (master of business administration) programme.

The TOPS supply chain focused on delegating value added activities and selecting preferred suppliers. Since at the start of the project none of the fresh goods suppliers performed the value added functions required (for example, sorting, washing, packaging), the project decided to build a new distribution centre that would also perform productive functions like quality control, washing, packaging and processing. This value added centre was a complete green-field operation located on the edge of Bangkok. The centre served as the locus for the project's work to improve supply chain performance for perishables. A number of noteworthy results were achieved:

- establishment of the fresh distribution centre in Bangkok
- reduction of the number of suppliers from 250 to 60, with 40 out of the 60 certified by the DoA and carrying the DoA label in 2001
- provision of training for quality control managers at the TOPS distribution centre and in the stores, with the service level increasing to 98 per cent
- development of a 'road map' (or in other words, a practical blueprint) to achieve trusted third-party certification for food safety assurance in emerging fresh markets
- reduction of the lead time from farm-to-fork from 68 hours to less than 24 hours
- reduction of post-harvest and shrinkage losses
- during the chain optimization process, the introduction of standardized crates, pallets and crate washing facilities. Most major players in the Thai retail industry (including leading suppliers) accepted the TOPS standard.

Small producers were involved in the TOPS supplier network in two ways: (1) via the network of contract farmers and buyers who became preferred suppliers because of their ability to exert backwards control on the supply chain; and (2) via a new phenomenon of informal farmers' associations. In these associations, professional growers within a family or village joined forces and exchanged experiences and farming knowledge. These groups seemed to meet all the preconditions for developing into fully-fledged growers' associations and engaging in long-term direct business relationships with retailers.

Although one of the goals of the preferred supplier programme was to reduce the total number of suppliers, it was not specifically targeting small producers as such. On the contrary, those small producers who could deliver volumes, consistent supplies and quality via contract farming schemes or new associations, were included in the sourcing portfolio of the supermarket. Those producer/suppliers who could not develop value-added activities and meet the above supply criteria were excluded from further deliveries.

Between 1998 and 2002, the emphasis of the supply chain development strategy gradually changed from chain optimization (reducing post-harvest losses, shrinkage, handling costs) to integral chain care (HACCP, good agricultural practices, certification). Chain partners established cross-border public–private alliances with international research institutes and ministries of agriculture to find ways to increase food safety assurance and improve certification, as well as to strengthen research and education capacity about and within the food chain.

The project became affiliated with the DoA's certification programme to increase public awareness and gain trust and to build the image of a reliable and responsible retailer. Chain leadership was in the hands of the retailer, the supermarket, which prioritized the interventions and set the pace for the process of change.

The main challenges the project encountered were intercultural barriers. For example, the preferred supplier programme ran up against the traditional Thai system of personal networks in agricultural trade. Buyers and suppliers customarily maintain personal relationships to create stability and continuity in trade, despite the fact that this is not always economically efficient. Consequently, there has been some resistance to the optimization of the supplier network. After Royal Ahold withdrew from the joint venture at the end of 2003 and disposed of its TOPS chain to its Thai partner CRC, the TOPS category managers for fresh produce started reverting from the new preferred supplier model to the traditional personalized buyer-seller relationships.

The TOPS case illustrates that: (1) globalization and the consolidation of the international supermarket industry brings integrated supply chain principles and concepts to all corners of the globe; the creation of value-added centres and new preferred supplier relationships are part of this development; (2) although at a disadvantaged position with regard to economies of scale, small producers can continue to be included in this segment by organizing themselves into specialized grower associations and focusing on labour-intensive crops and production methods, such as organic vegetables; (3) old habits and structures between buyers and suppliers are resistant to change; newly established preferred supplier models are vulnerable to old personal ties that deal with monitoring and compliance mechanisms in an alternative way.

The critical reader might remark that the supplier reduction from 250 to 60 is a clear indication of an ongoing process of exclusion of certain categories of producer/suppliers. However, there were various reasons for farmers/suppliers to exit the relationship with domestic supermarket chains. A small proportion moved upwards to the export markets (a few TOPS suppliers became suppliers of the Ahold subsidiary in the Netherlands). Another category started supplying competing supermarkets and others switched to traditional wetmarkets or terminated their business.

Conclusions

Hypermarkets have emerged as the major format in Thailand even though the sector is highly competitive in terms of price and margin. Modern retail business (hypermarkets, supermarkets and convenience stores) has had a significant and adverse effect on the traditional 'mom and pop' grocery business. This became a controversial issue, which led to zoning regulations imposed on large retail businesses.

Foreign retailing businesses have brought in capital, know-how and efficient retailing management, and these have lowered prices to consumers and also created employment. While these benefits are of value, there is a need to counterbalance the market power of foreign investors to protect local businesses. In the same light, there is an urgent need for local businesses to make some adjustments, build their capacities and equip themselves for the sake of their business and to benefit consumers, who should be the real beneficiaries of a competitive market.

On the demand side, Thai customers have responded very positively to hypermarkets and supermarkets and been encouraged, partly through stores' promotion programmes, to prefer the modern shopping style. With the growth of income, small family size, changing preferences and health concerns, Thai consumers have increased their purchase of small packaged rice and safe, or hygienic, vegetables from modern stores.

Consumers found it difficult to buy safe produce at the time and place of their convenience. They questioned why safe produce demands such a high price when the costs of chemicals have already been excluded. Evidently, both conventional and safe produce appear side by side in the modern stores despite the stores' professed safe food policy. The differences of both types of products are notable at retail as well as farm levels. However, the differences are insufficient to cover the extra cost of labour, especially in case of new farms growing chemical-free vegetables.

It seems clear that the marketing system should be studied in depth to provide consumers as well as retailers with information on the supply side. This is confirmed by the discussion at the national consultation meeting. Only price, which accurately reflects quality, can encourage small producers to continue growing safe produce and supplying it to the modern stores. Otherwise, the benefits of joining modern supply chains will only accrue to large-scale vendors and the chains.

To enter the modern supply chain, a supplier needs to have substantial capital, for two main purposes: (1) to pay for the entrance fee, stores' new branch fee and promotion costs such as advertising; (2) to maintain sufficient working capital because credit terms are 15 days for vegetables and 60 days for rice. Small vegetable grower groups do not find 15 days credit terms a major constraint in participating in the modern chain because they have other outlets for their products.

They agree with the store managers that they are lacking in management skills to overcome problems in meeting stores' requirements such as delivery of required quality and quantity on schedule. Skill in logistic management and production planning are seen as just as important as negotiation ability. Local government offices have not been involved in alleviating this problem. As for small-scale producers, the opportunity of participation is currently almost nil. Small producers of high-quality products are better advised to seek to supply local or Thai speciality stores rather than discount stores, hypermarkets and supermarkets.

To be optimistic, one may expect that high-quality rice and vegetables will be increasingly distributed abroad through the multinational companies' chain distribution systems, since they have selected Thailand as a procurement hub. There should be benefits to small producers as long as fair trade marketing is guaranteed by companies and/or supervised by government authorities.

After the controversial issue of modern retail's adverse effect on traditional retail stores, the Ministry of Commerce initiated ART in 2002 (see above). ART stores are expected to operate efficiently in serving the community and to compete with modern convenience stores. As such, an ART should also carry community food products and employ a strategy similar to that adopted by existing suppliers of 'Lemon Farm', sold at Bangjak gasoline stations.

To enhance small- and medium-scale producers' direct participation in the supply chain of modern retailing stores, the following policies are recommended:

1. The top priority is to encourage companies' management to contribute a small fraction to the development of the producers' business in network production-marketing in cooperation with government agencies.
2. Supermarket chains are urged to do away with their entrance fees (a fee paid for becoming a new supplier, typically 10 000 baht per product when a new store is opened). These are already illegal.
3. The payment period to suppliers should be shortened to 15 days.
4. The practice of purchasing fresh produce such as vegetables on a consignment basis should be reviewed, as it is unfair and not helping small producers/suppliers.
5. Supermarkets should help small suppliers with advice on logistics management and provide access to credit for new suppliers.
6. Organizations of farmers need technical assistance in terms of logistic management, production planning and sanitary certification. Vegetable producers should form a group to work as a network for efficient technology transfer. Logistic management for rice production needs to be improved.
7. Supermarkets require a minimum volume (for example, 40 kg of vegetables or 100 bags of rice per delivery). However, some stores order small, uneconomical amounts. Their suppliers are penalized when they fail to meet the volume requirement, yet the stores can do the same with impunity. Thus, there is a one-sidedness and not fair business practice.
8. Turning to public policy, the government should use the anti-trust law to prevent the use of monopolistic power. In this respect, the market share of a company should be calculated as the sum of the company's total value earned from all formats in which the company operates in the whole retailing system (that is, hypermarkets, supermarkets or convenience stores).
9. The existing services on sanitary certification should be extended to small-scale suppliers at a reduced cost.

References

ABAC and Krungthep Thurakit, 2002. Newspaper survey.

Boselie, D., and Van de Kop, P., 2004. *Institutional and organisational change in agri-food systems in developing and transitional countries: Identifying opportunities for small producers.* Regoverning Markets, Global Issue Paper. Available: www.regoverningmarkets.org.

Boselie, D., Henson, S. and Weatherspoon, D., 2003. Supermarket procurement practices in developing countries: Redefining the roles of the public and private sectors. *American Journal of Agricultural Economics* 85(5), 1155–61.

Paopongsakorn, N., 2004. *Impact of hypermarket on the suppliers of fresh produce.* Workshop on the Growth of Supermarkets as Retailers of Fresh Produce, 4–7 October 2004, Kuala Lumpur, Malaysia.

PlanetRetail, n.d. Thailand country report. Available: www.planetretail.net.

5 Philippines

Larry N. Digal and Sylvia B. Concepcion

Introduction

There have been notable changes in the Philippine retail food industry. The number of supermarkets has been increasing, including those that are owned by foreign investors, albeit more slowly than in other Asian countries. Moreover, there are increasing opportunities in private label products. Also, the share of supermarkets of total food sales has been expanding, including fresh produce.

KEY DATA

	2002	2003	2004
Population (millions)	78.58	80.02	81.45
Per capital GDP (US$)	990	997	1013
Urbanization (%)	60.2		
Agriculture as % GDP			14.8
Per capita total food retail sales (US$)	285	286	288
Modern food retail sales (US$)	87	86	87
Modern food retail sales as % total			36

Exchange rate (1 January 2006): 1 US Dollar = 53.14 Philippine peso

TOP CHAINS, 2004

Company	Ownership	Number of stores	Retail banner sales 2004 (US$ millions)	Market share (%)	Grocery sales 2004 (US$ millions)	Grocery market share (%)
SM Group	Local	161	1 013	11.3	471	6.2
Mercury Drug	Local	500	829	9.3	580	7.7
Robinsons	Local	192	511	5.7	126	1.7
Rustan	Local	165	401	4.5	208	2.8
SHV Makro	Joint venture	12	304	3.4	243	3.2
Sub Total		1030	3 058	34.2	1 629	21.6
Other			5 888	65.8	5 923	78.4

Source: PlanetRetail (www.planetretail.net)

Supermarkets are not widespread yet and the chains that have emerged so far are small by international standards. The market is still quite fragmented. The top five retailers have a combined market share of just over 27 per cent. Mercury Drug, SM Group, Rustan and the warehouse club Uniwide are the largest domestic players, all held by local family-controlled conglomerates.

Both Rustan and SM Group operate a variety of retail formats, while Uniwide is recovering from a period of poor sales, heavy debts and uncertainty regarding its future. Mercury Drug dominates the drugstore sector and is probably the best known retail brand in the country.

Foreign chains that meet government criteria have been allowed to invest in the Philippines since 2000. One interesting criterion is that the foreign chain must source at least 30 per cent of products from local suppliers. Now that retailing has been deregulated, more foreign chains are expected. Wal-Mart, Casino, Carrefour and Tesco have all shown an interest in the Philippines.

The foreign presence is small and dominated by the SHV Makro cash-and-carry operator (a joint venture with Ayala Land, Inc. and SM Investments), and 7-Eleven convenience stores (majority license ownership by the Taiwanese President Chain Store Corp). The US warehouse club PriceSmart pulled out in 2005. However, it seems likely that the list of leading retailers will change markedly in the coming years as the possibility of major foreign firms entering the market becomes a reality.

Case study 1: Supermarkets and fresh vegetables

Supermarkets have become increasingly aware of their need to upgrade the quality of the vegetables that are on their retail shelves. In turn, they try to demand these specifications from their suppliers. Farmers have been eased out from supplying directly to supermarkets because of the long credit terms that they have. In the Philippines, only a few supermarkets like the NCCC of Davao City are willing to pay their suppliers within the week.

Most supermarkets pay their suppliers of vegetables in 15 to 30 days. Farmers are not able to wait this long for their payment since many of them are very poor and rely only on their farm for income. Vegetables are also considered by the DoA as cash crops. Farmers are supposed to be able to get their short-term needs from these cash crops.

Many of the temperate vegetables recently demanded by consumers, such as romaine lettuce and broccoli, are vegetables that the Filipino farmers are not familiar with. Since they do not consume these temperate vegetables themselves, these crops do not add to the diet of the family. In fact, in interviews with farmers, they have asked the interviewer which part of the broccoli is eaten. It seems that the buyers that deal with farmers have not also taken the time to inform the farmer of the attributes of the product they are producing.

Varying types of arrangements for suppliers of supermarkets have emerged in the last five years. The first is outright purchase from suppliers. The merchandizing activities on this type of arrangement all rest with the supermarket. The supermarket has very high control over the placement and packaging of vegetables. Shrinkage and product spoilage are borne by the supermarket.

The second type of arrangement is full consignment, where the supermarket leases out the space to a vegetable supplier. The lessee takes care of the product selection, packaging, stocking, display and all other merchandizing activities. Most supermarkets give guidelines for operation to the supplier. For the SM chain of supermarkets, all the concessionaires have to pay a royalty on sales to the SM Management, as well as paying for the space used. The supplier bears the burden of risk of shrinkage and spoilage.

The third type of arrangement is modified consignment. The supermarket leases out the space to vegetable suppliers but also has some degree of control over the types of vegetables, the volume and the prices. The supermarket decides on most of the merchandizing strategies but the supplier is completely responsible for sourcing, stacking and packaging the vegetables. The supplier bears the risk of shrinkage and spoilage but the supermarket helps in the monitoring of sales.

Traditional marketing channels differ substantially from supermarket supply chains. With regard to product flows and exchange levels, supermarket supply chains are shorter and more condensed and involve direct delivery to centralized distribution centres in contrast to traditional multilevel and fragmented marketing systems. This has resulted in a streamlined supply chain.

In the northern part of the Philippines, Benguet Farmer's Federation, Inc. is one of the leading organizations in vegetable production and the Benguet Farmers Multipurpose Cooperative is one of the organizations trading vegetables.

In the southern Philippines, the Northern Mindanao Vegetable Producers' Association (NorMin Veggies) has collectivized efforts so that it can sell directly to retailers in Manila. In addition to the accessibility to ports and the more sophisticated cold chain facility, NorMin Veggies has a more aggressive and informed leadership that has gathered and organized the member-farmers into production and marketing clusters and managed to get the production schedule of the varying members coordinated based on the market demand. Post-harvest activities have also been coordinated to optimize volume, transport and post-harvest expenses. NorMin have managed to market their products as an association of growers in Metro Manila. Their clients include fast food restaurants like Wendy's.

The Vegetable Industry Council of Southern Mindanao (VICSMIN) has followed suit and it appears that its aim is to gather together small producers based on locality, regardless of the variety of their fresh produce, because of their common environment (infrastructure, public support and market systems and work cultural habits.) VICSMIN failed in an attempt to market its own vegetables two years ago because the association was not registered, as required by law, to sell vegetables. VICSMIN has been registered as a non-profit, non-stock association. It has recently renewed plans to do its own marketing by organizing a corporation with the legal authority to engage in business.

THREAT FROM IMPORTED VEGETABLES

Imported vegetables pose a new threat to Philippine vegetable growers (Macabasco, 2004), with imports having increased sevenfold between 1996 and 2002. This is mainly due to the reduction of tariff rates and the changing market dynamics of the vegetable supply chain. Imported vegetables are said to be cheaper by 30–50 per cent compared to some of the local produce. They are better packaged and generally of better quality. These attributes make them more attractive to the to the institutional markets and the supermarkets who cater for the high-end consumer markets.

LINKS WITH UPSTREAM AGENTS

In 2002, a survey of small-scale vegetable farmer households in Kapatagan, Davao del Sur was conducted by the University of the Philippines in Mindanao under a grant from the Australian Centre for International Agricultural Research. One of the findings was that out of the 207 vegetable farmers surveyed, 134 (65 per cent) grade their vegetables before selling. Grading appears to be more important in vegetables such as potatoes, tomatoes, carrots and cabbage. Actual data on the price received by the farmers particularly for cabbage, carrots, potatoes and tomatoes show a substantial difference in prices between graded and ungraded vegetables (Digal and Hualda, 2003, ACIAR, 2004) .

Farmers define quality according to the physical and biological characteristics of the vegetable such as weight, size, shape, colour, pest/mechanical and physical damage/defects, mechanical injury, cleanliness, freshness and firmness, while market intermediaries define quality not only in the attributes described by the farmers but most especially in terms of timely delivery and consistent supply (Concepcion and Montiflor, 2003). The optimum maturity of the vegetable, a result of timely harvesting, is important to the farmer but not to the market intermediary.

The use of refrigerated trucks in transporting vegetables is becoming wide spread. Local government has tried to help small-scale producers in various ways, providing refrigerated trucks, cold store buildings, and air-blast chillers. There are also support organizations such as the Small Business Guarantee and Finance Corporation, Quedan and Rural Credit Guarantee Corporation, Development Bank of the Philippines, and Land Bank Organizations that will extend financial support for small- to medium-scale farmers and agri-food entrepreneurs.

The industry, with the encouragement of the DoA, also frequently holds congresses and symposia to discuss and assess problems and issues. Policy recommendations are often presented to the DoA for their consideration. In the meantime, farmers' groups continue to consolidate in the hope of empowering farmers.

All through supply chains, sharing information is of crucial importance, particularly information about prices. Farmers need to know how to evaluate the information and use it on their farms.

Another challenge is the upgrading of the production and marketing systems of the vegetable industry so that its competitive edge can be increased. At the moment, the threat of cheaper and tastier vegetable imports looms over the heads of the farmers and threatens their very existence. While market intermediaries can still earn income from imported vegetables, farmers will be eased out of the picture. An upgraded production and marketing system would allow farmers to access modern markets in a sustainable way.

This is not to say, however, that the only way for farmers to go is to market to supermarkets. Accessing institutional markets directly is probably a better option, as shown by the Northern Mindanao farmers. Vegetable processing is possibly another option, but identifying the correct product–market mix would be another challenge. Overall, the prospects for vegetable farmers in the Philippines are rather bleak unless their capacity to become competitive is built though training and linkages.

Case study 2: Small-scale mango producers

Mango farming in the Philippines is dominated by small growers whose farm size is less than three hectares. Based on the latest census on agriculture conducted by the National Statistics Office (NSO) in 1991 pertaining to the distribution of mango farms by size of farm lot, 73 per cent of mango farms are owned by small growers, while 24 per cent operate farm sizes between 3 and 10 hectares. Those operating 10 hectares and above constitute only about 3 per cent. The fresh mango industry has some 2.5 million farmers and farm family members who provide raw materials for the varied product lines of the mango processing industry.

Historically the mango industry in the Philippines has not been dominated by multinational corporations, unlike the banana and pineapple industries where big multinational corporations such as Dole-Stanfilco (Philippines), and Del Monte have a virtual monopoly in exporting.

However, Dole Philippines and Lapanday Corporation, a large domestic agribusiness firm, have now ventured into mango production. A few years ago, Dole Philippines started with buying from traders and running an experimental farm. Now they contract supplies from a large mango farm where they provide technical assistance in terms of agricultural inputs and management practices.

A number of mango processors currently source mangoes on contract and some traders would like contracts with large plantations for the supply of high-quality mangoes. They are constrained from doing so by the Comprehensive Agrarian Reform Law (CARL). Agrarian reform has caused uncertainties that have constrained investments in agriculture and reduced market valuation of land such as in the case of the sugar industry. Regardless of the mode of resolving the issues, a price-setting mechanism that will lead to more acceptable contractual terms must be encouraged. It is important that the terms are acceptable not only to farmers but also to corporate growers so they will be encouraged to invest in improved efficiency.

Summing up, small-scale mango producers, supplying both the formal and informal marketing chains with fresh mangoes, need the understanding and attention of policy-makers. The natural instinct of supermarket chains, especially new ones attracted in over the next five years, will be to seek out mango plantations experienced in export and use them as preferred suppliers.

Conclusions

In the Philippines, the challenge is to make small-scale producers attractive to buyers so that new organizations of small farmers can market their produce to supermarkets. At the moment, this is not a problem because half the food supply system is through the traditional markets. Evidence from other countries further down the 'supermarketization' road is that unless steps are taken to organize groups now that have internal coherence and trust, the supermarkets will turn to the plantations.

References

ACIAR, 2004. *Improving the efficiency of the agribusiness supply chain and quality management for small agricultural producers in Mindanao.* Australian Centre for International Agricultural Research unpublished research document, ASEM 2000/101.

Concepcion, S. and Montiflor, M., 2003. *Perceptions of southern Mindanao farmers on the quality of temperate vegetables.* Paper presented at the 47th AAERES Conference, Fremantle, Western Australia.

Digal, Larry and Hualda, Luis, 2003. *Quality grading in the supply chain: the case of vegetables in southern Philippines.* Paper presented at the 47th AAERES Conference, Fremantle, Western Australia.

Macabasco, D., 2004. *A closer look at Philippine vegetable imports.* Agri-food Trade Service. Available: www.agr.gc.ca/ 2004.

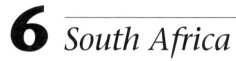 6 *South Africa*

*André Louw, Hilton Madevu, Danie Jordaan and
Hester Vermeulen*

Introduction

South Africa has a dualistic agricultural economy, comprising of a well-developed commercial sector and a predominantly subsistence-orientated small-scale sector. Agriculture is divided between approximately 46 000 commercial farmers and 2.5 million emerging or 'developing' farmer households (Development Bank of South Africa (DBSA), 2005: 68). This DBSA report specifically analysed the vegetable and dairy industries of South Africa and the issue of the emerging sector in these industries.

KEY DATA

	2002	2003	2004
Population (millions)	44.76	45.15	45.53
Per capita GDP (US$)	2331	3544	4305
Urbanization (%)	56.5		
Agriculture as % GDP			14.8
Per capital total retail food sales (US$)	467	709	861
Per capita modern retail food sales (US$)	186	261	318

Exchange rate (1 January 2006): 1 US Dollar = 6.34 South African rand (ZAR)

TOP RETAIL CHAINS, 2005

Company	Ownership	Number of stores	Retail banner sales 2005 (ZAR millions)	Market share (%)
Shoprite	Public company	881	29 965	20.5
Pick 'n' Pay	Public company	536	29 167	20.0
Massmart	Public company	212	25 843	17.7
Metcash (RSA)	Public company	596	14 705	10.0
Spar (RSA)	Public company	794	12 191	8.4
Sub Total		3019	111 871	76.6
Other			34 123	23.4

Source: PlanetRetail (www.planetretail.net)

SOUTH AFRICAN SUPERMARKETS AND GLOBALIZATION

No foreign retailers of size are currently present in the South African market. The country's remote geographical location away from industrialized regions, and the dominant position of its domestic retailers are two major contributing factors for this. The country's difficult sociological and political development and the lingering poverty in large parts of the country are further reasons why international retailers have shied away from investing in the country, and are likely to stay away in the near future.

South African supermarket chains have expanded into other African countries since apartheid ended and sanctions were stopped in 1994. Shoprite, Pick 'n Pay, Metro SA (Metcash) and Spar have been expanding enthusiastically into surrounding African countries.

Shoprite, Pick 'n Pay and Spar have opened stores in Botswana, Namibia, Zimbabwe, Malawi, Mozambique, Kenya and other southern and eastern African countries. With their strong operational experience, financial strength and concepts adaptable to local demands, South African retailers are well placed to explore and conquer these embryonic markets.

Shoprite is the most internationalized retailer, having entered four new countries over the past three years, with its operations now spanning a total of 14 African countries. By comparison, Pick 'n Pay operates stores in six other African countries. Due to the relative youth of the network, sales from foreign operations are still small, accounting for 8 per cent of Shoprite's sales and slightly less than 8 per cent of Pick 'n Pay's. In most countries, Shoprite has established its flagship eponymous supermarkets in cities and adapted them to the local clientele. Recently, it has created the Usave chain, a limited assortment format with 600 lines, inspired by European discount concepts. This format has been chosen as a major vehicle for expansion into southern Africa.

Metro SA (Metcash) is an important cross-border player with its network of cash and carries, supermarkets and neighbourhood stores. Since 1999, it has opened over 250 stores and now operates or services over 950 stores in nine African countries (apart from South Africa). Its cash-and-carry stores are an important vehicle for the development of modern retail formats in developing countries.

Spar is active in countries bordering South Africa only, unlike Pick 'n Pay, Shoprite and Metro who have ventured further afield. Spar is active in Namibia, Botswana and Swaziland.

Massmart is South Africa's sixth largest company in terms of retailing, but ranks third when its wholesale, distribution and buying alliance operations of general consumer goods are included. Its retail business consists of discount stores and it is also operating wholesale outlets. Massmart is planning to expand further across the rest of Africa. It is currently engaged in seven southern African countries with its wholesale operations. Massmart operates two major buying alliances, Shield and Furnex, alongside its wholesale network. Shield and Furnex both serve over 600 members and retail outlets.

Buying alliances play an important part in South Africa, as there are still a large number of independent supermarkets and especially corner shops. Their large numbers assure buying alliances and other wholesale operations a major standing.

Wholesale outlets, similar to buying groups, play a major role on the South African market, especially for the procurement of FFV. Shoprite has its own distribution wholesale network named Freshmark dedicated to the procurement of fruits and vegetables. Suppliers deliver mainly to wholesale or distribution centres where products from various suppliers are collected before being distributed to a chain or sold on to independents.

SMALL-SCALE PRODUCERS AND 'EMERGING' FARMERS

In South Africa, there is a category of small- and medium-sized farms with the potential to expand, called 'emerging farms' and farmers. These are seen as the farmers with the potential to be integrated into modern supply chains. As we note below, this will take a long time at the present rate of progress.

Currently there is little scope for small-scale producers or processors to compete with or to be integrated with large-scale food processors in South Africa supplying the modern food system. In fact, small-scale processors supplying traditional markets with products such as bread, traditional beer, rice, meat and dairy products are under pressure and in no position to challenge the large-scale food processors in terms of supplying large supermarkets with processed foods.

We looked in detail at the potential for emerging farmers to supply milk and found one promising scheme run by Clover, the largest dairy company in South Africa. However, overall the sophistication required to supply milk to dairy processors and supermarkets on a continuous basis is well beyond the current capacity of emerging farmers and consequently we do not discuss the South African dairy sector perspective in this chapter.

The only product category where we observed a potential for the integration of small-scale producers in South Africa into the modern system is in unprocessed (and minimally processed) vegetables. We propose that a sensible strategy for emerging farmers is to establish themselves as suppliers to large urban wholesale markets and then apply the experience gained to seek access to the more demanding supermarket sector. We envisage a gradual development as farmers learn through experience. For further information about the case studies below and similar initiatives in South Africa, see NDA, 2005 and 2006.

Case study 1: Vegetables to Johannesburg market

A readily available marketing opportunity for emerging farmers is to gain entry to wholesale markets such as the Johannesburg Fresh Produce Market (JFPM). This can provide a learning experience and allow emerging farmers to become gradually skilled at supplying good quality vegetables. A period supplying wholesale markets is a good preparation towards engaging in supply to a supermarket chain.

There is a well-developed system of traditional wholesale markets, informal retailers (spazas), traders, shops and hawkers or informal traders in South Africa. This is regulated and is expanding as population and urbanization increase. The requirements of urban markets are more demanding than village markets, street sellers and farm-gate sales to consumers, the outlets most emerging farmers are used to.

Grades are important and in traditional markets, the 'personal touch' makes the difference between the best and worst supplier. According to our sources in wholesale markets, the size of a producer is not necessarily a good predictor of the quality of vegetables marketed. Both small-scale emerging farmers and large-scale commercial farmers are able to comply with product standards.

If an emerging farmer can gain a reputation on a traditional market as a good supplier, this may help them get noticed by supermarkets. In South Africa, many potato processors (for example, McCain's, Simba and Willards) engage with contract farmers, but also procure first-grade potatoes from the national fresh produce markets to top up their raw material levels in cases of shortages or natural disasters. Other major business buyers on the market include Pick 'n Pay, Fruit and Veg City, Tiger Brands, Spar and Freshmark. The quality of produce procured by these buyers on the market depends on consumer needs, availability and market prices (C. Holtzkampf, personal communication).

The increase in the supply role of emerging farmers to the JFPM is proving to be an agonisingly slow process. Most of the fresh produce that is acquired from emerging farmers is coming from those who have mentors. There are certain particular success stories like the tomato producer Sam Mohale (see below), who operates in collaboration with ZZ2 (the largest tomato producer in South Africa and one of the largest tomato producers in the world) to gain access to economy of scale advantages in terms of production inputs. This case study is described below. Furthermore, the emerging citrus producers at Zebediela recovered to some extent after it nearly collapsed after being handed to a local community under a land claim. It is now delivering produce to the national fresh produce market (C. Holtzkampf, personal communication) as well as exporting.

Traders prefer to deal with as few suppliers as possible in order to reduce transaction costs. The interviewed market agent personnel indicated that emerging and large-scale producers were treated similarly in the trading environment. However, it was pointed out that there were definite advantages in dealing with fewer high-volume suppliers, especially due to reduced transactions costs. The importance of establishing a balance between the two types of producers was expressed; as one interviewee stated: '113 small farmers equals 113 potential problems, as compared to 10 large farmers with 10 potentially big problems'. Agents indicated that they assisted small farmers to familiarize themselves with quality standards, even though they did not get involved with any formal training and outreach ('extension') activities. However, the overall impression is that an emerging farmer who seeks to become a new supplier must 'sink or swim'.

According to Charlotte Holtzkampf of the JFPM, there are no formal entry barriers facing buyers and sellers on the JFPM. However, other factors do cause entry barriers for emerging farmers. These include: (1) marketing problems, including inadequate skills and funds for proper grading, packaging and branding; (2) lack of expertise and knowledge regarding production and resulting poor quality produce; (3) logistical problems, especially expensive transportation costs, even more so in cases where cold transportation is required.

Transportation is perceived by market agents as the biggest problem facing emerging farmers, causing quality losses, late delivery and consequently reduced prices. Many emerging farmers still have a 'semi-subsistence' mindset, ensuring household food supply as a first priority. Also they often lack enough land to rotate crops. Consequently, quality is compromised and market returns are poor. Further, many emerging farmers can only deliver produce for two or three months of the year and cannot achieve continuity on the market. They also typically face problems such as inadequate extension, poor credit access and poor infrastructure, especially in terms of telecommunications and road conditions.

Transport assistance could be a critical success factor for emerging farmers. The involvement of the Department of Agriculture will be vital in this regard. It was suggested that groups of emerging farmers could become involved in shared transportation of fresh produce to the market, in order to obtain economies of scale. The exploitation of emerging farmers (with transportation barriers) on the Makatini flats by wholesalers from Durban was also mentioned (C. Holtzkampf, personal communication).

One of the future development projects of the JFPM will be to construct a communal vegetable packhouse for emerging farmers. The farmers will then be able to deliver their produce in bulk to the fresh produce market, after which grading and packaging will be done in the communal packhouse. Thus, the farmers will not have to transport the packaging material as well (C. Holtzkampf, personal communication).

A way to mitigate some of the market entry barriers to emerging farmers may be through organizing them into producer and marketing associations. Such groupings could give the small-scale producers access to economies of scale and support channels. In addition, mechanisms need to be sought to provide market agents in fresh produce markets with incentives to acquire more fresh produce from emerging farmers.

Sources in the trade indicate that the fresh produce industry has a bright future and they anticipate future market growth. However, as regards emerging farmers, Charlotte Holtzkampf (personal communication) anticipates that their entry into formal markets will become even more difficult for several reasons.

First, the gap between consumers' requirements and the ability of emerging producers to satisfy consumers' needs is widening as consumer demand becomes more particular and complex in terms of issues such as food safety, organic food and genetically modified (GM)-free products. Second, the national fresh produce regulations are currently being revised and upgraded, with implied increased requirements and adherence costs. Most of the emerging farmers already struggle to adhere to the current national fresh produce regulations and thus serious problems could be anticipated in terms of emerging farmer compliance with new private standards such as EUREPGAP (a private sector standard for the certification of agricultural products for Good Agricultural Practices at the farm level, with a focus on food safety) and BRC (also a private standard, but applying to food processing, manufacturing and supply) in the domestic and export fresh produce markets. In addition to the revised fresh produce regulations of the national fresh produce markets, yet another hurdle will soon be facing emerging farmers. The JFPM is going to implement the HACCP system in the future. Again, this will increase the costs and difficulties facing emerging farmers.

Case study 2: Spar Thohoyandou

The integration of emerging vegetable farmers into a supermarket chain, as seen at the Thohoyandou Spar supermarket, is an important example for both South Africa and the larger context of this book.

During August 2004, a number of interviews were conducted in Thohoyandou in the Limpopo province to investigate the situation regarding the Spar supermarket in Thohoyandou and the emerging farmers supplying it with fresh vegetables. The managing director of the Spar supermarket was interviewed. Furthermore, two focus groups (with four emerging farmers per focus group) were conducted with emerging farmers delivering vegetables to the specific Spar supermarket.

The Spar supermarket in Thohoyandou opened its doors for trading in June 2002 to capture some of the enormous purchasing power present in the corridor area to the east of the N1 highway in the Limpopo Province. In June 2002, the supermarket market share in Thohoyandou was 72 per cent for the Shoprite supermarket compared with 28 per cent for the Score supermarket.

However, after the opening of the Thohoyandou Spar supermarket, a dramatic shift occurred in the supermarket market share within the area to Spar (66 per cent), away from Shoprite (28 per cent) and Score (6 per cent). The current area of the store is around 1100 m², which will be expanded to 7000 m² in the near future. The store is located between a taxi rank and a bus rank in the city business complex, which is a very strategic location given the fact that up to 95 per cent of the Venda people in that area use bus or taxi transport.

The major factor that contributed to the tremendous success of the Spar supermarket was the fact that it focuses completely on addressing the needs of the emerging market found in the Thohoyandou area in Venda, with a high level of community involvement.

An important component of the strategy was to fulfil the fresh produce requirements of its customers, since it was found that the competing supermarkets did not offer high-quality fresh produce. During 2004, typical daily fresh produce sales in the supermarket included 3700 cabbages (an important component of the Venda people's diet), 1500 spinach bunches, 1500 beetroot bunches, 2700 carrot bunches and 4000 apple pre-packs. The supermarket also invested in the biggest in-store bakery in South Africa. The supermarket sells 33 000 loaves of bread per day, adding up to 23 tonnes daily.

Other interesting characteristics of the supermarket include loose-served meat displayed to enable customers to choose what they want to buy. The hot food (take-away) department opens at 06:00 every morning and typically serves among, other things, 3 tonnes of maize porridge and 2 tonnes of fried chips per day. The supermarket also attracts customers with low prices on known value grocery items and allocates a lot of space for the big brand products.

The Thohoyandou Spar supermarket has a policy of procuring fresh produce from the local area, which is different from the procurement for the Shoprite supermarket that is done by Freshmark. Commercial farmers from the Limpopo province supply the store with most of its needs for fresh produce, such as potatoes, onions, butternuts, peppers and tropical fruit. Procurement of cabbages and spinach involves emerging farmers and commercial farmers. Dairy procurement is done through the commercial sources Clover and the Limpopo Dairy situated in Louis Trichard. High standards are required for dairy products sold in the supermarket. The criteria influencing the sourcing decisions of the Thohoyandou Spar between commercial and emerging farmers are of particular interest.

SPAR THOHOYANDOU AND EMERGING FARMERS

Emerging vegetable farmers produce cabbage, spinach, sweet potatoes, tomatoes, carrots, beetroot, butternuts and chillies. In addition to production activities, the farmers engage in sorting, washing and bundling of vegetables. Their marketing channels include the Thohoyandou Spar, hawkers and direct sales to consumers. In 2004, approximately 30 per cent of the vegetable procurement of this Spar store was from emerging farmers. The interactions between emerging farmers and the Spar store include: (1) providing interest-free loans (2500 rand per farmer) to emerging farmers who supply vegetables to the Spar, on presentation and approval of a proper business plan; (2) providing an unlimited market for the produce of the emerging farmers based on verbal arrangements between the farmer and the supermarket; (3) engaging in farm visits; (4) requiring progress reports from those who produce vegetables for the Thohoyandou Spar supermarket; and finally, (5) assisting farmers in training on required quality standards.

Prices are negotiated with the store, based on factors such as market prices, vegetable quality and the supply and demand prevailing in the supermarket on the date in question. Emerging farmers are paid promptly, once a week.

It is important to note that the interaction with the emerging farmers involves a very strong trust component. The Thohoyandou Spar needs the produce delivered by the emerging farmers. On the other hand, the farmers trust the Spar to give them fair market related prices and to engage with them in long-term relationships, given that they deliver quality produce to the supermarket.

According to the representative of Thohoyandou Spar, the vegetable quality standards enforced by the Spar store are attainable by emerging farmers. The biggest cause of quality problems is insect-related damage.

The procurement of vegetables from emerging farmers has certain benefits for the Thohoyandou Spar, including the fact that smaller quantities of produce are delivered more often, thus having positive implications for the freshness of produce sold in the supermarket. Community development occurs thanks to the injection of capital. Many farmers spend part of their earned income in the Spar supermarket after receiving payment on Fridays.

For the Thohoyandou Spar, the disadvantages associated with procuring vegetables from emerging farmers include: (1) dealing with larger numbers of small farmers (instead of smaller numbers of bigger farmers) causes pressure on administration and transaction costs incurred by the supermarket; (2) the inability of emerging farmers to deliver higher volumes throughout the year; and finally, (3) sometimes the quality of produce delivered to the supermarket is inadequate. Poor quality is particularly affected by: (1) climatic conditions in the local production area; and, (2) inadequate farming knowledge and primitive farming methods among many emerging vegetable farmers.

If the success at Thohoyandou Spar is to be replicated across South Africa, a number of improvements must be made. In particular, emerging farmers need:

- more access to training/extension services in terms of production, quality, marketing, business planning, financial and other relevant aspects
- better coordination in order to ensure schedules to supermarkets are met
- support to solve their logistical (transport) problems
- survival mechanisms to cope during periods of adverse climatic conditions – that is, it is not sensible to encourage emerging farmers to rely solely on sales to supermarkets. When harvests are poor and quality low, farmers need to have other ways of supplying their basic needs.

The complete 'shopping list' for emerging farmers is in reality much longer than this. There is a need for private and public sector involvement in order to improve the situation of the emerging vegetable farmers. Some argue that that private sector initiatives seem to be more successful than those driven by the government. This is just as well since the government is unlikely to finance input subsidies or credit schemes, though it might offer to carry out market research studies for groups of farmers.

At the inception of the Spar initiative financial institutions were reluctant to get involved. However, with its success, it has now attracted the interest of one of the large financial institutions, which recognizes a potential growth market in providing sound finance to small farmers through agribusiness establishments such as supermarkets, where there are also support services and market access. This highlights the need for bankers to rethink their model regarding 'bankable' customers. Concurrently finance providers are under pressure from Black Economic Empowerment (BEE) legislation to combine a profit target with a wider development approach. Businesses need to understand certain more non-traditional cultures and to adapt their financial norms accordingly without compromising profits. This creates new opportunities to develop products and services suited to new markets such as emerging farmers and the rental markets.

The ability of bankers to finance actors in supply chains with confidence indicates that an enterprise or project can be viable. Banks may, as an example, deal with the players in the supply chains rather than individual businesses. By doing this, their security is in the relevant stakeholders, the type of industry, cash flows and in soft collateral, such as trust.

Case study 3: Emerging farmers as tomato suppliers

During August 2004, an interview was conducted with Mr Philé van Zyl, the chairperson of the Tomato Growers Association and one of the co-owners of ZZ2, the largest tomato producer in South Africa and one of the largest in the world.

The Tomato Growers Association does not provide technical assistance. However, many of the emerging farmers do belong to the association. This could be a route through which these emerging farmers are reached in terms of extension services. Technical support for emerging farmers could be achieved by means of two routes: learning from experience (by working on other farms or own farm), and government extension. Many of the successful emerging farmers started off by working on commercial farms and building up their experience. In contrast, government extension is currently generally perceived as being worthless.

Land tenure is the most important problem facing emerging tomato farmers. Many of the emerging tomato farmers do not own their land, but only have permission to occupy. Consequently, the growth of these farmers is curtailed since they cannot use their land as security for financing. It is important for the government to complete the Communal Land Bill to allow emerging farmers to acquire security of tenure. Furthermore, structures could be put in place in order to render financial support to these emerging farmers' operations on tribal land.

Logistical and transport problems are the second most important set of problems facing emerging tomato farmers. Most of the small farmers have transportation problems. In the case of the Venda farmers supplying Indian businessmen, this problem is overcome because the businessmen collect the tomatoes from the farmers. The transport capacity problem comes down to a 'chicken and egg' situation. Farmers need the capacity to fill transport volumes, but cannot build capacity since they do not have transport for their current produce. A possible solution might be some sort of transport subsidy and cooperation between emerging farmers in order to increase transport volumes. Another possible solution could be the involvement of transport contractors.

If emerging farmers plant the 'right' seed varieties (for high-quality tomatoes), they could become more successful. However, the high-quality seed varieties are imported from the USA and are a very expensive input. Like the case described below regarding Steven Mohale and ZZ2, it might be worthwhile for emerging farmers to either associate with commercial farmers or associate with each other through farmer associations and cooperatives, in order to get some economy of scale advantages during procurement. Such farmer associations and cooperatives could also be a means of reaching emerging farmers with technical support.

Due to the risky nature of tomato production, there is little incentive for commercial farmers to get involved in joint ventures with emerging farmers. It is often viewed as an artificial structure that costs money and introduces more risk into an already risky business. However, private partnerships (like the Venda/Indian businessmen example) could make a tremendous contribution to the growth and development of emerging tomato producers.

Steven Mohale grew from an emerging farmer to a commercial farmer due to a number of success factors: (1) he worked on the ZZ2 farm for many years, gaining a lot of experience before starting his tomato production; (2) he established an alliance and long-term relationship with ZZ2; (3) he can procure seed, advice and fertilizer through ZZ2 in order to share in their economies of scale and high-quality seed and other inputs; and (4) he is able to deliver produce to the national fresh produce markets. Mr Mohale's annual turnover is 2–3 million rand (about US$ 400 000–500 000). Mr Mohale was 'mentored' by the large-scale company. The benefit for ZZ2 is to be recognized as demonstrating corporate social responsibility at little cost to itself.

Conclusions

Emerging farmers are not emerging fast enough in South Africa. This is because of the weaknesses of small-scale producers as suppliers to the modern food system on the one hand and the high degree of competition on the other. It will be a long time before the dominance of large-scale farms in food supply to the modern system is significantly challenged.

Nevertheless, farmers are emerging with government and private sector support. The best way to help them seems to be to train and finance them to supply wholesale markets in the big cities first. Once they have gained experience of the discipline of marketing to these outlets, supermarket supply will be easier.

On the other hand, the Spar experience of helping emerging farmers by using them as preferred suppliers of vegetables for one store suggests that supermarkets could emulate this and spread the example further in South Africa. Unless the supermarket companies are proactive and positively nurture emerging farmers as new suppliers, the speed of change is likely to remain glacial.

References

DBSA, 2005. 'Development report', in *Overcoming underdevelopment in South Africa's second economy*, Chapter 7. Midrand, South Africa: Development Bank of Southern Africa (DBSA).

NDA, 2005. *Trends in the Agricultural Sector 2005*. Pretoria: Directorate Agricultural Information Services, National Department of Agriculture.

NDA, 2006. *Crops and Markets: Report No. 296*. Pretoria: Directorate Agricultural Information Services, National Department of Agriculture.

3 *Country Studies:* Countries in Transition from State Control

This second set of country studies focuses on countries in transition from state control, where centrally planned economies have undergone rapid opening and liberalization. The three CEE countries – Hungary, Poland and Romania – share a Communist past with state-run food systems of different sorts. Two are now EU members and a third is scheduled to join in 2007 or 2008. All been through major restructuring of their economies and industry. Supermarkets are expanding quickly and the pattern of development follows western Europe, though at a much faster rate of change. The new retailers and food processors are faced with procurement options from an agricultural sector divided between large former state-run operations and small (in the case of Romania, micro) farms. The two Asian countries, China and Vietnam, remain ruled by Communist governments but both have seen market liberalization policies. Vietnam has just been admitted to the World Trade Organization (WTO), five years after China. Supermarkets and cash-and-carry operations have expanded rapidly, both local chains with varying degrees of state control, and foreign multinationals. Governments have generally encouraged these trends.

7 *Hungary*

Imre Fertő, Csaba Forgács, Anikó Juhász, and Gyöngyi Kürthy

Introduction

Hungary has moved from being a communist command economy through a free-for-all transition period to EU membership, all in 15 years. In some ways, Hungary is western Europe's gateway to CEE. Budapest (accounting for 18 per cent of the Hungarian population) has historic connections with the West that are being revived. The country occupies a central position and makes an obvious location for future investments in the food industry as borders become less important among EU member states. Partly as a result of this, there have been relatively high levels of foreign investment in both food processing and retailing.

In the broad set of Hungarian policies, there only a few that directly or mostly indirectly impact upon the integration of small farmers into vertical supply chains. Among them is support to create producer organizations (POs), mainly for joint marketing. Marketing-oriented producer organizations are common in the EU and most of the new CEE member states have introduced policies to encourage producer groups.

Food chains in Hungary have been deeply restructured since the early 1990s. The privatization of state owned, centrally managed retailing outlets at the beginning of the decade, giving rise to a proliferation of small retail shops was followed by the privatization of national food wholesaling and retailing as well as green field foreign investments in the sector. The relationship among market players within supply chains has also been transformed. These changes have very much affected both the small producers of agricultural raw materials and the food manufacturing companies.

The importance of super- and hypermarkets in food retailing has become crucial and is still expanding. We look at two products, onions and milk, to show how these changes have affected food chain participants. Milk is one of the most important agricultural products in Hungary, while onions play an important role in Hungarian cuisine.

KEY DATA

	2002	2003	2004
Population (millions)	9.22	9.88	9.83
Per capita GDP (US$)	6632	8337	9922
Urbanization (%)	65		
Agriculture as % GDP	3.2	2.8	3.3
Per capita total food retail sales (US$)	672	837	1014
Per capita modern food retail sales (US$)	513	628	832
Modern food retail sales as % total			82

Exchange rate (1 January 2006): 1 US$ = 212.6 HUF (1 Jan 06)

TOP CHAINS, 2004

Company	Ownership	Number of stores	Retail banner sales 2004 (US$ millions)	Market share (%)	Grocery sales 2004 (US$ millions)	Grocery market share (%)
Tesco	Foreign	69	1932	16.7	1364	16.3
CBA	Local purchasing organization	2996	2866			15
Co-op Hungary	Local purchasing organization	4487	3575			12
Metro Group	Foreign	26	1710	14.8	839	10.1
Louis Delhaize	Foreign	211	1224	10.6	913	10.9
Reál Hungária	Local	1840	1998			8
Tengelmann	Foreign	198	963	8.3	664	8.0
SPAR	Foreign	153	932	8.1	689	8.3

Source: Authors' calculations from yearbooks and monthly bulletins of the Central Statistical Office (CSO) 1998–2004, Statistical Yearbook of 2004, and issues of Mai Piac (trade magazine, 1998 and 2003), PlanetRetail (www.planetretail.net).

STRUCTURE AND TRENDS IN AGRI-FOOD CHAINS

The political and economic transition at the beginning of the 1990s and privatization had significant effect on Hungarian food trading. It was attractive for investors, especially foreign investors. Several international supermarket chains started operating in Hungary, either by reconstructing old stores or with green field investments. Supermarket chains of Hungarian ownership were also created, some of which developed very quickly, also expanding abroad. In spite of this, most of the Hungarian trading businesses are small and medium-sized enterprises (SMEs), and short of capital. We have identified four periods for the Hungarian food trade:

1. Spontaneous privatization: 1989–91.
2. Privatization: 1992–95.
3. Concentration begins: 1996–2000.
4. Accelerated concentration: 2001–.

The period of spontaneous privatization happened in 1989–91, when the smaller shops were privatized and a significant number of private shops were established. Therefore the number of food retail shops started to grow.

During the period of privatization (from 1992 to about 1995), the owners of the larger food retail chains changed. Most of the shops in the favourable areas became the properties of multinational chains. Some of the small private shops continued to develop, but some of them went bankrupt. The first part of this period was characterized by the launch of so-called 'forced'[1] enterprises, a lot of them only remaining in business for a short time. Therefore, at the beginning of the 1990s, there was a big increase in the number of food shops. Within this, the number of shops operated by sole proprietors also increased. Their share of the total was highest in the middle of the decade.

---

1   After the change in the political system, unemployment increased drastically. Thus, thousands of people started their own small businesses mostly employing only themselves or the members of the family.

A period of concentration began in 1996, although at the same time (until 2000) the number of shops and even the number of stores operated by sole proprietors still increased. Based on 2003 data from the CSO, the value of sales of the food and mixed retail business was 2263 HUF billion (US$ 10.9 billion). The sales of the retailers almost doubled in the given period, while the number of stores showed only a mild increase. Although this trend may have resulted in part from inflation and the growing purchasing power of the Hungarian consumers, it may also indicate an increase in the size of the stores, which can be interpreted as a form of concentration. This strengthening competition and concentration among the top-10 food retailers is illustrated in the data shown in Table 7.1.

Table 7.1   The importance of the top 10 food retailers

	1997		2003	
	Sales (million USD)	Stores (number)	Sales (million USD)	Stores (number)
Food retailers	5435	47 384	10 082	51 082
Top-10 food retailers	3019	8943	7623	11 324
Top-10 food retailers (%)	52	19	89	22

Source: Own calculation from yearbooks and monthly bulletins of the CSO 1998–2004 and issues of Mai Piac (1998 and 2003).

The ratio of sales of the top-10 retailers also shows the ever increasing pace of concentration in the Hungarian food retail business. Between 1997 and 2003, the ratio of the largest 10 food retailers from total branch sales increased by 37 per cent. In both 1997 and 2003, the top-10 retailers' share of total sales (52 per cent and 89 per cent) was realized in around 20 per cent of the stores, which means that the top-10 retailers had captured a larger market share without considerably increasing the number of stores.

Although the 90 per cent of sales with 20 per cent of stores data means a high concentration level, the number of retail shops remains surprisingly high in the period examined, especially compared to other countries. When we look for the reasons we have to take into account an important characteristic of the Hungarian food retail sector. In Hungary, of the top-10 retailers, one (Co-op/ÁFÉSZ) in 1997 and four in 2003 (Co-op Hungary, CBA, Honiker, Reál) were so called 'procurement associations', some of them operating almost as a franchise system, comprising a considerable number of relatively small stores (mostly 51–200 m²) with independent ownership or forming mini chains. In 1997, two more chains (Hungarotabak and Tobaccoland) had the same type of small shop structure.

These associations with Hungarian ownership have proved viable and although Co-op Hungary lost some of its market share, the other associations have kept on growing in the last decade, now taking an important share of the Hungarian food retail market. The key to their success is twofold: (1) they behave as retail chains with the producers and the processors (central procurement, increased negotiating power); and (2) they have maintained the consumer-oriented aspects of the smaller traditional food retail stores (being present in smaller settlements and inner areas of towns and keeping personal contact with the consumers). We think that the presence and development of the buyer associations are the main reason for the much slower decrease in the number of stores than the pace of concentration would lead us to expect.

Aside from the small stores, other important store formats are supermarkets and discount stores (mostly 201–400 m² and 401–2500 m² respectively), but the absolute winners of the last decade have been hypermarkets (2500 m²). Of the top-10 retailers in 1997, not one company operated hypermarkets. By 2003, three (Tesco, Auchan and Cora) had opened hypermarkets. In 1997, five hypermarkets existed and accounted for about 5 per cent of food retail sales. By 2003, the number of hypermarkets had reached 64, accounting for 24 per cent of total food sales. The trend to this large size format is the main reason for the concentration trend.

Retail chains are even more concentrated on the procurement side. From the top-10 list, Spar and the wholesaler Metro form the buyer group METSPA with more than US$ 1,800 million sales. Also from the top-10 list, the last two, Cora and Csemege (Match, Smatch, Profi, Alfa), have founded the PROVERA buyer group.

Companies operating cash-and-carry stores such as Metro and Interfruct are registered as wholesalers and thus are not part of national retail statistics. But Metro operates almost like a hypermarket.

WHAT TRANSITION MEANS FOR SMALL-SCALE PRODUCERS

In the pre-reform period, Hungarian farming was dominated by large farms. Around half of gross agricultural output was produced by cooperatives, one third of production came from small-scale farming, mainly the household production of cooperative members and less than one-fifth of output was produced by state farms. Small-scale production had been deeply integrated by cooperatives where the latter provided their members with inputs and marketing the products mostly at cost price level.

Small producers did not have to deal with marketing their products, as it had been taken over by production coops and in some cases by marketing cooperatives. Large firms, in addition to crop production and animal husbandry activities, were allowed to run so-called non-agricultural activities (services and industrial production) in order to produce enough profits. Industrial activities were more profitable than agricultural production and were used as a source for further investments in plant and animal production.

The agricultural reform has the following main components: price liberalization, cutting of agricultural subsidies, trade liberalization, privatization, and land reforms. The period from 1989 to 2004 can be divided two phases: first, a period of transformation (1989–93) and, second, a period of consolidation and solid recovery.

Agricultural policy during the transformation phase focused on building up the legal and institutional framework for the market economy. The second, consolidation phase of agricultural reform concentrated on two issues. First, agricultural policies stabilized the domestic agricultural market by establishing a market regulation office, improving the activity of such institutions and increasing production support. Second, the policies harmonized the legal environment for agriculture towards EU accession.

Where any type of production contract does exist, agricultural producers face problems with hold-ups (for example, delayed payment for delivered products; Gow and Swinnen 1998). In principle, the legal system makes it possible for transactions to be carried out smoothly when contracts are incomplete. However, in Hungary, parties to transactions sometimes cannot enforce contracts because of the time-consuming and expensive legal process in the courts. Consequently, the delay raises the cost of market exchange leading to strong barriers to establishing new market institutions.

Empirical evidence suggests that foreign direct investment (FDI) in food industries encourages the resolution of these problems mainly through long-term contracts, in dairy products rather than the onion chain. However, it must be noted that in some cases where multinational firms have dominant market positions, they create a new type of problem, for example, ex-post reduction of contract price. In other words, supermarkets agree a price with suppliers but then unilaterally pay a lower one when payment becomes due. The supplier may decide to accept the price cut rather than protest in order to remain a listed supplier to the chain.

With regard to processing, two phases can be distinguished in privatization. The first phase (1990–92) was dominated by FDI. More than 50 per cent of privatization revenue stemmed from privatization of the food industry. In the second period (1993–97), the pace of privatization slowed. The government adopted the concept of decentralized privatization in order to accelerate the process. As a result, by the end of 1995, foreign ownership already exceeded 50 per cent in the food industry.

FDI has played a dominant role in the Hungarian food industry. Although the number of foreign-owned companies has decreased between 1995 and 2002, their role in owners' equity is more than 70 per cent, and their share in net sales exceeds 50 per cent. Two-thirds of the capital in food processing is foreign owned.

BUYING GROUPS

In Hungary, hotel, restaurant and catering (HORECA) networks are well established. While earlier, the headquarters allowed each outlet belonging to a chain to order goods from suppliers as they wanted, more recently they have introduced a new policy. Namely, the headquarters negotiates centrally with the suppliers, agrees on a product list and fixes the prices for all goods for one year. Once the deal is finalized, they pass this product and price list to their outlets in the network. Hotels belonging to a chain can order only from those suppliers that are on the list at a price negotiated. This is a highly centralized purchasing system, while decentralized as far as physical delivery is concerned.

Hungarian HORECA networks are interested in reducing the number of suppliers because of it makes negotiations easier and it forces all suppliers to reduce prices if they would like to be on the supplier list. Companies in HORECA are large, and order a wide range of products, significant in terms of both volume and value. A small producer cannot act alone but can supply through a Producer Organization (PO). However, prices tend to be lower for suppliers because profit must be shared with the HORECA business.

The foreign element has also caused changes in retail practices. For instance, the German cash-and-carry firm Metro operates in Hungary and provides seven day per week delivery, which makes it challenging for other wholesalers to keep their clients. This is a very competitive phase of the vertical chain, as foreign businesses are tough competitors. If food imports are significant, there is a need for wholesalers to assemble the needed composition of goods for customers. At this point, international chains have advantages in comparison with domestic ones.

Hungarian-owned buying groups have proved viable and although the largest group (Co-op Hungary) has lost some of its market share, other associations have kept on growing over the last decade, accounting today for an impressive proportion of the Hungarian food retail market. The presence and development of the buyer associations are the main reason for the much slower decrease in the number of stores than the pace of concentration would suggest. According to the market research company GFK Hungary, these small shop networks are characterized by high (69.6 per cent) penetration and frequency of shopping (35.3) but consumer spending per shopping trip is low (1200 HUF or about US$ 6). The typical consumer is the housewife alone, going to the shop on foot or by public transport on working days and during the day. The over-represented groups are the low-middle-income Budapest or large city consumers. This retail type has shown a steady decrease in recent years.

Case study 1: POs supplying onions

In 2003, small-scale private farmers accounted for 90 per cent of onion production in Hungary and 70 per cent of fresh vegetables. Three POs accounted for 70–80 per cent of onion marketing. One of them, Makó, was founded in February 2003 and registered in November in the same year with a profile of vegetable production. The owners include: small producers (10 per cent), entrepreneurs (20 per cent), and partnerships (70 per cent). Makó manages 500 hectares, of which 300 hectares is onion production. The total number of producers involved amounts to 140 with a total annual turnover of 500 million HUF (about US$ 25 million), of which 300 million HUF (about US$ 15 million) is accounted for by onion production. To improve their bargaining power, Makó has joined forces with 20 other POs in a joint stock company.

In the future, it is expected that POs will receive subsidies under the EU Common Agricultural Policy which will amount to 3 per cent of total turnover (12 million HUF or about US$ 60,000 per PO). This amount of money is badly needed to build cold storage capacity that will make Makó more competitive in the marketing chain. At the same time, due to market needs, the technology also has to be improved so that Makó can produce products for final consumption in small units.

If small producers want to become stable partners in the marketing chains, they have to increase their efficiency within the chain. The latter can be managed, for instance, by new investments in irrigation. However, it is rather costly and most small producers cannot afford such investments. Another possibility for them is to improve their willingness to cooperate with POs or even to join POs. Areas where intervention by upstream agents is required are: the varieties of seed and baby onion to sow; and the quality requirements of end consumers/customers who provide feedback through other players in the marketing chain such as POs, buying companies and middlemen.

There is very little information on private sector policies to support small- and medium-sized farms. This case study illustrates that today in Hungarian agriculture, marketing cooperatives can solve some of the problems arising because of the lack of market institutions or their embryonic state (Fertő and Szabó, 2004).

The Mórakert Purchasing and Service Co-operative, Mórahalom, is a successful so-called new type cooperative built on the Danish model. Its strength is in carrying out marketing activities on behalf of its members, and it has the capacity to accomplish its basic objective: to help farmers to sell their agricultural produce and/or to purchase input materials on their behalf at the most favourable prices in a market that offers long-term security. Provision of information is also very important with respect to the success of the cooperation between the cooperative enterprise and its members. The cooperative runs according to what is known as the 'cost principle'. After the subtraction of deposits and cost from the surplus made annually, the cooperative reimburses members in proportion to their turnover with the cooperative.

The cooperative itself has no machinery or land title connected with agricultural production. The input side of members' activities was organized first, as this was a simpler task. Coordination of sales began later. The cooperative had 52 founding members in April 1995; by April 1998, membership had increased to 66, by October 1999, to 134, and in 2002, the cooperative had 289 members. All members have their own land property and assets for farming. The cooperative has 23 employees, which is of great significance, since work is otherwise rather scarce and cooperative employees enjoy relatively high salaries in comparison with the local average.

Seventy per cent of the produce purchased from members is sold on the domestic market and 30 per cent abroad (Estonia, Latvia, Lithuania, Czech Republic, Slovakia and Slovenia). The cooperative brands onions, potatoes and peppers with its own label, and wants to increase the range of products of this kind. About 90 per cent of the products distributed on the domestic markets by the cooperative are sold to retail chains. Wholesale markets are avoided, where possible, to shorten the marketing chain. Some products are sold on a contractual basis at weekly prices.

The increase in both the membership and the turnover of the cooperative demonstrates that it is operating effectively. This is partly due to the favourable approach of the local authority, the various sources of capital derived from funds for development, and above all, the human capital and resources within the cooperative, particularly its leadership and its managing director. The cooperative plans to form a secondary cooperative to be able to exploit countervailing power.

Case study 2: Dairy products

The dairy sector presents a challenge for farmers and policy-makers alike. As in many CEE countries, there are large dairy farms at one extreme and many tiny producers at the other. The policy question is this: should Hungary encourage small-scale producers to organize themselves into groups in order to access the modern food system? Or should the government concentrate on rehabilitating the old large-scale dairy farms and accept that conditions no longer favour small-scale dairying in the EU? Or perhaps it should attempt to create a new stratum of medium-sized farms? The Amal cooperative in India offers an example of the first strategy, western member states of the EU provide examples of the second and South Africa's 'emerging farmers' provide an example of the third.

The number of farms producing milk is in decline in Hungary. At present, an estimated 20 000–25 000 farms and smallholdings keep cows. Three types of dairy farm can be identified. There are 700–800 large-scale farmers with 300–600 cows who sell milk on contract to processors. Another 4000–6000 farms have 10–30 cows, selling to processors and other outlets, often through milk collectors. Nearly all the other farms have a few cows and sell milk in the traditional market system. As far as looking for 'small-scale producers' the target group for policy-makers must surely be those with 10–30 cows.

Large-scale enterprises can be made viable by investing in technology and improving the management of the dairies to comply with strict EU hygiene standards. Even so, low procurement prices make a number of these enterprises unprofitable.

As far as we can see, the problem group are farmers with 10–30 cows. They are too big for direct sales and procurement prices are too low to be profitable – processors are their main customers. On the other hand, most have already invested significant amounts in the development of their dairies so they are too much involved in production to stop it.

The third group, farmers with a few cows each, will diminish, with survivors selling raw milk locally. Some may be able to interest processors as milk suppliers if they can form organizations and meet EU hygiene standards. At the moment, the demand for raw milk is increasing following consumer suspicion about adulterated 'milk-like' products.

Concentration in the milk processing sector started to become significant in the middle of the 1990s. There are still too many uneconomic processors but the top-10 companies now account for 80 per cent of milk processing and the top-5 have over 50 per cent. One of the critical issues is the bargaining power of small scale processors. They only receive 30–40 per cent of the retail price of milk. Increasing their share of the retail milk price requires them to organize and match the scale of the top-10.

The influence of foreign milk processors operating in Hungary has been significant during the transition. First, they have raised standards. Second, they have made close supply chain partnerships with large-scale dairy farms. Third, they have introduced more complex, quality-related payments for milk. Fourth, they sell to supermarkets and these are moving towards central buying.

Foreign-owned milk processors have also introduced internal systems to aid quality control in contrast to small local companies. This has limited the latter's ability to export and they will face increasing difficulties on the domestic market as Hungary adopts EU food laws as part of the process of accession.

Foreign supermarket companies have also introduced new ways of working in Hungary. Their investments have led to developments along western European lines: introducing and developing warehouse point distribution, own brands and systems for electronic data interchange (EDI). This is used for determining the size and frequency of deliveries as orders are based on actual buying patterns rather than estimates. Suppliers have been pressed to introduce systems to handle EDI. This has favoured foreign-owned processors and further marginalized small dairies.

In these ways, Hungarian milk supply channels increasingly mirror practices in western Europe. Excluded agents (micro-producers and small-scale Hungarian dairy processors) are involved in informal channels of distribution characterized by self-consumption or sale to village neighbours and small traders.

Conclusions

During the transformation period, agriculture and food processing were declining sectors within the Hungarian economy. Although the total and manufacturing GDP have increased considerably since 1994, agriculture shows only slight growth. Total labour productivity has not improved significantly in either agriculture or the food industry.

We have looked at onions and milk in detail in this chapter, two products of importance to private farms, which have had differing experiences during the transition. The share of individual farms in onion production reached almost 90 per cent in 2003, indicating the dominance of small-scale farmers. Milk production shows a different picture of moderate concentration. Both onion and milk producers earn low profits.

We find that in both the dairy and fruit and vegetable processing sectors there is growing concentration and a predominance of multinational firms. Small- and medium-sized firms focus mainly on regional markets and niche markets.

It is important to recognize that particular groups of agricultural producers use different vertical coordination mechanisms to connect with the food industry. Large agricultural enterprises and cooperatives usually have a production contract, sometimes long-term, with the food industry. They are rarely involved in closer vertical integration offered by food industry companies. These farms can also sell their products through organized spot markets. Products from smaller, individual farms are purchased mainly via spot markets, but they sometimes have production contracts. Market-oriented part-time farmers sell their commodities basically through spot markets. Subsistence part-time farmers do not sell their products.

It can be seen that only a small number of agricultural producers have stable linkages with the food industry. Furthermore, the majority of farmers face significant market uncertainties with little scope for risk reduction. It follows from this that the situation of many farmers has not stabilized even after 15 years of transformation.

There are also non-economic factors in vertical coordination. Our case study of the Mórakert cooperative shows that marketing type cooperatives can be very useful. However, we do not expect much expansion of marketing cooperatives and other such producer organizations in the foreseeable future.

Future opportunities for onion and milk producers will arise less from growth in the market and more from niche market development based on growing income inequalities in Hungarian society. While supermarkets in Hungary have so far focused upon medium- to high-income consumers, low-income families continue to provide a large informal market, encouraged by a tax system that tends to favour the black market. Furthermore, increasing imports after EU accession will increase competition for milk producers and processors.

In spite of difficult conditions such as quantity and quality requirements and long-term payments, super- and hypermarkets have become attractive partners for food processors and producers. This phase of supermarket growth in Hungary still leaves access to plenty of non-supermarket markets for farmers. But if small producers do not develop horizontal linkages (marketing cooperatives and other producer organizations), it will be increasingly difficult for them to access routes to the higher-income consumers who are the particular target of supermarkets.

The problems of farmers cannot be solved simply by government subsidy. The starting point is that without establishing and developing efficient and transparent market institutions there will not be sustainable growth in the agri-food sectors. The disadvantages experienced by small-scale farms stem from transaction costs. Therefore, the focus of government activities should move from income and price support to interventions that decrease transaction costs. Also policy should take a problem-oriented, supply chain approach. Measures that increase information, reliability of quality standards and transparent prices will all help to reduce transaction costs.

A number of useful policy options exist to help manage change in the Hungarian food supply system:

1. A programme of investment in the rural infrastructure will improve the access of small-scale farmers to both input and output markets.
2. Policies that encourage private investment in post-harvest activities (storage, manipulation and packaging) and intermediary organizations (marketing cooperatives and producer organizations) will reduce exchange costs between farmers and their partners (processors and retailers).
3. The government should help food companies develop reliable contractual forms that build up trust between supply chain partners, are enforceable and avoid hold-ups.
4. Action needs to be taken to increase collaboration between milk producers, something for which EU subsidy schemes are available. Similar action is required among medium-sized milk processors, which otherwise have little economic future in a free market.

5. The small and very small producers need policies to allow them to withdraw from uneconomic production entirely. The EU also has a number of programmes that are relevant here.
6. For the surviving milk producers, policies are required to help improve milk quality, management, safety certification and environmental management.

As a result, the milk sector will become more efficient and will be more likely to survive in a business environment characterized by increasing competition and stable demand.

References

Fertő, I. and Szabó, G.G., 2004. Transaction cost economics and agricultural cooperatives: A Hungarian case study. In H.J. Bremmers, S.W.F. Omta, J.H. Trienekes and E.F.M. Wubben, eds. *Dynamics in Chain and Networks*, Wageningen: Wageningen Academic Publishers, pp. 245–51.
Gow, H. and Swinnen, J., 1998. Agribusiness restructuring, foreign direct investment, and hold-up problems in agricultural transition. *European Review of Agricultural Economics*, 25(4), 331–50.

8 *Poland*

Jerzy Wilkin, Malgorzata Juchniewicz and Dominika Milczarek

Introduction

During the past 15 years, the Polish economy has been transformed and prepared for accession to the EU. The road from centrally planned economy to open market economy has required profound changes in almost all institutional structures of the economy and society. These changes have also affected the agro-food sector. Agricultural and food products were first in the process of market liberalization that started in 1989. In 2003, over 95 per cent of food processing was in private sector hands.

The process of institution building in the agri-food economy has been very complicated and is not yet finished. Three factors have played especially important roles in this process: growing competition due to the opening up of the economy, an inflow of foreign capital, and preparations for membership of the EU, which was achieved in May 2004. Restructuring, and modernization of the food economy have accelerated in the second half of the 1990s and in the first years of this decade. Polish agriculture is still dominated by small producers, but their position is weakening year by year.

We look at two products in this chapter, apples and pigs. Poland is the largest producer of apples in CEE and one of the largest producers of pigs.

KEY DATA

	2002	*2003*	*2004*
Population (millions)	38.62	38.60	38.57
Per capita GDP (US$)	4913	5364	5723
Urbanization (%)	63		
Agriculture as % of GDP			2.9
Per capita total retail food sales (US$)	997	1083	1146
Per capita modern retail food sales (US$)	634	697	740
Modern food sales as % total			64

TOP CHAINS, 2004

Company	Ownership	Number of stores	Retail banner sales 2004 (US$ millions)	Market share (%)	Grocery sales 2004 (US$ millions)	Grocery market share (%)
Metro Group	Foreign	90	3852	8.2	2013	5.2
Tesco	Foreign	78	1430	3.1	1028	2.6
Jerónimo Martins	Foreign	725	1426	3.0	1212	3.1
Ahold	Foreign	198	1333	2.8	926	2.4
Schwarz Group	Foreign	173	1298	2.8	1009	2.6
Other			37 490	80.1	32 889	84.2

Source: PlanetRetail (www.planetretail.net)

FOOD RETAILING IN POLAND

Food retailing in Poland is characterized by an overwhelming western dominance with a number of global players having brought a wide range of modern store formats into the country, such as hypermarkets, superstores, modern discount stores and cash-and-carry stores.

The share of modern distribution channels has been increasing rapidly, from 18 per cent of food retail sales in 1998 to 32 per cent in 2002. The proportion is expected to rise to 50–60 per cent of retail sales by 2006–07. In 2002, the largest turnovers were achieved by foreign-owned retail chains Metro, Jerónimo Martins, Casino, Carrefour, Auchan, Tesco, Rewe, Ahold and Tengelmann. In the period 1996–2000, 112 hypermarkets began operations in Poland. Recently, hypermarkets operating in Poland have started to export Polish food products, mostly fruit juice and FFV to their chain stores in other countries. Metro Group has 40 Polish suppliers who export their products through the group's channels.

There have been two stages in the expansion of retail chains in Poland. During the first stage, new stores were established and supplied through international channels with imported products. In the second stage, which is the situation today, the chains are building their supply chain systems within Poland itself.

The expansion has lead to local opposition and action to limit the operation of supermarkets, such as restricting Sunday opening. For this and other reasons, local shops continue to survive in small city and country niches. They also survive in the form of tens of thousands of small independent shops sourcing from a combination of western-owned and domestic cash-and-carry outlets as well as local wholesalers. Even in the large cities, where modern formats play such an important role, significant parts of the independent sector have managed to hold on to their niches. It is also important to note that, due to the largely rural structure of the country, village shops can combine to form a truly heavyweight sector and will do so for some years to come. Food shops selling from 300 m² or less still account for 98 per cent of all food stores in Poland. This is also the reason why market concentration here continues to be low when compared with more advanced CEE economies.

APPLE MARKETING

Fruit and vegetable production is an important branch of the agricultural sector in Poland and amounts to around 12 per cent of total agricultural production for sale. Arable land under fruit and vegetable growing covers around 640 000 hectares (4 per cent of total farmland in Poland) including orchards of 270 000 hectares (around 1.6 per cent of total farmland). Apple production is dominant and is conducted on over 50 per cent of the orchard area.

According to the Agricultural Census conducted in 2002, there are around 320 000 farms (around 11 per cent of the total number of farms in Poland) with an orchard. Most of them (over 65 per cent), have less than 5 hectares and cover 34 per cent of total orchard area. Large fruit-growing farms of over 20 hectares constitute less than 5 per cent of the total number but account for around 15 per cent of orchard area. Most apple production is concentrated in small- to medium-sized orchards operating from 5 to 15 hectares of farmland (27 per cent of the total number of apple-growing farms) and covering almost 50 per cent of the total area under apple production. Virtually all orchards are on private land.

Farmers with apple orchards are diversifying their production and only around 10 per cent of farmers with apple orchards specialize in apple production. This is a rational response to the unstable nature of the apple market in Poland, the result of fluctuations in supply and prices.

For processing apples, the main distribution channel is through local trading companies and small wholesalers. The profit margins of trading companies are usually in the region of 10–20 per cent. In areas of high production and concentration of fruit processing, such as the central region of Poland, producers also sell directly to processing companies.

The role of trading companies in table apples is very small. Small fruit growing producers usually sell table apples directly at local street markets (around 40–50 per cent of table apple sales) and to grocery shops. They usually have verbal contracts, and sales and prices depend strongly on seasonal conditions.

Larger fruit growers and members of POs tend to sell table apples directly to large purchasers such as super- and hypermarket chains or exporting companies. They usually have written short-term contracts that require more stable deliveries and provide higher prices in comparison with other marketing channels. Usually, in the case of table apples, farmers receive around 70 per cent of the final price. However, they have to adapt to long payment periods and high purchaser requirements such as quality and tight delivery deadlines. Such contract terms are a reflection of the relative bargaining power of supermarket chains over producers.

Despite the existence of many branch organizations and associations, there is a very low level of economic cooperation between producers in fruit and vegetable markets. Current producer associations and horticulture cooperatives very often have organizational and financial problems and they do not fulfil their statutory tasks. The situation of small farms could be improved if well-organized POs were created. However, a number of problems have hampered the creation of POs: (1) slow process of preparing legislation for the creation of POs; (2) negative attitudes of farmers – lack of trust for common activities, fear of being cheated and unwillingness to bear high organizational costs; (3) insufficient information on how important groups are to the functioning of markets within the EU.

In 2000, two important acts were passed: a law setting down rules for the organization of POs and their associations, and an act concerning the organization of fruit and vegetable markets, hop markets, tobacco markets and dried fodder markets. These acts are based on similar regulations in other EU countries. They define organizational rules and support for POs in these markets. Apart from these regulations, apple producers do not receive any specific support.

There are around 1300 fruit and vegetable processing companies in Poland. Most of them (90 per cent) are small firms employing less than 50 people. Large companies with more than 100 employees constitute around 2 per cent of companies. Most fruit and vegetable processing companies are located in central Poland, though the processing industry is also well developed in the southern and eastern regions of Poland. In all branches of fruit and vegetable processing (except pickled and dried vegetables), foreign capital is becoming a dominant force. Super- and hypermarket chains provide good opportunities to large fruit and vegetable producers and producer groups to increase production and sales.

Case study 1: POs for apples

A producer group in Łęczeszyce is located in Grójec Powiat in the central region of Poland where apple production is concentrated, sometimes called the 'largest orchard in Europe'. According to data from the CSO, there are 40 000 hectares of land under fruit farming in the Grójec region. Annual average production in 2000 amounted to around 700 000 tonnes, 30 per cent of total apple production in Poland. There are around 750 000 farms producing apples, which have an average size of 7 hectares including 4.2 hectares of orchards.

The producer group in Łęczeszyce was created in 2001 as a limited liability company with nine founder members operating a total 80 hectares of orchards. In October 2002, it gained official recognition. In 2003, three new members joined the group. Currently, farmer-members of the group operate around 100 hectares and produce 2500 tonnes of apples per year (and 500 tonnes of other fruit such as cherries). They own shares according to their area of farmland.

The group was founded at the beginning of the 1990s as an informal group of family and friends (five farmers). They started to sell fruit to small vegetable shops. Before then, the five farmers were members of a very large fruit production cooperative. The most important factor in creating a new producer group is trust. Other producers were reluctant to create POs because they were afraid of being cheated.

Currently, a number of services are available to members of the producer group in Łęczeszyce. These include joint marketing, discounts on farm supplies, credit, and legal services. According to the agreement, all members are obliged to sell 80 per cent of their apples through the group. The group has annual written contracts with supermarket chains and with a foreign (Norwegian) trading company. A small part of the apple production is sold to a local fruit processing company. The group is also seeking to associate with other POs so they can tender for larger contracts.

THE FRUIT PRODUCERS' PROTESTS

The Polish Fruit-Growers Association is the largest association of fruit producers in Poland. It was founded in 1999. One of the main goals of the association is to present the needs and interests of fruit producers. Because of a sharp decline in fruit prices, farmers (mostly of cherries and berries) decided to organize protests in autumn 2001 and 2002, blocking access to several fruit processing companies in many regions of Poland, and publicized their opinions in the media. According to representatives of the association, low prices were a result of collusion between brokers and fruit processing companies. The association gained the support of the Senate and organized a meeting with the Minister of Agriculture and representatives of fruit processing companies, who agreed to price negotiations. It was successful in negotiating minimum prices for apples for processing during the season 2002-03.

According to the Minister of Agriculture, Wojciech Olejniczak, and agricultural experts, the current problems of fruit producers arise from over-production, an unwillingness to create POs and an unwillingness to sign long-term contracts. The Minister decided to apply to the

European Commission for support for fruit producers who would receive payments for the sale of fruits for processing (similar payments have been negotiated during EU accession negotiations for tomato producers). Fruit producers also wanted protective tariffs because of the high level of imports of Chinese fruit to the EU. However, the WTO forbids minimum prices or import barriers for these kinds of fruit.

SURVEY OF APPLE PRODUCERS

A number of growers in different parts of Poland were asked for their views on various issues in 2004. Most farmers interviewed felt that the liquidation of cooperatives during the transformation period was a mistake and wanted them restored. The most important advantage of cooperatives from the farmer's point of view was that they provided an assured and steady market, and availability of packing and transport services. Producers also did not have to worry about fruit storage.

For farmers who were members of producer groups, an additional problem was a high level of competition during the transformation process. This could explain why they decided to join POs to improve their market position. Producers started to sell directly to supermarket chains and to fruit processing companies. Hortex, a state-run organization in the pre-1990 period had a monopoly in exports of fruit from Poland. Since 1990, Hortex has declined in the face of competition. Currently, in the central region of Poland there are around 300 fruit exporting companies that compete strongly. However, apple producers do not perceive it as a positive change since, according to their opinion, Hortex was a professional organization and now it is difficult to reach agreement with so many new and unprofessional export companies.

All those interviewed were trying to adapt to the new conditions. Some of them perceived necessary changes as quite radical. They had all invested a lot in their farms, financed mostly from savings and also from preferential credit (nobody took commercial credit). The investments included: construction of (cold) storage buildings, irrigation systems, purchase of new machinery such as sorting and grading machines, change of apple variety, new plantings, and purchase of additional farmland. Farmers were also taking part in training and were looking for information on new technologies and marketing. Several of them travelled abroad to compare practices and learn from western fruit growers.

Small-scale orchards (operating around 5 hectares) and independent producers felt they were worse off in comparison with other producers. On the other hand, large producers operating around 15–20 hectares of farmland and members of POs who had modernized their farms saw themselves as much better off in comparison with other apple producers, thanks to them having more possibilities for financing investments, allowing them to increase product quality and marketing. All respondents agreed that small farmers have no chance to survive and develop fruit production because their low incomes do not allow for the necessary investment.

Membership of a producer group allows for more stable production and marketing conditions. A farmer member of a producer group has a written contract and the group undertakes to market the apples produced. Farmers are obliged to sell a given share of their production through the group (usually 80 per cent). Producer groups tend to sign contracts with large companies such as supermarket chains, exporting companies (both foreign and national) and fruit processing companies. Usually these contracts are for one season with an option to extend cooperation.

According to members of POs, the most important problems with purchasers are connected with long payment periods and high quality requirements. They feel that they can influence contract terms and that they could easily apply for a court judgement if necessary. However, at the same time they told us that supermarket chains and large fruit processing companies dictate conditions and have greater market power.

The supermarket chains' requirements illustrate their relative power over producers. Producers must be timely when delivering products and must provide their own transport, pay high costs for advertisements and expect that there will be a large share of the delivered product's value deducted to cover spoiled fruit.

In addition, there are high quality requirements. For example, several supermarket chains organize inspections in orchards. Stable demand and regular purchases seem to be an important advantage for producers so they agree to the supermarkets' restrictive terms. On the other hand, POs can always look for better conditions and try to influence the buyers.

Independent farmers, not associated with a producer group or cooperative, usually have no written contracts. They sell very often to casual purchasers, such as trading companies, and on the basis of verbal contracts. They need to look for purchasers and, as one farmer said, this is very stressful. Therefore, small independent farmers evaluate their position as very weak; they cannot influence terms of contracts and do not see any sense in applying for a court judgement. In their opinion, market conditions are dictated by supermarket chains, fruit processing companies, large apple producers and POs.

THE APPLE PROCESSORS' PERSPECTIVE

Fruit processing companies were reluctant to give interviews, partly because of the protests mentioned above (farmers were dissatisfied with low procurement prices and stopped deliveries to the processors). Two interviews were conducted in the central region of Poland. Both companies were of medium size and employed 50 persons as well as seasonal employees. One company was established two years ago by a German investor. The second one is Polish and was founded at the beginning of the 1990s.

Both buyers complained about the dispersed production system, which results in fluctuating quality and unstable deliveries. One said: 'You never can be sure what kind of apples will be delivered.' The second complained: 'Producers deliver apples when it is convenient for them rather than when we need fruit.'

Naturally, buyers are not very sympathetic to the difficulties facing farmers. These two buyers criticized farmers in several ways. First, farmers fail to estimate their likely volume of production, or how much will be available for sale to processors. As a result, planning their processing businesses was difficult and inaccurate.

A second criticism was the continual complaints of farmers that the price they were offered for apples was too low. The buyers said that farmers were unrealistic and did not want to accept the rigours of the market.

In both companies, contracts with brokers are signed for one year (season). These companies do not want to have longer contracts because of uncertainty. Brokers cannot guarantee given amounts for several years because this largely depends on the weather conditions and the available supplies of apples that they can purchase from producers.

Contracts guarantee payments by bank transfer within 14 days after delivery. Contracts also contain delivery periods and quality requirements – these are internal quality requirements; in one company they were based on HACCP and International Standards Organization (ISO). None of the companies offers any support for producers. According to them, it is too costly to build storage buildings or to organize transport. One of the companies plans to start cooperating with producers and hopes to support them in producing specific varieties of apples suitable for juice extraction. This support could include training, provision of credit and provision of seedlings. However, in return, producers would have to guarantee supplies to the juicer.

Usually, if cooperation is good, contracts are prolonged. In one of the processing companies, suppliers are evaluated annually (also on the basis of fulfilling quality requirements) and a reference list is created. If suppliers from the reference list cannot fulfil requirements, the processing company looks elsewhere for apples. The company that cooperates directly with farmers signs long-term contracts (usually for six years) with them. These are mostly farmers who have invested in a given kind of production.

Case study 2: Procurement from pig producer groups

The liberalization of the Polish economy led pig producers to turn from contract sales to processors and instead use the new free market and sell by auction and by direct marketing. However, after a few years of 'free-for-all', we saw a restoration of contract sales to processors. In the space of a decade, the Polish market for pig meat moved from one sort of regulated marketing to another with a brief experience of free market forces in between. Large, state-owned companies and centrally organized cooperatives dominated the meat market in Poland during the era of central planning. A high level of concentration characterized this structure. Pig producers had little freedom to choose a purchaser and also relied for their inputs on their contractual links. This meant a close integration of pig producers with meat processing plants.

The profitability of pig production depended upon the price relationship between pigs on the one hand and feedstuffs, such as grain and potatoes, on the other. Keeping food prices low created a very large demand for agricultural products, including meat and processed meat. Chronic excess demand resulted in a good economic situation for both small- and medium-sized farms. Farmers had little incentive to introduce new technology and the lack of a competitive market meant that it was pointless for them to cut costs or improve the quality of their products.

The reforms in 1989 quickly changed all that. State-run systems of contracting, the administration of prices, distribution of inputs and the subsidizing of production and consumption ceased. As a result, per capita pork consumption fell and later stabilized at around 40 kg per person.

Changes also occurred in the organization of the meat processing sector, with the most important tendency being adjustment to the market determined by demand factors – a shift from fixed, low prices and a shortage economy to flexible, higher prices and a 'demand-pull' market. As a result the integration of pig production and meat processing based on contracts collapsed in the early 1990s.

Another factor in the demise of integrated pig/pork production was the privatization of state-owned and cooperative retail outlets (such as Samopomoc Chłopska, Społem, Państwowy Hurt Spożywczy), which hitherto had dominated the distribution of agri-food products in Poland. Small trading companies sprung up from the ashes of cooperative and state-owned outlets and new ones were formed. New distribution channels and small slaughterhouses and processing companies developed in the new unrestricted market.

Entrepreneurs were free to make the most of the lack of entry barriers for new entities and of better access to a dispersed retail network. As a result, the state sector lost its dominating market position in a very short time. Within a few years, contracted supplies of pork amounted to only 45 per cent of production. However, from the mid-1990s there was a growing tendency, especially by large meat-processing companies, to restore contracting relationships. Registered purchases, in other words contracted supplies, increased from 41 per cent in 1994 to 65 per cent in 2002.

At the same time privatization continued rapidly: by 1998, the state accounted for only 5 per cent of meat-processing. A group of leading sector companies has now emerged both from privatized companies as well as from the small and medium companies that were created during the first phase of transformation. This was also the period of large investments, inflows of foreign capital and improvements in the finances of private companies.

Recently, in the so-called 'second restructuring' phase, meat processing companies have started to remove redundant resources and to limit production. In the years 2002–03, they also accelerated investments to meet sanitary requirements in the EU, to implement quality systems, and to extend integration with pig producers. With increased competition since the mid-1990s, contracting in the pig sector has increased. Currently, the best meat processing companies use contracting to stabilize deliveries and to improve the quality of pigs for slaughter. The meat industry once more organizes its own source of raw materials, and influences the development and reorganizing of agricultural structure. The results of a survey show that over 70 per cent of farmers interviewed entered into agreements with purchasers. Among them, 40 per cent had long-term written contracts, 40 per cent had one-year written contracts and only 20 per cent had oral contracts.

As contracting has been re-established, so the role of auction markets has declined. By the end of the 1990s, their number had significantly decreased and there were only six to eight regional auctions left. Another effect has been a growth in the importance of POs.

PIG PRODUCER GROUPS

Pig POs are being created, although their current share of production is marginal. They are an example of the horizontal integration of the pig meat market. However, their growth has been slow and halting. Legal regulations in force since September 2000 have been a hindrance and by 2003 there were only 37 officially registered POs. The Information Centre of Extension Services for Agricultural Producer Groups created by the Rural Cooperatives Foundation know of more groups than this and estimate that 413 POs (both registered and unregistered) are currently operating. There are five registered POs and 93 unregistered ones in the pig market.[1]

Several factors explain the slow process of the organization of POs. First, a high level of distrust exists based on past experience. Second, strong farms are unwilling to cooperate with weak farms. Third, there is little tradition of cooperation patterns in rural society and few farming leaders who are prepared to undertake the organization of POs.

The advantages of joining a pig group are demonstrated by Knoblauch and Lizińska (2003). They found that members of pig POs are in a better position to negotiate with meat-processing companies than independent farmers. The terms of contracts of members of POs are more beneficial since they are preceded by negotiations. Independent farmers, who also sign agreements, usually have to take what they are offered. The results of our own research confirm this. All the independent pig producers we interviewed who had signed contracts with meat-processing companies told us that they had no influence on prices paid to them by the processing companies.

---

1   See www.fsw.pl.

It should also be remembered that production and export subsidies, as well as other types of support used in the EU, are available only for POs. In addition, POs provide conditions that favour vertical integration. Joining subsequent agro-business networks strengthens the competitive position of a producer group and improves its bargaining position on the market. If vertical integration is not based on a foundation of horizontal integration, farmers will become more dependent on their market partners.

Conclusions

Polish agriculture remains dominated by small producers. Most count themselves as among the losers of post-Communist transformation and market reforms although this attitude will probably change as new projects begin and more EU money flows in. The biggest problems which farmers face are poor institutionalization, especially in the area of self-organization, and very limited access to modern knowledge and technology. As a result, thousands of farms have reduced their links with the market and now produce only for the needs of the farm household. Overall, there is a lack of well-defined and efficient public support for small producers.

Since EU accession, we can observe a very fast increase in the share of foreign trading companies in the marketing of food products. Big international retail chains account for over 30 per cent of all food product sales and it is estimated that this share will reach 75–80 per cent in 2010.

The rapid modernization of the meat industry has been a result of many factors, but two of them are the most important: an inflow of FDI and the introduction of EU norms and standards. In the mid-1990s, over 20 per cent of FDI in Poland went to the food processing industry, now (2002–03) it is down to about 10 per cent.

Small-scale pig producers have less access to the market than large-scale ones. There is a lack of well-organized POs, particularly in the fruit and vegetable sector. Cooperation between farmers in the form of POs or cooperatives is developing very slowly. In 2003, there were only five registered POs in pig production. Another 20–40 groups have been established but are not registered yet. Producer groups are supported now from EU funds and support for POs is the only form of public support after EU accession provided for the fruit and vegetable sector. Strong individualism and the slow progress towards cooperation between farmers in Poland is partly a result of their bad experience with collective farms during the communist era.

There are several positive signs that a new era has begun for agricultural producers in Poland thanks to the implementation of the EU support within the Common Agricultural Policy. In October 2004, the first direct payments were made to Polish farmers. These payments will gradually increase over the next decade. Farmers can also now benefit from other forms of support available under the Common Agricultural Policy (CAP) regime. There is a growing interest by farmers in investments to modernize their farms as a result of the improved outlook for farm profitability. EU accession has given Polish farmers and food producers better access to the Single European Market and 450 million consumers. This alone will have an important impact on the operation of the food economy in Poland.

References

Knoblauch, L. and Lizińska, W., 2003. Grupy producenckie alternatywą dla polskich producentów żywca wieprzowego z województw północno-wschodnich (Producers' groups as an alternative for pig producers in the north-eastern region of Poland). In *Prace Naukowe Akademii Ekonomicznej*, Wroclaw

9 Romania

Dinu Gavrilescu, Mariana Grodea, Camelia Serbanescu, and Crina Turtoi

Introduction

Despite a continuous economic growth since 2000, Romania lags behind other large CEE countries according to most economic and social indicators. Therefore, it is not surprising to find few supermarkets and limited examples of a modern food system. Even so, there are signs of dynamism in Romanian agri-food, illustrated by case studies in this chapter.

In 1990, Romania bade farewell to the centrally planned economic model and welcomed (again) the market model. During the pre-transition period, production and distribution were mostly state owned, and only a small share was cooperative. Private trade was forbidden except for some agri-food products that were sold in local markets.

Transition in Romania led to high unemployment and many people moved back to ancestral land and attempted to take up semi-subsistence farming. They invested much labour into this but because of limited management skills, expertise and capital, the yields were low. As a result there is a high degree of dislocation in Romanian farming at present.

KEY DATA

	2002	2003	2004
Population (millions)	21.8	21.7	21.7
Per capital GDP (US$)	2102	2742	3479
Urbanization (%)	53.3	53.4	54.9
Agriculture as % GDP	11.3	11.6	13.0
Per capita total retail food sales (US$)	476	575	684
Per capita modern retail food sales (US$)	194	232	278
Modern food retail as % total	41	40	41

Exchange rate: 1 USD = 1 old lei (ROL) 33055.5 (2002); 33200.1 (2003); 32637.6 (2004)

or

! USD = 1 new lei (RON) 3.31 (2002); 33.20 (2003); 32.64 (2004)

TOP CHAINS

Company	Ownership	Number of stores	Retail banner sales 2004 (US$ millions)	Market share (%)	Grocery sales 2004 (US$ millions)	Grocery market share (%)
Metro Group	Foreign	28	1628	24.3	1074	20.8
Rewe	Foreign	26	664	9.9	556	10.8
Carrefour	Franchise	4	329	4.9	230	4.5
Louis Delhaize	Foreign	22	150	2.2	96	1.9
OMV	Foreign	680	71	1.1	53	1.0
Other			3868	57.6	3154	61.1

Source: PlanetRetail (www.planetretail.net)

STRUCTURE AND TRENDS IN FOOD RETAILING

Food market concentration in Romania is relatively low and the Metro Group is the only real heavyweight, with a share of 20 per cent of food retail sales (2004). There are few significant domestic players active in the Romanian market, and the pace in food retailing is set by western European companies. This is despite the fact that foreign investment in Romania is easier in theory than in practice thanks to a number of bureaucratic hindrances.

After transition, retail was the first sector of the economy to restructure and privatize. Several factors contributed significantly to this process: the increased autonomy of the production enterprises (which were no longer obliged to sell to specific customers), the emergence of a private production sector, the liberalization of prices, the freedom to travel abroad and the relaxation of foreign trade restrictions (very low import tariffs and discontinuation of import bans).

New private retail businesses were mostly kiosks or small shops because of the lack of capital and of premises, added to unclear ownership structures and processes. Even so, the number of retail units tripled in the years between 1989 and 1994. The ownership structure changed quickly: by 1994, 77 per cent of the total number of retail units were privately owned, while the number of public-owned and cooperative shops dropped by one third each.

By the mid-1990s, local domestic independent small-format supermarkets emerged in the big towns, many of them with foreign investment. The very first modern supermarkets emerged in Bucharest, and were joint ventures with Lebanese and Greek capital. In 1996, the Metro Group opened the first cash and carry. Since then, other international chains have invested in Romania and opened supermarkets, cash and carry, discount stores and hypermarkets. At the same time, the trend in the number of shops reversed: after the explosion of the first few years, a process of concentration started: by 2002, the total number of shops had decreased by one-third compared with 1994.

The trend could be easily seen: wherever a supermarket emerged, most of the specialized surrounding small shops closed within months. Yet, this trend has mainly been restricted to large cities. In smaller cities, as well as in the rural areas, very few supermarkets have emerged, and most of the domestic trade is still going on in small specialized shops. Today, local agri-food markets are selling mostly FFV, but also other food products, as well as cheap, low-quality non-food products.

There are several reasons for the low prices of the products sold in the small independent shops and in the local agri-food markets: the shops are buying the products directly from the producers, or from small-scale processing units that are producing unsophisticated food products of poor quality and with poor packaging.

Kiosks in local agri-food markets incur low costs, much lower than those incurred by supermarkets. Therefore, kiosks sell at low prices and consequently local markets are not badly affected by competition from the emergence of nearby supermarkets. On the contrary, most of them have recently benefited from investment from local authority budgets; as a result they have significantly improved in terms of presentation of products, freshness and cleanliness. As a result, they represent a good opportunity for small-scale producers to sell their fresh products.

Currently, the absence of marketing cooperatives and/or wholesale markets for fruit and vegetables is resulting in the fact that these small farmers, who are producing the largest share of the total output of these products at national level, are able to provide only small quantities of fruit and vegetables with inconsistent quality, and therefore the big supermarkets refuse to deal with them.

When looking at the top players in the Romanian grocery trade, things may at first glance look the same as elsewhere in CEE: there are quite a number of foreign companies playing in the top field. However, the situation is fundamentally different from markets such as Hungary, the Czech Republic or Poland, where western multinational retailers have carved out substantial market shares. In Romania, there is only one grocer with a market share of more than 15 per cent. Most foreign grocers – including Carrefour, Delhaize Group, Gima, Louis Delhaize, Caprabo and Intermarché – have all started securing a few retail sites but are still in a waiting position. This because Romania has a large population by CEE standards and is characterized by low incomes and weak spending power.

Supermarkets started off selling expensive imported products to high income groups. Later, Romanian products that were able to match foreign products in terms of packaging and quality started to be sold there too, but their prices were at least 20 per cent higher than in other retail shops. In time, sales have increased, and the general level of the prices of the food products sold in these supermarkets has decreased.

This has led to new groups of consumers being attracted into supermarkets, those of medium income. Low-income consumers and pensioners continue to shop for cheap products in small independent shops and in local agri-food markets, as well as the small government-owned domestic operation called Economat. Founded in December 2001, Economat shops sell basic foods (mostly groceries) at prices between 10 and 30 per cent cheaper than regular food stores. However, low-income consumers have more recently also started to shop in the hypermarkets and supermarkets, attracted by the aggressive advertising and the opportunity of numerous occasional discounts offered for various food products. A feature of the food market is that imports have recently risen strongly because of continuing domestic supply problems.

THE EFFECTS OF THE TRANSITION ON PRODUCTION

Romania has experienced two dramatic changes in agri-food since 1992. First, the transfer of ownership of land and livestock to the private sector, virtually completed by 2002. Second the collapse of livestock numbers in 1992–02 with the withdrawal of subsidies and the bankruptcy of specialist state-owned producers. Livestock numbers fell by more than half in Romania.

These changes have resulted in a pattern of land ownership that is fragmented and chaotic. Plainly, the vast majority of micro-holdings of land are not commercially viable. Ways have been sought to farm land cooperatively even though it is owned in a multitude of fragments.

However, a lack of equipment and money for investment means that much of the agricultural potential of the country lies idle. Romania is one of the few places in the world where the poorest farmers have switched back to using horses for tillage and transport.

Case Study 1 illustrates how transition brought in foreign capital under various schemes. This modernized some vertically integrated farms such as the one in the study and allowed the business to bounce back. The old structures, freed from bureaucratic constraints and obsolete methods and payments, have been reborn in more favourable circumstances. But the conclusion is that, for grain at least, there is no place for small-scale producers in the modern Romanian food system. More scope is found for small-scale milk producers, the subject of Case Studies 2 and 3.

Case study 1: Supply chain for wheat and bread

Pombis is a private agricultural company which has farms producing fruit, arable crops, young cattle and milk. It also has storage facilities, a mill, two bakery and pastry factories, and a commercial complex with a chain of shops in Bistrita-Nasaud town.

Most of the wheat the company is producing is not sold directly onto the wheat market but is used in the company's bakery and pastry factories. The wheat is transported from the field to the farm storage facilities, then, as needed, to the mill, and to the bakery and pastry factory. All the transportation is done with the company's fleet. The factory processes the wheat flour, producing and marketing bread, bakery and pastry products at both the wholesale and retail levels.

The wheat comes entirely from the company's farms. Each year, the company takes care that the necessary quantity of wheat for making flour and afterwards bread, bakery and pastry products can be covered from its own production. Moreover, the company is interested in making all the effort necessary to produce wheat of the best possible quality, so that the bakery produce is as good as possible.

Because the bread and bakery factories belongs to the company, according to the law, the wheat delivery is considered to be 'inner consumption' and the company is eligible to receive support for wheat production. The mill was built and started operating in 1997 using a US\$ 50 000 credit from the State Ownership Fund. The bread and bakery factories were built using the company's own financial resources, as well as a European Bank for Reconstruction and Development (ERBD) credit and began working in October 1993. The investment was made in cooperation with an Italian firm, which supplied the equipment (of the up-to-date technology), assisted in the installation and provided the instructions for the use of the equipment. The storage facilities for raw materials in the factory are quite limited, with reserves only for a few days' production. The purpose of these investments was mainly to make the entire wheat chain more fluid, from wheat flour to bread, bakery and pastry products, thus eliminating problems linked to continuity of supply along the chain. Thus, complete vertical integration has been realized for these products.

The bread and bakery factories are producing bread on a daily basis plus more than 15 kinds of bakery and pastry products, including cakes. The company studied carefully the local demand variations according to the day of the week, the season and religious feasts; therefore the total output varies accordingly, in order to minimize the losses.

The output of the factory is sold in the local area in Bistrita town, through the factory's own shop, which is located in the same building as the factory (25–30 percent of the output), through three shops and 10 small distribution points belonging to the company (about 20 per cent), through institutional buyers such as boarding schools, and military units, and to other clients, especially private shops.

Plombis managers are confident that they have a winning formula for the future; a combination of vertical integration, low costs, value added, good quality products, increased exports, rapid response to prices (that is, switching in and out of store) and close relations with business customers and final consumers.

Case study 2: Montana milk supply chain

The company Montana was set up in 1989 with private capital and issued shares. Its headquarters are in the town of Piatra Neamt. The company buys milk for processing into butter, cheese, milk powder, ice cream and other products. It is a medium-sized business by current Romanian standards, with assets valued at US$ 5.6 million. This includes assets purchased with a World Bank loan. The company has a chain of shops, and its products are retailed through these as well as sold to retailers in urban areas. Montana runs three factories making dairy products and operates a milk collection network with 509 collection points and over 9000 producers (see Table 9.1)

Table 9.1   Organization of milk collection

Name of the centre	Communes allocated	Collection points	Number of producers
Piatra Neamt	29	126	2013
Roman	26	76	1474
Targu Neamt	75	307	6121
Total	130	509	9608

Source: S.C. Montana S.A.

About 90 per cent of the milk comes from small-scale producers, the rest from one large-scale farm. Milk collected by Montana declined by 68 per cent between 1989 and 2000. This occurred for two reasons. First, the disruption of the agrarian economy described above. Second, the proliferation of small local milk processors. Before the small-scale processors emerged in the mid 1990s, Montana accounted for 80 per cent of the local retail market. Now this is down to 20 per cent.

The decline of large processing plants in the face of competition from small-scale processors has been widespread in Romania. Before 1990, there were 46 large state-owned milk and dairy processing enterprises, one per county. After 1990, the dairy processing sector was among those where privatization of state-owned enterprises progressed slowly; in 1999, only 75 per cent of the state-owned enterprises in the sector were privatized. The privatization process in the sector was completed by the end of 2000.

In the same period, a large number of new private small and medium-sized enterprises for milk and dairy emerged. In 2002, the milk and dairy processing sector comprised a total number of 835 enterprises with 16 202 employees and another 640 unpaid staff.

Case study 3: Danone milk collection network

Danone entered the Romanian market in 1996, marketing yoghurt imported from other CEE countries. In 1999, the company bought, rebuilt and modernized the present headquarters factory and started up a production line for yoghurts and dairy desserts.

In 1998, the company started building its own milk collection chain. The quantity of milk collected has increased from 20 tonnes per day to 140 tonnes per day. In the beginning, the milk came from surviving state farms, each with an average of 200–300 cows. However, the supply was insufficient and Danone continued to import most of the products sold in Romania, despite a high import tax.

When more small-scale dairy farmers went into business in the late 1990s, usually with only around three cows each, Danone began a collection scheme. After identifying a suitable place for a collection centre, the company now provides the tanks and the cooling facilities for the collection centre. It makes a contract with a local milk collector, a person who becomes the local manager of the collection centre. The manager must have a truck to collect milk from individual small-scale producers twice a day. A collector typically collects 600–800 litres at a time and has a tank capacity in the collection centre of 2 tonnes.

The company sends its own refrigerated lorries every evening to transport the milk to the factory. Thus, the company does not have direct contracts with individual small-scale farmers. However, Danone does pick up milk directly from farmers with 50 cows or more; in the Romanian context these are specialist dairy farms.

Presently, Danone has about 70 suppliers (large farms plus collection centres). At arrival at the Danone factory, a sample of 2 litres of milk from each tank is sent to the laboratory where a quality test is performed. All the rules regarding the traceability of the milk are strictly observed. If the test reveals a quality problem, the tank is not unloaded and the milk is sent back to the collection centre or farm of origin.

The contract stipulates the quantities and the quality requirements for the milk to be delivered. The price is negotiated periodically, depending on the inflation rate. During the summer, 45 per cent of milk is collected from large specialized farms and 55 per cent from collection centres. During the winter, 70 per cent of milk is collected from specialized farms and 30 per cent from collection centres. But this does not solve the problem of seasonality of production. In winter, the milk supply decreases considerably due to the two calving months, while in summer the supply is excessive and the milk surplus is transformed into powdered milk, but the price is higher than the EU price, which is supported by export subsidies.

In an attempt to ease the pressure on prices in these critical periods and avoid compromising quality, the company has proposed a scheme for an increased subsidy for summer milk, or for summer stocks, to the government.

Small-scale farmers like dealing with Danone because they have several benefits. First they get paid more than elsewhere. Second, payment is made within 30 days, also an improvement on other buyers of raw milk. Third, the company has a scheme for helping farmers upgrade their equipment (New Technology Access Programme) and provides free advice on agronomy and machinery, and free veterinary services. Fourth, a special price premium is provided for meeting or exceeding standards. These are measured in milk protein content, consistency in delivery, meeting animal welfare standards, good agricultural practices and cow identification. In this way, the company is raising technical and managerial standards among dairy farmers.

Conclusions

The case studies illustrate the ways in which the Romanian food system is being restructured. There has been a place for small-scale producers in milk supply because there was a shortage of milk and unemployed workers turned to farming as a means of semi-subsistence living. However, in the case of wheat, the mills can get supplies from large farms and there is no need or place for small-scale farmers. The question is, as milk yields rise on specialist dairy farms with 50 or more cows, and as private standards become more stringent, will small-scale dairy producers be squeezed out?

The impact of Romania's entry to the EU in 2007 is constrained by a number of transitional arrangements. In particular, the first pillar of CAP will not fully apply for several years (the level of direct payments). Nevertheless, the extra funding available for new member states and their farm and food sectors will have a major impact on these hitherto capital-starved sectors in Romania. Extra funding coming from the national program for setup of producers' groups and associations, from SAPARD pre-accession funds and from rural development projects in the second pillar of CAP will certainly contribute to a fast development of the commercial farms. The pattern of development seen during the 1990s in Hungary and Poland will probably be repeated over the next decade in Romania.

In our opinion, the following could make a favorable contribution to the establishment and development of competitive markets and of food chains by product:

- The establishment of supply organizations through the development of rural cooperation in the take over, acquisition, processing and sale of agricultural products. The emergence and development of modern rural cooperation in our country, in conformity with the operation principles and the organization modalities practised in western European countries is conditioned both by the adoption of Rural Cooperation Law (Law of agricultural cooperatives) and by financial support from the state in the initial stages through establishing production and marketing infrastructure.
- The establishment and consolidation of forward and futures markets, as well as of stock markets.
- The facilitation of the establishment and consolidation of farmers' professional associations by products/groups of products.
- New measures to encourage competition, help new businesses enter agri-food markets and discourage the formation of monopolies.
- The development of longer-term contract-based relations between farmers and processors, as well as the establishment of common enterprises along different links in the agrifood chain.
- Actions to provide improved market transparency, in the first place through the creation of an information system regarding specialized markets; this should include making data available for farmers in a systematic manner and through the intermediary of the National Agency of Agricultural Consultancy (ANCA).
- The establishment of a market control system as regards quality standards and product origin control.

We cannot end this chapter without mentioning the problem of establishing and developing financial markets in rural areas. This is the main constraint on farm operation, because in a situation where farmers are decapitalized, there is very little possibility for capital formation.

10 *China*

*Xiang Bi, Xiaoxia Dong, Jikun Huang, Dinghuan Hu and
Scott Rozelle*

Introduction

China's agri-food market has experienced a gradual liberalization. The markets have been
moving from a state-owned system to a more diversified system, where private sectors have
been taking over the market since 1985. China had a restrictive state-run food system in
the cities from 1950 until 1980. Some foods were available at fixed prices, others required
ration cards. In rural areas, traditional markets and street trade were much less affected. Since
1980, the state system has been dismantled. In its place is a fast-expanding modern sector of
supermarkets and a flourishing system of wetmarkets. The supermarkets are now expanding
into towns in west and north China. Thus there are at the moment two retail systems operating
and growing in parallel, the modern and the traditional. Already there are plans to convert
some wetmarkets into supermarkets.

Both systems are supplied by small-scale producers, but the modern system is supplied
from producers organized together into production bases by specialist wholesalers or
processors.

KEY DATA

	2002	2003	2004
Population (millions)	1295	1305	1315
Per capita GDP (US$)	992	1101	1276
Urbanization (%)	39	41	42
Agriculture as % GDP	15.3	14.4	15.2
Per capita total retail food sales (US$)	255	273	292
Per capita modern retail food sales (US$)	60	66	71
Modern retail food sales as % of total	23	24	24

Exchange rate (2002–04): 1 US Dollar = 8.277 Chinese Yuan Renminbi

TOP CHAINS, 2004

Company	Ownership	Number of stores	Retail banner sales 2004 (US$ millions)	Market share (%)	Grocery sales 2004 (US$ millions)	Grocery market share (%)
Lianhua	Public company	3149	4194	1.3	3041	1.0
Hualian Supermarket	Public company	1607	2755	0.9	2087	0.7
China Resources Enterprise	Public company	2524	2717	0.8	1655	0.6
Carrefour	Joint venture	226	2010	0.6	1220	0.4
Beijing Hualian	Public company	70	1931	0.6	983	0.3
Other			308 505	95.8	281 847	96.9

Source: PlanetRetail (www.planetretail.net)

THE CHANGING STRUCTURE OF FOOD RETAILING

Since the 1980s, China has liberalized its market and gradually relaxed controls on foreign investment. Supermarket development in China is phenomenal and has changed the retailing system as well as the agri-food marketing system. Unlike the gradual development of supermarkets in other parts of the world, the explosive growth of China's supermarkets within three to five years is particularly impressive. In the early 1990s, supermarkets first developed in south and east coastal China, such as Guangdong, Shenzhang and Shanghai. They spread to major northern cities, such as Beijing, Tianjin and Dalian in the second half of the 1990s, then to inland cities, such as Wuhan in the late 1990s and 2000s, and finally into the western region and small cities in the last one to two years. However, the movement of supermarkets to western China is still incipient; 82 per cent of supermarkets are still concentrated in eastern China, 15 per cent of them in central China and 3 per cent in west China. The number of stores has increased dramatically, especially from 1998 to 2002, with an annual growth of 20–30 per cent (Hu, et al., 2004). There were 2500 supermarkets in 1995, expanding to 53 100 by 2002. Supermarket sales were only 0.18 per cent of the national total retail sales in 1995, but they increased to 11.2 per cent by 2002.

In the early stages, supermarkets in China were small. When the government began to promote supermarket development, the main focus of supermarkets was food (CCFA, 1990–2000, 2001, 2002). In 1995, Carrefour first established two hypermarkets in Beijing and Shanghai, which triggered the transformation of the sector from traditional small-scale food supermarkets to large-format hypermarkets. By 2002, approximately 36 700 stores in China were large format (supermarket, hypermarket, discount stores, club stores), which is 70 per cent of supermarkets in China, and 16 400 were chain convenience stores (Hu, et al., 2004). Within three years, China's supermarkets entered a period in which large-format stores were dominant.

Supermarkets started in richer, middle-income neighbourhoods and commercial zones of the largest cities. With profits gained from this segment, they invested in expanding their store units and penetrating smaller cities. This investment usually comes from FDI in China. By December 2004, FDI constraints on retailing in China were completely removed, and domestic chains rushed to build market share in secondary cities before more FDI flooded into

China's retail market. Today, the cities of China are characterized by both foreign and locally owned retail chains

Large storage facilities and bulk merchandizing give supermarkets an advantage over small shops in selling processed, packaged and bulk foods, such as edible oils, grains, noodles and condiments. Supermarkets first quickly penetrated the processed dry foods markets in the 1990s in urban China. They then quickly moved into processed semi-fresh foods, such as dairy products, tofu and processed meats. The slowest market penetration is of fresh foods, such as fresh fruits and vegetables (FFV), meat and fish. Fresh produce sales in supermarkets (fruits, vegetables, meat, and so on) were almost zero before 1995, but have shot up in recent years. In 2001, 20 per cent of fresh products in big and medium cities were sold in supermarket chains (Fang, 2002).

Interestingly, the wetmarkets (*nonggaichao*) have not yet declined and in fact have grown in parallel with the expansion of modern retailing (see Table 10.1) in contrast to the experience of other countries where supermarkets have displaced traditional markets. In part, this reflects the dualistic economic development in China, with a growing affluent urban middle class and a less affected poor rural and urban population.

Table 10.1   Wetmarket expansion in China

	1980 Number of wetmarkets	1980 Annual turnover (US$ billions)	2002 Number of wetmarkets	2002 Annual turnover (US$ billions)
Rural	37 890	12.5	55 969	130.6
Urban	2919	1.4	26 529	182.4

Nevertheless, government policy has explicitly promoted supermarkets and is encouraging a shift away from wetmarkets. For example, based on the 2002–08 plan of Agricultural Products Marketing of Beijing, Beijing plans to increase fresh products sales in supermarkets and neighbourhood markets to 70–80 per cent by 2005, while decreasing morning market and wetmarket sales to 20–30 per cent; by 2008, wetmarket sales are planned to drop to 10 per cent and supermarkets and neighbourhood markets to rise to 90 per cent.

The wholesale market is still playing a dominant role in the inter-provincial trade of fresh produce, as an intermediary between producers and retail markets. In Beijing, 90 per cent of agricultural products are first distributed in wholesale markets, then retailed via all types of wetmarkets (BNCGZWYH, 2001). Li (2003) estimated that 70 per cent or more vegetables consumed in the cities were sold wholesale via wholesale markets. In addition, wholesale markets also sell directly to group and institutional customers, such as the military, schools and restaurants.

The few state farms that exist have mostly been privatized and some have become the basis of new 'production bases' operated by specialist wholesalers and supplying the new supermarkets. There are insufficient large farms to allow supermarkets to choose these alone as their preferred suppliers. Therefore there has been the development of group action by small-scale producers to supply the modern food system.

VEGETABLE PROCUREMENT

In rural areas, farmers either sell their vegetables directly to the nearby local market or to an intermediary or wholesaler. In this marketing channel, there is evidence that the producer gets 30 per cent of the retail price and the wholesaler and retailer share the remainder. Evidence from interviews with wholesalers suggests that their share amounts to 15–25 per cent of the retail price, from which they obtain profit rates of 5 to 7 per cent of the retail price.

Marketing by farmers themselves involves considerable costs (time, transportation etc). When farmers have easier access to nearby wholesale markets, they can load their products on their vehicles (tricycles) and drive to the markets in the early morning for sale, and then return to tend to their crops afterwards. But when farmers live in more remote areas, marketing activities are more constrained. There are some full-time intermediaries who help wholesalers with collecting vegetables from vegetable farmers at a charge of 0.04 yuan (0.5 US cents) per kilogram of transaction between producers and wholesalers. Mutual trust rather than written contracts link people at the village level.

Both farmers and wholesalers consider it efficient to use a 'middleman' and value the information this person can transmit. On the other hand, there is the belief that in some cases middlemen collude to conceal from farmers what wholesalers are willing to pay. After collecting products at farm gates, long-distance traders (some just transporters, others both transporters and wholesalers) market food products from one wholesale market to another.

It is evident that marketing in China's traditional food system is a tough job, usually carried out as a family business so that the heavy labour, bargaining and long distance transportation can be shared. Mostly such businesses are run by a man with the help of male relatives; wives rarely work with the men. Women, on the other hand, play an important role in retailing fresh food at the wetmarkets while men fetch supplies from the wholesale market.

PORK PROCUREMENT

Pork marketing is different from vegetable marketing in the sense that, since 1997, all pigs must be slaughtered in a designated factory/slaughterhouse before being sold. Pigs used to be slaughtered by a butcher in the village and sold in local wetmarkets.

Pigs are collected by traders either as live animals or after slaughter, and then are shipped to designated slaughterhouses/processing factories. After processing, pork is sold to the wholesale market or to local wetmarkets. In the rural areas, periodical markets or daily wetmarkets are still the main places to purchase pork. In the cities, small butchers shops have disappeared and supermarkets compete with wetmarkets on the sale of pork. When wholesalers and retailers at wetmarkets procure pork from the slaughterers, some have written contracts. Also, some do not pay the whole price in cash but only pay a deposit to the slaughterer.

MODERN FOOD PROCUREMENT SYSTEM

An interesting development in marketing food has been 'Dragon Head' companies. A Dragon Head company is a facilitating company, part logistical and part venture capitalist. It provides a mix of capital, technology assistance and marketing expertise to build loose or tight contracts with farmers and create an integrated supply chain. These are companies that elsewhere are sometimes called 'second level logistic companies'. They make contracts with producers, slaughterers and supermarkets and handle the logistics, or contract this out to others. For example, in Chengdu, Sichuan province, there are three types of contract used by buyers:

- Procurement contracts: enterprises sign procurement contracts with farmers with prices higher than the market prices, and provide technical assistance to contracted farmers, including management and supervision on use of feeds and veterinary medicines.
- Contracts for poor farmers who cannot afford to raise pigs: the company provides inputs and piglets, and farmers are charged 30 yuan per head by the company when selling to the company.
- Contracts with multiple parties, including specialized pig farmers, large farming enterprises, local financial cooperatives, and local governments: the enterprises provide technical assistance and local financial cooperatives provide credit to specialized farmers. Specialized pig farmers are required to sell to the enterprises, and the enterprises pay the farmers via the farmers' accounts in the financial cooperatives. The cooperatives deduct credit charges from the farmers' accounts to cover credit given to the farmers during the process.

In the early 1990s, when wholesale markets thrived and supermarkets were quite small, buyers from supermarkets went to wholesale markets themselves or contracted with a broker to purchase fresh products. Each store found its own supplies and supermarkets mainly sold dry, processed foods. In recent years, supermarkets have shifted to centralized procurement and they choose dedicated suppliers instead of wholesale markets as their suppliers of fresh products.

The rapid rise of supermarkets has required steady supplies with large quantities at minimum cost. The leading chains are setting up regional procurement centres and distribution centres to gain more bargaining power and reduce transaction costs. Signing contracts with dedicated suppliers, instead of bargaining on the wholesale markets, can reduce transaction costs and dedicated suppliers usually provide logistics to each chain store, which also saves costs for the supermarkets. Products from wholesale markets are not graded and quality control and food safety cannot be guaranteed. Supplies from dedicated suppliers, on the other hand, require quality inspection and some even have 'green food' (that is, pesticide residue-free) status. This means that the processor and grower have passed stringent inspection and use only permitted chemicals.

Regional or centralized procurement and distribution greatly increases the bargaining power of supermarkets and thus lowers their costs. However, the move to centralization does not always occur simultaneously for all products, but is often implemented gradually. Generally, fresh products (that is, leafy vegetables and fresh meat products, live fish and some processed food such as tofu, bakery and cooked meat) and cut vegetables are still sourced locally. Vegetables that can be stored and readily transported, such as Chinese cabbages, onions, potatoes and winter melons, are sourced inter-regionally from a central depot.

Some supermarket chains, such as Wu-mart, have their own regional procurement and distribution centres, but their DCs find it hard to handle perishable products. Wu-mart started to use its own DC to source shrimps, but it proved too difficult and costly. Fresh produce distribution requires timing, quality control and cool chain facilities, whereby the product is kept cool right through the supply chain to the retail shelf. This is too expensive for a Chinese supermarket chain such as Wu-mart at present. Instead, Wu-mart uses a logistics company, which has a cool chain, to transport and store fresh agri-food products like shrimps.

Other supermarket chains, such as Lianhua, do have distribution centres for fresh products. Lianhua established a processing and distribution centre for FFV in 2001 in a suburb of Shanghai. This investment includes a cool chain. Other companies are also building cool facilities. For instance, the Shoulian supermarket group plans to build a distribution centre for fresh products in a suburb of Beijing, as a joint venture between Shoulian and the Shunxin Company (Hu, et al., 2004).

Our interviews indicate that procurement officers at the centre directly negotiate with suppliers, avoiding the involvement of any intermediate agent to reduce costs. After signing contracts, suppliers deliver the products to each chain store according to the quantity and timing required by the store. Each of the stores checks the quality (usually appearance and freshness) of the delivered products, and the cash payment is made by the centre to the supplier.

Contracts between supermarkets and suppliers are renewed annually. Suppliers receive orders (exact prices, quantities) from each store a day before (afternoon or evening), then they deliver the products to each store by the next morning. For example, Carrefour requires delivery before 07:30 every day, other supermarkets require two deliveries every day, that is early morning between 04:00 and 05:00 and in the afternoon.

As well as a fee for providing logistics, some supermarkets, such as Carrefour, require an entrance fee. In our interviews, suppliers reported that entrance fees vary from $240 to $1 200 in one case, 2 000 to 10 000 yuan in another (1 US$ = 8.277 yuan). There are also shelf fees charged, for instance, 2 000 to 3 000 yuan for each variety of vegetable or fruits. A new product may be charged another fee of, say, $120. If a supermarket has a promotion, they may charge the supplier a promotion fee. The level of such fees is one measure of the difference in bargaining power between the supermarket and the suppliers.

The profit shared between supermarkets and suppliers differs between both food products and regions; for instance, the Sanlu vegetable company of Beijing (see below) obtains a profit of 10–15 per cent when selling to supermarkets. The value added from procuring to selling is about 70 per cent, though it can be higher. For instance, a small-scale peach trader who supplies a supermarket purchases peaches for 80 Chinese cents per kilogram at the farm gate, obtains a 40–60 Chinese cents price margin and sells to supermarkets for 1.00–1.20 yuan per kilogram. The supermarket sells to final customers for 1.80 yuan per kilogram.

Some suppliers rent shelves, others form a partnership with a supermarket and send out a member of their staff to work in the supermarket as an informant (Interview with Xiaotangshan vegetable company). Every day, the informants call the suppliers' sale centres and inform them what products and quantities are needed by the store they are working at. The supplier takes responsibility for keeping the shelves full. Any excess product that cannot be sold is regarded as the responsibility of the supplier (Fang, 2002).

Usually, a supplier sources their fresh products from a mix of growers. Typically a supplier might buy from both local out-growers and wholesale markets or through wholesalers acting as their agents. Some wholesalers, though not many, might grow themselves in what is termed their 'production base'. For example, the Xingcheng Food Company in Shanghai (see case studies below) sources 50 per cent of their vegetables from contracting with local farmers, 30 per cent from wholesale markets in the production region, and 15–20 per cent is grown by them on rented land. These integrated agri-food enterprises supply not only to supermarkets, but they also export and supply to other groups (that is, institutional consumers).

Consider the example of a supply company based in Shanghai. Zhengyi Horticulture Ltd can produce 4100 tons vegetables and as well as supplying to supermarket chains, Zhengyi also delivers to hotels and government departments. Lianhua supermarket company has long-term contracts with both of these suppliers. Fang (2002) estimated that 30 per cent of fresh vegetables supplied in Shanghai supermarket chains are via contracted suppliers with their own production bases. Suppliers with integrated production bases and processing have obvious advantages when competing in the market: better quality control and the ability to grow and process exactly what customers want. This has proved successful for Shanghai Xincheng Food Ltd (see case studies) and Zhengyi.

Smaller, specialized suppliers also tend to establish their own production base, in order to reduce transaction costs and secure good-quality supplies. ShijiKaitai Ltd, a company in Beijing, is a small supplier to the supermarkets compared with Zhengyi and Xincheng (ShijiKaitai has sales income of 2 million yuan, while Zhengyi and Xincheng have sales incomes in excess of 50 million). In 2004, this small company sourced one-third of fresh peaches from its own production base, a rented 3.3 hectare orchard, and two-thirds from nearby peach farmers. Unlike Zhengyi and Xincheng, this company does not sign procurement contracts with nearby farmers, but relies on trust. The company has a reputation for paying a premium price to farmers and paying quickly.

A problem for large companies is how to ensure discipline among out-growers. The Xiaotangshang vegetable company prefers to deal with the local town government rather than negotiate separately with every contracted farmer. This implies that farmers are still not able to organize as a single force and take a unified position in negotiations. Making contracts via local government officials helps secure the contracts because farmers who break their contract risk losing the support of their local government.

IMPLICATIONS FOR SMALL-SCALE PRODUCERS

A supplier to supermarkets is required to hold certain qualifications. First, the supplier must be registered and be able to issue invoices (VAT invoices that can be submitted to the tax office). Second, it must have a number of official permits and approvals. Third, it needs vehicles for logistics, and must be able to afford the high entrance fees, shelf fees and other payments required by the supermarkets. Furthermore, supermarkets do not pay by cash, but by cheque. A supplier has to wait for 45 days, sometimes even up to 90 days, for payment, which is very demanding in terms of working capital for a small business.

Food safety and quality control and inspections are the other barriers for small enterprises. As discussed above, producers need to have their production environment tested and checked, and provide production records and inspection reports in order to be a certified 'green food' or 'safe for public consumption' agri-food producer. 'Green food' sells for up to five times as much as other food when sold in supermarkets. Supermarkets signing contracts with big producers of vegetables with 'green food' certification know that this reduces the risk of food poisoning as well as leading to greater profits. As a result, supermarkets are moving to bigger suppliers who are able to offer certification and away from wholesalers and small suppliers.

Individual farmers and SMEs might be squeezed out of the market as supermarkets take over from the traditional procurement system. Most farms in China are very small. The average size of a farm in China is only about 0.5 hectares, with 2.8 labour units and 4.1 persons per holding. On average, a farm provides about half of farm household income, while the rest comes from off-farm activities. With the family size getting smaller and farmers spending less time working on the farm, farmers require more extension services in the areas of marketing, information provision and technology. Some SMEs have begun to expand by building a production base and contracting farmers as their suppliers; and there is also evidence that POs and professional farmer associations are gaining bargaining power with supermarkets by acting together.

PRODUCER ORGANIZATIONS

A small farmer must join a group to have any chance at all of gaining a place in a supermarket supply chain. The farmers' professional association (FPA) is the only vehicle available at the moment. For this to be effective, it is important to have the active support of the local authority, which can act as a guarantor and support the FPA in negotiations with supplier companies. However, FPAs also need to become much more effective than they are at present. Membership of FPAs seldom accounts for more than 4 per cent of local farmers. Most FPAs interviewed (290 in all) were set up by local government, led by government officials and unable to provide marketing or technical services to their members.

Arrangements to link farmers to supermarket suppliers are going to be of increasing importance in China as the food market develops. For example, in Shandong province, research found three types of relations between producers and the markets: (1) contracts with out-growers; (2) FPAs; (3) specialized wholesale markets contracting supplies from farmers. The diversity of institutional arrangements is likely to grow as new regions are drawn into supermarket supply. In the major vegetable production region, research found several types of organization. They include Dragon Head companies – that is, those that encompass both supply and trade functions in a supply chain – as well as different types of FPAs.

The government has formulated policy in favour of the liberalized agri-food market through two publications. In 2002, The State Council issued the document 'Suggestions for boosting the agri-food processing industry', in which it announced government plans to increase the infrastructure investment in the agri-food processing industry, and promote technology innovation and improvement investment in leading companies. In 2004, the central government issued the 'No. 1 Document', which exclusively deals with agricultural and rural development. This document specifically noted that FPAs, farmer wholesalers, and farmer intermediaries should be encouraged.

The policies proposed in the 2004 'No. 1 Document' are worth setting out in full, although it remains to be seen how they are implemented; the word 'encouragement' is used but the means of encouragement to be used are not yet clear. Given the strength of market forces in China today, it is likely that any measures will be supporting trends rather than attempting to resist change. The policies are as follows:

1. The government plans to increase the infrastructure investment in the agri-food processing industry, and promote technology innovation and improvement investment in leading companies, including Dragon Head companies.
2. Agri-food processing companies will be encouraged to set up production bases, carry out research and development (R&D), improve technology and extension services, and impose quality standards. There may be government finance to do this.
3. Banks will be encouraged to lend to farmers who are in production bases.
4. Small- and medium-scale processors will also receive encouragement.
5. The government will encourage the establishement of FPAs, farmer wholesalers and farmer intermediaries.
6. There will be new services providing information, technology, training, standardization and certification, and marketing services, mainly accessible through FPAs.
7. At production bases, FPAs will be encouraged to manage new storage and processing enterprises. There will also be government loans for transport and handling equipment.

8. The government will encourage agri-food chain stores, supermarkets, and logistics companies. Wetmarkets will selectively be converted to supermarkets where it is appropriate, and Dragon Head enterprises set up to link together supply chains.

This document makes clear that the government sees small farms as part of rural development and wants to see more farms growing for supermarket suppliers.

Another development in 2004 was the publishing by the Ministry of Commerce of a comprehensive policy outline (the first of its kind) to act as a guide to establishing a national marketing system for food. According to a report, this states: 'Convenience stores, discount stores and small and medium supermarkets should be encouraged in urban and in rural areas.'

Apparently some local governments have already taken action. The Department of Commerce and Finance in Beijing has decided to provide three years of subsidies for newly opened chain supermarkets and convenience stores in the suburbs of Beijing. The subsidies range from 15 000 to 30 000 yuan. A newly opened supermarket in a town can receive 30 000 yuan; a newly opened convenience store in a village can receive 15 000 yuan. The subsidies are also available where a supermarket chain upgrades village and town shops.

Many of the points raised above are illustrated in the four case studies we deal with next. The size of China and rapidity of change make it difficult to say how typical these four cases are, but at least they provide us with a flavour of the developments under way.

Case study 1:Beijing Sanlu Vegetable Ltd

Sanlu began to supply to domestic supermarket chains in 2000, and since then, their sales have increased 30 per cent annually. Sanlu sources its fresh vegetables through contracted farmers in Daxing district, Beijing. These out-growers provide 50 per cent of Sanlu's supply. The rest they obtain by direct procurement in the production region (30 per cent), and procurement from Xinfadi wholesale market and Gu'an county market (20 per cent). Note that Sanlu does not grow anything itself (that is, it has no production base).

Even though Sanlu has contracts with farmers, it still faces the usual problems of small-scale producers everywhere – low quality being rejected, contracts not complied with, and farmers chasing high prices and not fulfilling contractual obligations.

In order to build up trust between the farmer and the company, Sanlu provides information on vegetable demand and supply, varieties and seeds. The company also provides technical assistance. Standards are specified in the contract and all vegetables produced according to these standards are accepted and purchased. The company also gives 'protected', or minimum prices, to contract farmers.

Case study 2: Shanghai Xincheng Food Ltd

As a leading agri-food supplier, Xincheng has nine agri-food production bases, four of them for vegetable production. Xincheng has signed contracts with farmers on their production bases, and provides them with greenhouses, seeds, fertilizer and pesticides. It also sends technicians to work with the farmers and the farmers must follow the instructions from technicians.

Many of their contracted farmers are from other provinces. When procuring from these farmers, Xincheng company deducts the costs of greenhouses, seeds and other inputs. In total, Xincheng buys from 4200 farmers.

Case study 3: Xiaotangshan Vegetable Company (XVC)

XVC sources its vegetable supplies from contracted farmers (50 per cent), wholesale markets (30 per cent) and a production base of its own (20 per cent). XVC contracts farmers that are 65 km from Beijing, who specialize in vegetable production. Farm gate prices are 50 per cent higher than selling to the local wholesale market, but quality is higher. XVC provides technical assistance to these farmers. Centralized processing is conducted through hired labour near Beijing. Contract enforcement is coordinated by the local government. The group mainly supplies 'green food' to the supermarkets.

Case study 4: Zhejiang Plum Association (ZPA)

ZPA was founded in 2002 and now has 180 members, including several large-scale producers, some companies, research institutes and small farmers. Producers must grow at least 4 hectares of plums to become a member, though smaller farmers can join together and have joint membership.

The association has established product standards for members to meet and provides information on varieties, production and inputs. Technical assistance is provided by the universities, extension services, and research institutes, who are also members of ZPA. The association organizes marketing for members, which increases their bargaining power.

Eleven members have been selected as an 'elite' group of growers. Their plums are marketed under the same brand, for which they receive prices four times higher than the price of bulk, non-branded plums. The association uses various media to advertise their products and their brand. They grade, package and ship plums to the supermarkets. Each season ZPA negotiates with supermarkets. As product quality is standardized and consistency guaranteed, the ZPA plums are in high demand from supermarkets and consequently ZPA can negotiate reduced fees.

Conclusions

Supermarkets are having a positive impact on rural China by encouraging the establishment of FPAs and prompting farmers to raise quality standards and fulfil contracts. The main beneficiaries are farmers and processors who are part of the production bases near urban areas. However, there are also negative effects. Contracted farmers have weak bargaining power, especially when they supply the modern food system with 'green food' and 'organic food' that are difficult to produce and are produced to a particular supply chain's standards. The standards needed to become a production base producer are exacting and most of China's micro-scale growers cannot meet them. For them the wetmarkets remain the main market opportunity.

The current structure of the market will undoubtedly change. More fresh produce will be sold through supermarkets in the future and the market share of wetmarkets will decline.

Supermarkets are already setting up their own distribution centres to further decrease their procurement costs and this will have a major impact on wholesale markets and the agri-food market as a whole.

Based on a recent study (Yu, 2003) on income and probabilities of shopping in the supermarket, around 30 per cent of the population in Beijing currently shop for fresh products in supermarkets, and around 14.7 per cent of the population in urban China. Probably the percentage of fresh agri-food sales in supermarkets in urban China will grow to 50 per cent by 2020, assuming urban incomes increase by 7 per cent per annum. According to the same assumptions, by 2020 people in rural China will buy 20 per cent per cent of their fresh produce from supermarkets. Overall, the country will buy 35 per cent fresh agri-food consumed at home from supermarkets by 2020.

Therefore, the market is a good one for better-placed small farmers to aim for, despite the difficulties. The government has indicated it is willing to help small producers, both farmers and processors, and has suggested several measures. City authorities are committed to the dominance of supermarkets and are probably equally concerned to guarantee supplies of the right quality of food products. Foreign chains are expanding and looking for good suppliers. All that is needed is the establishment of efficient associations of farmers and processors, helped, perhaps, by well-managed Dragon Head companies. While these opportunities are only open to a minority of China's vast rural population, they are real enough.

References

Beijing Nongcun Gongzuoweiyuanhui (BNCGZWYH), 2001. *Beijing shinong chanpin Liudong tixi 2002-2008 Fazhan Guihua* (Development plan 2002–2008 for Beijing agricultural products marketing). Publication of Rural Work Committee, Beijing Commerce Committee, Beijing Development and Reform Committee. Available: www.bjnw.gov.cn.

China Chain Store and Franchise Association (CCFA), 1990–2000, 2001, 2002. *China Chain Store Almanac, (annual 1990–2002)*. Beijing: China Commerce Press.

Fang, X., 2002. *Shengxian Gongyinlian Xianzhuang yu Fazhan Fangxiang* (*The development of fresh agri-food supply chain*) Available: www.hypermarket.com.

Hu, D., Reardon, T.A., Rozelle, S., Timmer, P. and Wang, H., 2004. The emergence of supermarkets with Chinese characteristics: Challenges and opportunities for China's agricultural development. *Development Policy Review* 22(9), 557–86.

Li, Y., ed., 2003. *Nongchanpin Liutong Chuangxin Yanjiu* (*The innovation study on agricultural products marketing organization*). Beijing: China Agricultural Press.

Yu, H., 2003. *Research on management of fresh food in supermarkets in China*. Unpublished MSc Thesis, Chinese Academy of Agricultural Sciences, Beijing.

11 *Vietnam*

Phan Thi Giac Tam

Introduction

The opening up of Vietnam's economy has brought significant changes to Vietnam. The economy has been growing at an average rate of 6 per cent for the past 15 years. At 7.1 per cent, GDP growth rate in 2003 is one of the highest in the South-east Asian region. Even Vietnam's FDI has been increasing for the past five years, while the rest of its neighbours' FDI growth rate has been declining for the past three years.

Vietnam is relatively rich in natural resources and its economy is still predominantly agricultural. The country's cultivated land totals about 12.2 million hectares, classified as arable (21 per cent), forest and woodland (28 per cent) and used for other purposes (51 per cent). Vietnam's principal agricultural product is rice, and the country is the second-largest rice exporter in the world. Other major exports include coffee, tea, rubber and fisheries products, while other principal agricultural products include maize, sweet potato, peanuts, cotton, cashews and soybean. Agriculture's share of economic output has declined, falling from 42 per cent of GDP in 1989 to 17 per cent in 2003.

Small-scale producers of fresh vegetables supply supermarkets by joining cooperatives or contracting to private companies. In milk supply, 'backyard' producers have replaced state farms as suppliers to processors. A particular concern for Vietnamese consumers is pesticide residues in foods such as fresh vegetables. Many consumers seek 'hygienic' vegetables and this is also considered in this chapter.

KEY DATA

	2002	*2003*	*2004*
Population (millions)	80.28	81.35	82.42
Per capital GDP (US$)	407	438	471
Urbanization (%)	25		
Agriculture as % GDP	18.02	17.34	16.58
Per capita total retail food sales (US$)	143	154	164
Per capita modern retail food sales (US$)	25	27	29
Modern retail food sales as % total			18

Exchange rate (1 January 2006): 1 US$ = 15 904 Vietnamese dong (VND)

TOP CHAINS, 2004

Company	Ownership	Number of stores	Retail banner sales 2004 (US$ millions)	Market share (%)	Grocery sales 2004 (US$ millions)	Grocery market share (%)
Metro Group	Foreign	4	176	6.2	107	4.3
Saigon Co-op	State-owned cooperative	13	107	3.8	54	2.1
Casino	Foreign	3	46	1.6	28	1.1
Other			2517	88.4	2328	92.5

Source: PlanetRetail (www. planetretail.net)

FOOD RETAILING

The Vietnamese retail sector is highly fragmented and there are few chains of any note. The only two major foreign entrants are Casino (through its 70 per cent stake in Groupe Bourbon/ Vindémia, expected to become 100 per cent at the beginning of 2007) and Metro Group, although each hold less than a 5 per cent share of the modern grocery distribution sector. The two largest domestic chains, both based in Ho Chi Minh City (HCMC) are Saigon Co-op, a state-owned supermarket chain with around 13 stores, and Maximart.

FRESH VEGETABLES

Prior to 2000, the fresh food sector in supermarkets was rather small and vegetables in general were bought from wholesalers. Since then, the fresh food sector has gradually grown as a result of increasing investment and the efforts of supermarket managers to improve and expand as the demand for 'hygienic' vegetables has been increasing (see below).

The market share of modern retailers was estimated to be just 7 per cent of all fresh and frozen food sold in HCMC (Cadilhon et al., 2003). In other parts of Vietnam, the proportion is lower. The proportions of supermarket shoppers from poor and non-poor groups were 60 per cent and 99 per cent respectively from a recent survey of the more affluent areas of HCMC. The main reason quoted for this trend was higher prices in supermarkets. In addition, some consumers are doubtful of the real quality of so-called 'hygienic' vegetables in supermarkets. Therefore, it will take more effort from both public and private sectors to develop and enhance the certification process for hygienic vegetables and consequently to build consumer confidence.

However, supermarkets are trying to rectify this negative image and become the trusted source for pure, hygienic vegetables. Supermarket buyers seek preferred suppliers who can provide under contract guaranteed (and inspected) hygienic vegetables. The supermarkets make agreements with farmers' organizations and create production teams. To assemble and transport the products, they include in the supply chain trusted 'collectors' (that is, specialized wholesalers).

Most supermarkets build relationships with a few selected suppliers and adopt flexible purchasing arrangements. The purchase arrangement is covered by a relatively simple written contract between a supermarket and a supplier, stipulating only the period of contract (usually one year), method and terms of payments, method of product delivery, and the need for official receipts. The volume and prices are not specified in the contract and are arrived at verbally.

Supermarkets are careful to have more than one supplier for each product so that they can buy at low prices, thanks to the competition generated. The supermarkets do the same with purchases from wholesalers. Again the aim is to build good relations with preferred suppliers and also to leave room for competition among suppliers.

Supermarkets usually maintain the same price levels to suppliers *in a week*, a big advantage for farmers, even if they find they have little to sell in some months. We found out that the average load of vegetables and frequency of deliveries by one agricultural cooperative to the Big C supermarket chain (Casino) was about 2 tonnes every three days.

The products distributed through supermarkets have to be of good quality and/or of new varieties. Some supermarkets have their own standards and require their specialist wholesalers to use only farmers who satisfy the following criteria: (1) completion of grade 9 education (that is, schooling until 15 years old); (2) evidence of both innovation and discipline, ability to use technology to produce hygienic vegetables; (3) a track record of loyalty to a farm cooperative.

Only about one-third of farmers who take out a contract are able to maintain their position as a preferred supplier in the long-term. In a niche, luxury food market, supermarkets have less choice of suppliers and it is easier for a small-scale producer to gain access. Of course, the standards required are much higher. In each supply chain there is someone responsible for collecting together loads of vegetables. The collector may be a farmers' organization or a large-scale farmer. This person needs to invest in communication devices (such as computers, fax, and telephone), transportation and the costs of inspection, and laboratory testing of vegetable samples. They likewise have to bear the costs of business registration since modern retailers will only deal with registered businesses.

Two positive aspects of supermarkets are the higher prices they offer suppliers and the incentives they provide for farmers to upgrade their produce. A number of trade companies and cooperatives have recently been established to enable them to supply supermarkets and other organizations that deal only with officially registered organizations. The company owner or cooperative founder is usually a large-scale farmer, who has experience in trading and has some training in cooperative or company management. A successful cooperative structure in respect of supermarket supply chains seems to be this: several small farmers, a few large scale farmers and one experienced farmer accepted as the leader.

A cooperative often starts when a large farmer is unable to meet all the requirements of a supermarket. He contracts other farmers to provide sufficient produce. The cooperative cannot rely solely on the supermarket buyer though. Traditional wholesale and wetmarket outlets are needed to dispose of second-grade produce not wanted by the supermarket. Thus traditional markets experience the spill-over effects of the supermarkets' efforts to upgrade product standards and to advertise new products as well. In this way, positive benefits can come to other farmers. They may find they can get better prices and more sales in the traditional market because the standard of produce is higher.

It is a fact that a small farmer in Vietnam could not individually be integrated into a modern supply chain without being a member of an organization such as a farmers' organization or an agricultural cooperative. In terms of gender, most members of an agricultural organization are male as opposed to traders, who are female.

When farmers join a cooperative they get other advantages such as better access to government extension services, credit and a subsidized laboratory testing service. In the same manner, cooperative membership affords them access to training programmes that are free of charge to farmer-members of cooperatives.

The main constraint in supplying supermarkets is the limited amount of vegetables that are sold by supermarkets. The food prices in supermarkets are higher than at wetmarkets because of higher marketing margins, making supermarkets less popular with customers. Also, housewives who are older, of low-income or not highly educated are not attracted to buy at supermarkets at all.

Another constraint is the capacity to deliver to individual stores on a frequent basis. All suppliers are asked to deliver produce directly to supermarket branches and this has to be frequent since few supermarkets have storage facilities. Some retail chains operate temporary distribution centres where all products are gathered, inspected, collected and then transferred to individual stores.

The situation in HCMC is subject to rapid changes. Since October 2004, it can be seen that fresh food, particularly vegetables, is sold in most supermarkets at a cheaper price than in wetmarkets. In addition, market information has been broadcast daily on mass media (radio, television) to guide consumers to specific outlets. This trend needs to be studied to investigate the impacts on consumers, traditional traders and producers.

Case study 1: Hygienic vegetables

An interesting aspect of fresh vegetable marketing in Vietnam is the issue of food purity and safety of the products. The increase of food poisoning incidents in Vietnam in the period 1994–97 has drawn much government attention, leading to the 'Temporary Regulations on Vegetable Safety' issued 28 April 1998 and efforts to control the quality of crops at the production stage. The hygienic vegetable programme was first endorsed by HCMC authority in 1996 and further strengthened in 2002. Pilot programs on hygienic vegetable technology started both in HCMC and Hanoi in 1998. An important component of these programmes is to expand the number of market outlets. Modern distribution chains are considered appropriate outlets for these hygienic food products.

The former Vietnamese director of a Bio-organic company, Dr Nguyen Ba Hung played an important role in the innovation of safe production techniques in Dalat in 1997, through the financial assistance of the Department of Science, Technology and Environment. This technology was recognized by the UN Food and Agricultural Organisation (FAO) and was then disseminated among farmers through the agricultural extension services. As a result, many farmers have adopted new production practices and five hygiene vegetable cooperatives have been formed. This was also a response to the increasing demand from exporting companies and supermarkets in HCMC and others. Dr Nguyen Ba Hung together with Bob Allen, set up their own business to provide vegetables, particularly to five-star hotels that have been increasing in number in Vietnam since 1995.

This is a good example of innovative private enterprises gaining greater market access through technological breakthroughs. Recently, Dr Nguyen Ba Hung established another company – Hung Thien – to supply organic, high-class vegetables complying with Euro-Retailer Produce Working Group Good Agricultural Practices (EurepGAP) standards for export and domestic markets.

Another variety of hygiene vegetable supply chain was the one established by the Sao Viet centre, a branch of the An Giang Plant Protection Service. This centre has its own experimental units and contracts with farmers in both HCMC and Dalat. Through the contract, the centre provides technical assistance and quality management and buys the vegetables back from farmers. The vegetables are then sold to 26 outlets broken down into four supermarkets, seven shops and the rest are agents operating within the trade centres of HCMC.

Case study 2: Milk supply

Small-scale milk producers have been successful in taking over from state dairy farms. Between 1980 and 1990, dairy cows were kept on large state-owned farms. After 1980, these farms extended their production by contracting with a few backyard raisers, mostly farm employees. During this period, only one milk processing company (the predecessor of Vinamilk) existed, with a limited procurement network. The company's main product for sale was condensed milk. Most private dairy farms during that time manually processed the condensed milk or sold milk fresh to private traders who pasteurized the milk and made some into yoghurt, selling both locally.

From 1990 to 1997, dairy cow production became predominantly a backyard enterprise with two to three dairy cows per household. There were two companies, Vinamilk and Foremost, which each set up collection points to buy milk from backyard farms. Only one sample of milk from each collecting point was taken for testing and this allowed poor quality milk to get into the system. Some farmers mixed their milk with water and other substances to increase volume. Such cheating led the companies to stop buying from local farmers and, from 1997, to import powdered milk instead.

To address this issue, the HCMC authority formed a committee and agreed a solution; each individual farmer's milk was tested on arrival at the collecting points. This has increased cost but helped strengthen the contracts made between the companies and farmers, and enhanced farmers' awareness of the need and importance of maintaining the high quality of their milk products. From 1998 to 2004, the number of dairy farms increased rapidly, with most of the new producers keeping three to five cows in their backyards.

The three leading milk processing companies that buy milk from backyard farms are Vinamilk (Vietnamese), Dutch Lady (Netherlands–Vietnam Joint venture), and Nestlé. Other milk processors include Lothamilk (Taiwan–Vietnam Joint venture), Nutifood, Hanoimilk, Tribeco, Vixumilk, BIFO, BABIO and many other small, local factories. All the above-mentioned companies except Hanoimilk and one Vinamilk plant are located in HCMC, South Vietnam. The total daily purchase is estimated at about 365 tonnes per day.

Almost 90 per cent of fresh milk produced from all farms is sold by contract to Vinamilk and Dutch Lady, the two competing milk processors in the dairy industry. However, the number of medium- and small-scale processing factories in the industry has recently increased. This is partly aided by a government resolution to enhance the marketability of products by ensuring a link between production and processing (as well as consumption).

The medium-scale farms usually deliver milk directly to the Dutch Lady processing plants, while small farmers contracted by Dutch Lady deliver milk to collection points by themselves. Most farmers supplying Vinamilk sell to intermediaries who are also milk producers. These intermediaries have contracts with Vinamilk and deliver to designated collection points.

Dairy products from processing plants are delivered to consumers through three marketing channels. The main channel of the processing companies is their own agent network (for example, about 70 per cent of total Vinamilk products are delivered through this channel) that spreads out to over 63 cities/provinces. For example, Vinamilk aims to establish at least two agents for condensed milk and powdered milk at each province in the country. These agents supply to various traditional independent retailers/grocery stores in their designated coverage areas. The second important channel is through a modern retailer such as Metro. The lowest percentage share is products delivered directly to institutional clients such as hospital canteens, schools, factories, hotels and restaurants, or through company shops (about 10 per cent of total products from Vinamilk).

A number of medium-scale farms and an agricultural cooperative in HCMC have tried to process pasteurized milk and yoghurt and sell them in their locality or community. However, they also sell a portion of the fresh produce to processing companies by contract, as in the case of an agricultural cooperative selling to Vinamilk or as the case in Long Thanh, Dong Nai province selling to the Lothan company. Maintaining both outlets simultaneously is a strategy to stabilize and increase their profit given the fact that individual sales are low when there is heavy rain.

It is very rare that a medium-scale dairy enterprise owner is successful in directly selling to the supermarkets.

Although they enjoyed relatively stable profits from dairy cow production, the dairy producers now are facing profit shrinkage because of a relatively low milk selling price and continually increasing input prices. Efforts of producers to air their complaints with the assistance of mass media (newspapers, television, radio) paid off and processing plants recently agreed to increase the milk purchasing price by about 10 per cent.

In spite of this, the dairy producers are still complaining about the big mark-up between the purchase and the retail price of milk (3800 VND per kilogram delivered at the processing plant and 14000 VND per kilogram at the retail outlet) as well as the price difference between Thai dairy farms and Vietnamese ones (4600 VND equivalent per kilogram of milk in Thailand as compared to 3800 VND per kilogram in south Vietnam). As a result, the dairy cow population by farm tends to decline. Some farmers shift to raising cows for meat as avian flu is still a threat.

Conclusions

The development of supermarkets in terms of retailing fresh vegetables is still in its infancy. However, a number of positive impacts on farmers can be identified as follows:

- Farmers who are involved in this modern supply chain are obviously better off. They get incentives to improve their produce. In fact, these farmers are continually looking for new varieties for niche markets, for off-season production and new technologies to increase the yield of hygienic vegetables and increase their proportion of higher grade produce. Suppliers of supermarkets nowadays are often trade companies that were newly established by well-off farmers. Some farmers have likewise become traders and in the process obtained a better income.
- While maintaining good prices to loyal suppliers, some supermarkets try to introduce quality standards to farmers involved in the supply chain. Others seek to contract directly with farmer groups and provide them with technical assistance to farmers as well as in-field quality control inspection.
- The spill-over effects of quality improvement initiated by supermarkets can be seen in wetmarkets. The unabsorbed volume of supermarket-contracted supply usually finds its

way to wetmarkets, or other outlets, as supermarkets buy only first-grade produce. That unabsorbed volume is of better quality than the traditional produce in wetmarkets.

The development of the dairy industry in Vietnam is an example of a successful policy formulation that has benefited small farmers in several ways:

*   The policy initiatives on developing the dairy industry and linking production with processing have helped generate stable income for small producers and encourage more efficient utilization of agricultural by-products and residuals.
*   The dairy industry is one with successful cases of contract farming in Vietnam. This achievement is attributed to two factors: the development of processing plants with their extensive procurement system as a necessary condition; and the application of enhanced management techniques.
*   Government interventions are highly important in the integration of various small farmers with modern, large-scale processing plants. However, it seems that government is not as successful in integrating small dairy processors in the modern distribution chains. Government seems less powerful in resolving contract negotiation problems between a small group of big plants and a large group of small producers.
*   The development of the technical capabilities of small producers is important in assuring the quality of their dairy products. The farmers also need technical tools such as quick testing devices for milk samples and even for chemical residues as in the case of vegetables. A credit programme is also an urgent need.

Reference

Cadilhon, J.-J., Fearne, A., Moustier P. and Poole N.D., 2003. Modelling vegetable marketing systems in South East Asia: Phenomenological insights from Vietnam. *Supply Chain Management: An International Journal* 8(5), 427–41.

4 Country Studies:
Countries with Emerging Modern Supply Chains

This third set of country studies focuses on countries where modern supply chains are emerging but markets are fragmented, and the traditional and informal market sector is still dominant. The fragmentation of these markets can, however, make them very attractive to global chains looking for their next source of growth. Since these chapters were written, the situation in India, where retail is still 97 to 98 percent in the hands of neighborhood shops has changed remarkably. In November 2005, Wal-Mart announced a joint venture with an Indian partner Bharti Enterprises. This news followed closely after announcements by Reliance Industries, the country's largest business group, that it is to spend $5.5 billion on opening thousands of new shops over five years. Sunil Mittal, chairmam of Bharti, said in an interview: 'Brazil is done. China is done. This is the last Shangri-la of retail. Where will Tesco or Wal-Mart get their growth? Here.' In these markets, it is often national and regional players who have the skills and connections to develop successful formats for low-income areas. South African chains are the first movers in Africa. Furthermore, it is often the middle of the chains – the processing and cash and carry sectors – that become concentrated much faster than retail. Another feature of these countries is the important role of trade policy, with the liberalization of imports presenting domestic food producers with perhaps a stronger challenge than the restructuring of domestic food chains. The very large proportion of populations involved in agriculture, and the powerful voice of small producers and small shopkeepers in policy making, mean that international businesses must be seen to be partners in national development, or risk losing their franchise to operate.

CHAPTER

12 *India*

K.K. Upadhyay and Raghwesh Ranjan

Introduction

The Indian economic system has witnessed a significant change during the last decade and a half. With economic liberalization, the economy has moved from a public sector-oriented system towards more of a free market regulated system with much greater participation from private enterprises. During this period, the economic growth rate has also surged from the so-called 'Hindu rate of growth' of 3.2 per cent (1947–91) to more than 5 per cent during the period 1991–2004. With a GDP of US$ 568 billion (US$ 3.096 trillion at Purchasing Power Parity (PPP)), India has now become the world's 12th largest economy (and the fourth largest when adjusted for PPP). However, the large population means that the per capita income is quite low. In 2003, the World Bank ranked India 160th in real terms and 143rd in terms of PPP per capita income among 208 countries.

Along with the economic changes, Indian society has also undergone a change in the last two decades. The middle class has boomed and the degree of poverty has seen a decline from 36 per cent in the early 1990s to 26 per cent in 1999–2000. The Human Development Index has moved from 0.416 in 1975 to 0.590 in 2001. At the national level, during the 1980s, the index had improved by nearly 26 per cent and by another 24 per cent during the 1990s. The increase has been marginally more in rural areas in comparison to urban areas, resulting in a narrowing of the rural–urban gap. Nevertheless, more than one out of every four Indians is poor.

The main conclusion that could be drawn from all this is that while, on the one hand, there is a much greater participation of private enterprises in the production and trading arenas, on the other, the surge in demand for all kinds of commodities has meant that small producers also have a chance to benefit immensely from the opportunity.

Agriculture (including food production and processing) accounts for 26 per cent of India's GDP and for more than 60 per cent of its employment. However, with the rapid growth of the manufacturing and service sectors, the importance of agriculture has been in decline in recent decades.

Around the world, because food is central to a nation's economy, it is one of the first areas to reach a high level of development. This is not true for India, though, where the value addition to food production is only 7 per cent as compared to 23 per cent in China, 45 per cent in Philippines and 188 per cent in the UK. With the new policy of allowing corporate entry into the food production and processing sectors, this situation may change, as the market for value added food products in India is set to grow from 800 billion INR in 1999 to 2250 billion INR by 2005.

KEY DATA

	2002	2003	2004
Population (millions)	1050	1066	1082
Per capital GDP (US$)	471	531	599
Urbanization (%)	28		
Agriculture as % GDP			
Per capita total retail food sales (US$)	164	185	206
Per capita modern retail food (US$)	32	36	31
Modern retail food sales as % total			18

Exchange rate (1 January 2006): US$1 = 45.195 Indian rupee (INR)

TOP CHAINS, 2004

Company	Ownership	Number of stores	Retail banner sales 2004 (US$ millions)	Market share (%)	Grocery sales 2004 (US$ millions)	Grocery market share (%)
Margin Free Market	Cooperative	370	312	0.7	281	0.7
Pantaloon	Local	76	255	0.5	56	0.1
Dairy Farm	Joint venture	124	114	0.2	97	0.2
Subhiksha	Local	142	61	0.1	52	0.1
Metro Group	Foreign	2	51	0.1	36	0.1
Other			46 681	98.3	41 352	98.8

Source: PlanetRetail (www.planetretail.com)

TRENDS AND DRIVERS IN THE RETAIL SECTOR

Retailing is a high-growth industry in India. Retail sales amounted to about 7400 billion INR (US$ 166.9 million), equivalent to 44 per cent of GDP in 2002, and expanded at an average annual rate of 7 per cent during the period 1999–2002. Food sales account for 63 per cent per cent of the total retail sales. The number of retail businesses grew by 26 per cent in the past five years (1996–2001). Growth of food and food service outlets has been 33 per cent, and that of non-food outlets has been less than 30 per cent. Across the country, retail sales in real terms are predicted to rise more rapidly than consumer expenditure during 2003–08. The forecast growth in real retail sales during 2003–08 is 8.3 per cent per year, compared with 7.1 per cent for consumer expenditure. Most of this rapid growth will be in the large cities.

Modernization of the Indian retail sector will be reflected in rapid growth in the sales of supermarkets, department stores and hypermarkets. Sales from these large format stores are to expand at growth rates ranging from 24 per cent to 49 per cent per year during 2003–08, according to a recent report by Euromonitor International (2004). Urbanization, working spouses, increasing household disposable incomes and the convenience of one-stop shopping have been the drivers of growth of modern retailing India. The Indian retail market is, however, one of the most fragmented in the world with just 2 per cent of the entire retailing business being carried out in the organized sector.

In India, most consumer expenditure is on basic necessities, especially food-related items. The share of household spending on food is one of the highest in the world, at 48 per cent of income. Indian consumers are increasingly spending more on eating out as compared to five years ago, which clearly indicates that there is high potential for food service players. Market liberalization and increasingly assertive consumers are sowing the seeds of a retail transformation that will bring bigger Indian and multinational players on to the scene. October and November of 2005 saw delegations from Wal-Mart and Tesco travelling to India to lobby the government to open the vast domestic market to overseas supermarket groups. But opposition from Communist coalition partners and the 9 million domestic shopkeepers has forced the government to move slowly.

The entry of multinational companies such as Metro (which, as a cash and carry company, was not subject to FDI restrictions) has certainly transformed this sector. The supply chain and consumer interest and awareness in branded products have been built from scratch. In January 2001, the Indian government announced a partial liberalization, allowing single-brand foreign retailers into the country. Also, foreign groups setting up 100 per cent-owned wholesale operations need no longer go through the cumbersome process of seeking permission from the Foreign Investment Promotion Board – this should allow Wal-Mart's Sam's Club to enter the market.

High-income urban consumers are willing to pay a higher price for having the choice of quality products and the complete shopping experience in the large retail stores; but the low-income urban and rural consumers will go for the low-price products that are easily available in the smaller stores located nearby. The markets in both categories are very large and hence there is little direct competition between the two retail sectors.

Case study 1: Milk supply

From chronic shortage of milk in the 1970s, India has emerged today as the largest producer of milk in the world, at 80 million tonnes per annum. Co-existence of formal structures, such as cooperatives, and informal structures makes it an interesting case to be studied and analysed. Although there has been a remarkable revolution in the dairy sector in India through the famous White Revolution, the whole transformation as perceived by a small producer was seldom recorded. Therefore, the inclusion of dairy in this study was an attempt to identify the satisfaction and grievances of those who are often talked of, but seldom included in the decision-making or policy-framing processes.

Milk and milk products constitute an integral part of the daily diet of all Indian households, without exception, across all regions and all social and economic categories. However, consumption levels vary considerably, depending on income levels. Rising incomes countrywide and the high disposable incomes of the top 20 per cent of the urban Indian population are rapidly changing milk consumption patterns. The per capita availability of milk has increased from 110 g per day in 1968 to almost 225 g per day in 2002. This has been achieved largely through a small producer economy in which Operation Flood, one of the world's largest dairy development programmes, played an important role.

Until 1991, the Indian dairy industry was highly regulated and protected through quantitative restrictions and stringent licensing provisions. In the early 1990s, India embarked upon the liberal policy framework, which was reinforced with the signing of the Uruguay Round Agreement on Agriculture in 1994. The dairy industry was de-licensed in 1991 and the private sector, including multinational companies, was allowed to set up milk processing and product manufacturing plants.

However, in 1992, controls were brought back through the Milk and Milk Products Order (MMPO) with the aim of having 'orderly growth' in the dairy industry in India. As per the provisions of this order, any person or dairy plant handling more than 10 000 litres per day of milk or 500 million tonnes of milk solids per annum needs to be registered with the registering authority appointed by the Central Government. The main objective of the order is to maintain and increase the supply of liquid milk of the desired quality in the interests of the general public and also for regulating the production, processing and distribution of milk and milk products. The opening up to foreign trade has increasingly exposed the Indian dairy sector to world markets, which have been distorted by high subsidies and support in developed countries.

The importance of Europe as a key exporter of dairy products is likely to diminish with the reduction in subsidies under the WTO regime. This is likely to provide India, which offers no subsidies and has competitive milk production cost, with a chance to develop export markets for its dairy products.

The organized dairy industry in India had a turnover of almost 145 billion INR (US$ 3 billion) in 2001, and various estimates expect this sector to witness a compound annual growth rate of over 13 per cent, to reach a size of 240 billion INR (US$ 5 billion) by 2005.

INDIAN SMALL-SCALE MILK PRODUCERS

Indian dairy farming is basically a small-producer production system, characterized by milk production by the masses rather than the mass production of milk. More than 80 million households (about 73 per cent of rural households) keep some type of livestock. The base for Indian dairying is provided by millions of landless agricultural labourers and marginal and small farmers, who maintain one or two milch cows of low genetic potential for milk production, primarily fed on crop residues and by-products, and reared with the help of under-employed family members, mostly female workers. Although dairying is becoming more commercialized in some areas, it predominantly remains secondary to farming, constituting a complementary or supplementary enterprise to crop farming, with regular sales of surplus production.

Dairy farmers in India are by and large illiterate, resource poor (with an average land holding of less than 1 acre), and low risk-bearers. They often exhibit a low level of farming innovation; in the majority of cases, they are either non-adopters or late adopters of modern technologies. Their average family size is moderate at around five persons. The marketable surplus of milk is about 60 per cent of total milk production in rural areas. The rest of the milk produced is used for household consumption, as milk is an integral component of Indian diet.

In the future, the changing policy environment will have some impact on the organization of the dairy production and processing sectors. The small-producer production system will face many constraints; therefore, some policy strategies are needed to involve small producers in the decision-making process and the development of the Indian dairy sector.

Some of the constraints faced by small producers are as follows.

- The progressively shrinking farm size and fragmentation of land holdings will make dairy farming unviable and drive out a large number of dairy farmers at the bottom end of the small producer spectrum.
- Timely and adequate institutional credit at the farm level for dairy production is not available because of procedural complexities, high interest rates and other problems.

- Inputs and livestock health and breeding facilities for milk production are mainly in the domain of the public sector, and are generally inefficient and of poor quality. India has many animal diseases and control of these diseases is a low priority for the government, resulting in substantial losses.
- The demand and supply balance of animal feeds and fodder is worsening, which puts enormous pressure on natural resources.
- Liberalization of the Indian economy and implementation of WTO commitments has opened up global competition in the dairy sector, which exposes the small producer producers to unfair and distorted trade competition due to distortions in world dairy markets.
- The legal and regulatory framework has not kept pace with changes in the domestic policy environment and global trade regime. The MMPO Cooperative Societies Act continues to be restrictive rather than enabling.
- Food safety issues have become more important and consumers are looking for assurances that there will be no long-term effects from new practices, processes or products.

ROLE OF THE FORMAL AND INFORMAL SECTORS

Like nearly all developing countries, India has co-existing 'organized' and 'unorganized' sectors for the marketing of milk and dairy products. Sometimes called the 'informal' sector, the unorganized sector may be more usefully thought of as the traditional milk market sector, comprising the marketing of raw milk and traditional products such as locally manufactured ghee, fresh cheese and sweets.

The organized or formal sector is relatively new in historical terms and consists of western-style dairy processing based on pasteurization, though adapted to the Indian market in terms of products. In some cases, the traditional sector is quite well organized, with a complex net of market agents, and shows variation in numbers and roles of market intermediaries. It should be noted that, unlike some countries, the Indian government has generally adopted a *laissez-faire* approach to the informal sector, which has allowed it to expand with the growth in demand, and serve both small farmers and resource-poor consumers.

THE FORMAL (ORGANIZED) SECTOR

The formal or organized sector comprises dairy cooperatives. The cooperative movement began at Amul Dairy in Gujarat and is now replicated in 70 000 villages in about 200 districts of India. The cooperative societies are federated into 170 District Milk Producers' Unions, which further get integrated into 22 State Cooperative Dairy Federations. The village milk cooperative is a society of primary producers formed under the guidance of a supervisor or milk supply officer of the Cooperative Dairy Union (a district level cooperative owning the processing plant).

A milk producer becomes a member by buying a share from the cooperative society and agreeing to sell milk only to the society. Each society has a milk collection centre where farmers take their milk in the mornings and evenings. The number of farmers organized into village milk producers' cooperative societies is now over 1 million, and the daily procurement of milk by the cooperatives is 13 million litres per day. The cooperative is a no profit–no loss institution, which shares whatever profit gained amongst its members under the rules of the Cooperative Laws.

Small producers were interviewed during the course of the study in Anand and Baroda districts of Gujarat state. The dairy movement started from Gujarat in India, therefore Gujarat was an obvious choice. The majority of milk producers, especially the weaker section (monthly household income less than 1000 INR), identified milk societies as a source of better income from sale of surplus milk and an important source of income for their livelihoods.

Small producers in cooperatives are satisfied with their marketing channel because cooperatives pay on time. Also, there is an array of services that cooperatives provide to the small producers, such as animal husbandry support, training on livestock management, providing high nutrient cattle feed on nominal payments and insurance facilities.

Another instance of an initiative that gives small producers access to markets is Food Specialities Ltd (Nestlé India), based in Moga, Punjab. This company collects milk from nearby villages and transports it to the plant (capacity 800 000 litres per day) in Moga district. The firm follows a two-fold contracting strategy: (1) indirect procurement of milk through agents; and (2) direct procurement from producers.

In the case of an indirect contract, the firm enters into a legal agreement not with the individual producers, but with a local person who acts as an intermediary/agent between the firm and the milk producers for the collection of milk. The agent facilitates the distribution of information, inputs and services to the producers from the firm. This is the dominant mode of milk procurement. Such an arrangement reduces costs of information, negotiation, monitoring and enforcement to the firm. The firm also enters into contract with individual producers generally having a dairy herd of 25 and above.

Village agents collect milk from members who commit to supply milk to Nestlé. The agents are paid 4 per cent commission for milk collection. Veterinary officials from Nestlé check the quality of milk and verify the services at collection centres built by the company. In remote areas, small chilling centres with 2000 litre capacity are established.

All facilities are provided including a generator, solar lamp and so on to collect milk once a day. Computerized milk collection is arranged for the farmers and Milko Testers (electronic testing devices to speed up measurement of fat content) are in operation. In areas with no chilling facilities, milk is collected twice a day and the agents are responsible for the quality of milk supplied. If the milk is found to be doctored in any way, the agent's services are terminated by Nestlé.

Company village agents visit farmers and offer them advance payments for milk and also provide a buyer for milch cows. Also, a network of veterinary services is maintained by Nestlé. Milk payments are made regularly on the 2nd and 17th of every month. Around four to six village agents collect milk in each village. Each agent collects 100–400 litres of milk per day and is responsible for transporting the milk to the main dairy. Each village agent then delivers to a sub-contractor or a contractor.

Contractors are paid by the company on the 5th, 15th and 25th of each month. They each collect 150 000 to 450 000 litres per day. Prices paid to the producers depend upon two factors, fat content and solid not fat (SNF). Therefore there is no fixed price paid per litre of milk, rather the price ranges from 200–230 INR per kilogram of fat.

THE INFORMAL (UNORGANIZED) SECTOR

The informal or 'unorganized' sector includes producers, traders and contractors (intermediaries). There are large regional variations in the types of private operators and their modus operandi. There are four main types of milk suppliers in the informal sector:

- Those who keep one or two cows in a shed on the outskirts of urban areas. They produce and market as little as 50 to 500 litres of milk per day.
- Traders who procure milk from villagers, dilute it with bought skimmed milk and sell it.
- Traders who buy skimmed milk, dilute it even further and sell low-fat milk to low-income customers, tea stalls and restaurants for use in whitening tea or making curd (yoghurts).
- Milk contractors who purchase milk from livestock keepers on behalf of their principals.

Producers associated with unorganized procurers such as vendors and contractors complained of exploitation in terms of the price paid to them, as well as the fact that support services are almost non-existent and the chain runs on credit. Some of the associated dairy farmers also tried to conceal information initially, thinking that we were associates of their procurers, but the moment we could convince them, what emerged was a saga of manipulation and exploitation.

Small-producer dairy farmers are confronted with numerous issues in their farming situations that need to be dealt with. Since small-producer dairy farmers provide the basis for the Indian dairy industry and prospects for the dairy industry in India are dependent on the prospects of millions of small-producer dairy farmers spread across the country, their views merit attention. Small producer dairy farmers are resource poor in terms of land, capital, and management skills.

Because of the emphasis on attaining self-sufficiency in the production of food grains in the country, several incentives such as input subsidies and high minimum support prices are provided by the government for producing wheat and paddy. Consequently, most farmers are producing wheat and paddy crops, leaving a very small area for fodder production. This translates into shortages of fodder and also a decline in community lands for grazing.

Compared to that of food grains, the incentive for milk production is declining because the increase in demand and prices of food grains is many times higher than for milk products.

COOPERATIVE MILK PROCESSORS

The importance of the cooperative sector in milk processing has not lessened in spite of the entry of private enterprises, including the multinational and domestic corporations, after partial de-licensing of the dairy sector as a part of the macro-economic reforms in the early 1990s. In fact, the delays in project approvals under the MMPO reveal that there is state intervention in countless ways, even though there is constant demand for the government to remove licensing requirements and leave it to the markets.

Some of the important issues facing the private sector managers are as follows.

- There are a number of clearances – statutory and non-statutory – to be obtained before setting up a milk processing plant.
- Under the MMPO, the requirement for registration with the MMPO and the renewal of licences every three years used to be a major problem. However, the requirement for renewal of registration after three years was abolished in August 2001, which was a positive step towards the liberalization of the Indian dairy industry.
- The powers given to the Milk Controller under the MMPO to carry out inspection of milk processing units was also considered a problem by the private sector units. The Food Controller is appointed by the Government of India and has powers to enter, inspect and seize and the processors complained that they demanded hush money otherwise the processors would face false allegations and penalties

- The condition that each registered unit collect milk only in specified quantities and only from its registered milk sheds outside the existing cooperative/private sector dairy milk shed areas is a major problem faced by the new private sector dairies. These restrictions have serious implications for economies of scale and scope in the processing sector.
- The increased competition in domestic markets from cooperatives, the informal sector, and subsidized imports is perceived to be a major issue by the private sector.

Cooperative processors have several complaints about the system. First, the free rider problem: private sector processors do not invest much and poach on the territory of the cooperative sector where there have been big investments. Second, centralized procurement pricing controlled by the state federations/government prevents district cooperative unions from responding actively to competition from the private sector and informal channels, thus reducing the competitiveness of the cooperative sector plants. Third, there is a problem of over-staffing with an inefficient work force that leads to low efficiency and high overhead costs in the cooperative sector.

A fourth complaint is that the bureaucratization of some of the state federations, together with political interference, the absence of marketing and the commercial orientation of top management are major concerns for the cooperative sector. Finally, the absence of a level playing field makes these organizations less competitive. There are many government restrictions, such as the need for permission from the registrar, cooperative societies, and other government functionaries for petty things.

Case study 2: Fresh vegetables

The chapter concludes with an example based on a report from within a supermarket chain, presented by VP-Merchandizing from the FoodWorld supermarket chain to a regional workshop on supermarkets and fresh produce (Radhakrishnan, 2004) and subsequently also by PWC and CII (2005) (see the box below). FoodWorld began as a Joint Venture between RPG – one of India's largest business conglomerates – and Hong Kong-based Dairy Farm International. In late 2005, Dairy Farm announced that it was entering into new joint venture agreement with Arko Ltd following the withdrawal of RPG.

Although this case requires external evaluation, it points to what can be achieved when a supermarket accepts small-scale producers as partners. The example comes from areas where there has been farm consolidation leading to a group of 5-acre (2 hectare) farms specializing in fresh fruits and vegetables (FFV). Note that the farms are some distance from the supermarket stores and despite high losses, farmers consider the trade worthwhile.

Radhakrishnan (2004) points out:

There is no contractual relationship. For the time being the company has agreed to purchase everything its farmers produce, although if quality considerations begin to override quantity requirements this may not last. Prices are set on a daily basis with reference to the prevailing wholesale market price and the method of calculation is fully transparent. Farmers deliver from up to 50 km away to a consolidation centre which, in turn, is up to 300 km from the stores. There is no cool chain so losses are high, although significantly less than in the traditional supply chain.

There is a suggestion that the supermarket business provides security for suppliers of credit who would otherwise ignore small producers with little or no collateral. "Foodworld has negotiated with seed and fertilizer companies on behalf of the farmers and to ensure that the correct varieties are supplied. Farmers receive loans from these companies. At present, Foodworld plays no role in loan repayment although it would cease buying from farmers who fail to pay back their loans (this has yet to happen). Discussions are presently under way with banks to set up a quadripartite arrangement, whereby the banks finance the inputs supplied to farmers and Foodworld repays the banks out of the farmers' earnings."

Foodworld and FFV Procurement In Tamil Nadu

To manage the issue of the fragmented and multi-layered commodity supply chain in India, FoodWorld had set up a distribution centre at Hoskote, in Tamil Nadu, primarily with an objective of sourcing directly from farm producers and thereby removing multiple intermediaries in the supply chain. Today FoodWorld sources directly from about 150 farmers. Many of them are the first generation free of debts, thanks to FoodWorld's guaranteed and predictable off-takes, fair price and cash purchase. A few other examples of how FoodWorld has made a difference to the farmers are as follows:

- Improving productivity through adoption of better practices

  - Carrot farmers typically used to cordon a ditch and wash the carrots in ditch water, by stamping on them. This obviously affects the quality of produce. FoodWorld introduced the practice of using washing trays to wash carrots, thereby reducing wastage and improving shelf-life and quality.
  - A typical cauliflower farmer used to plant 12,000 cauliflowers per acre, resulting in 30 per cent wastage of produce and poor quality as well. FoodWorld insisted that their suppliers plant 9,000 cauliflowers per acre, thereby reducing wastage and improving quality. The increased size of the cauliflowers and reduced wastage actually increased the net yield for the farmers. As a result, this practice is now being widely adopted even by farmers who do not supply to FoodWorld. Wholesalers are also insisting that the farmers follow these standards.
  - FoodWorld has contracted millers for grains and spices. By adopting updated machinery, the millers have been able to save at least 15 per cent on cost of spices.

- Creating market access for farmers

  - FoodWorld markets tamarind paste in its stores. The best tamarind in India is grown in the Tumkur region of Karnataka. FoodWorld has been successful in branding the paste as 'Tumkur' tamarind. This not only builds brand equity for the Tumkur tamarind growers, but also benefits customers, who get to use high quality tamarinds. Similarly, Latur is known for its toor dal and Tenali for urad dal. FoodWorld has thus been able to build brand equity for regional farmers.
  - About 40 per cent of FoodWorld's merchandise is sourced from about 500 local small scale industries, which provides vital market access to these vendors, which would otherwise have been almost impossible in India's fragmented distribution system. A few examples of FoodWorld's impact on some of the vendors:
    o Ready-to-cook idli batter manufacturer – A former employee of RPG who wanted to turn entrepreneur was assisted by RPG to set up a business supplying idli batter to FoodWorld. His annual turnover today is about Rs 9 million.

> ○ Jam manufacturer – a small local vendor started supplying jam made in his aunt's kitchen to FoodWorld, and then diversified into making mango pulp. His annual turnover today is Rs 25 million.
>
> While creating market access for small vendors, FoodWorld has actually increased consumption and market size of certain categories, rather than eating into the share of national brands. In jams, for instance, private labels account for about 45 per cent of total category sales. This growth has not come at the expense of existing brands. However, FoodWorld has managed to expand the category itself, by attracting first-time consumers with lower price points and providing greater choice for existing consumers.
>
> *Source*: PWC and CII, 2005

Conclusions

The overarching strategic direction in the dairy sector will be to develop new, higher-value products and markets, which involves a focus on:

- understanding the market and preparing itself to respond to emerging market trends
- improving farmers' access to institutional credit through measures such as simplification of procedures and reduction in interest rates
- ensuring that the products are safe, free from residues, and are not impacted by trade barriers, animal welfare or animal health issues, and that they meet the range of functional and sensory quality standards that consumers demand
- restructuring the government regulatory and legal framework to enhance competitiveness of the production and processing sectors through vertical coordination in production, processing, value addition and marketing of products in domestic as well as global markets
- more emphasis on new production technologies, supported by efficient extension services for technology transfer
- restructuring and revitalization of government animal husbandry departments, reorienting their mandate from curative veterinary care to preventive veterinary care, moving delivery of livestock services away from government, progressive privatization of services, and the creation of a disease-free zone to improve institutional efficiency, exclusive to dairy
- reorienting the priorities of research institutions and encouraging greater participation of different stakeholders such as farmers and industry in the decision-making process
- manufacturing eco-friendly products.

References

Euromonitor, 2004. *Retailing in India: A nation of shopkeepers*. Euromonitor Plc, London.

PWC and CII, 2005. *The rising elephant: Benefits of modern trade to Indian economy*. PriceWaterhouseCoopers and Confederation of Indian Industry. Available: www.pwc.com/extweb/pwcpublications.nsf/docid/D13AC5F4FD6E7F5C852570C7006E2E7E.

Radhakrishnan, K., 2004. *Building a fruits and vegetables supply chain for supermarkets in India*. Presentation to FAO/AFMA/FAMA Regional Workshop on the Growth of Supermarkets as Retailers of Fresh Produce, 4–7 October, Kuala Lumpur, Malaysia. Available: www.fao.org/ag/ags/subjects/en/agmarket/docs/afmaklrep.pdf.

13 *Pakistan*

Syed Qasim Ali Shah, Mosharraf Zaidi, Muhammad Ijaz Ahmed and Huma Nawaz Syal

Introduction

Pakistan has made significant progress under various strategic policies aimed at improving the economic outlook of the country. However, much of the progress has been marred by factors such as floods, droughts, political instability, policy inconsistency, and weak implementation of policies and related legislation. Two decades ago, Pakistan embarked on the path to market-oriented economic reform. Even though Pakistan has received strong financial assistance, there remains scope for greater improvement. GDP per capita has improved for the period 1999 to 2002 and was expected to grow by 5.3 per cent in the fiscal year 2003–04.[1]

Today there are few restrictions on foreign investment, but a lack of potentially profitable opportunities means there is little sign of inward investment by international retailers. In fact, we cannot list the 'top five' food retailers – instead there's a 'top one' and that is a minnow by world standards. However, global cash and carry chains are preparing to expand rapidly in the country.

Agriculture represents the traditional foundation of Pakistan's economy. Despite gradual increases in the share of manufacturing and the services sector in national product, agriculture continues to be the single largest sector and the touchstone for growth and development. It accounts for 24 per cent of the GDP and employs 48 per cent of the workforce.

Agriculture's contribution in real terms extends far beyond farm output and includes its role as a supplier to industry as well as a market for industrial products and a significant portion of Pakistan's export earnings. Of Pakistan's population, 67.5 per cent inhabit rural areas and the livelihoods of the vast majority of the rural populace are directly or indirectly linked with agriculture. Any improvements in technology or increases in productivity, therefore, not only facilitate overall economic growth, but also have immediate micro-economic benefits for the large rural segment of the population.

Land distribution and ownership in Pakistan is indicative of the massive socio-economic inequality that exists, not only between the urban elite and the rural poor, but perhaps more importantly between rich and poor within rural areas. The total number of privately owned farms in the country is 6.62 million with an area of 50.43 million acres. There are another 170 state-managed farms that cover an area of 0.08 million acres. Out of 6.62 million private farms, 58 per cent are less than 5 acres, but the area of these farms is only 16 per cent of the total farm area. On the other hand, farms of 25 acres or above in size are only 6 per cent per cent of the total, but they command 37 per cent of the total farm area. The average farm size by farm area is 7.6 acres and by cultivated area it is 6.2 acres.[2]

---

1   Forecast by the Economist Intelligence Unit.
2   All data from Pakistan Agriculture Census, Agriculture Census Organisation, 2000.

The food system reflects the level of development and this provides us with some interesting insights. Pakistan today is an example of a country in which emerging supermarkets and food processors have not yet constructed supply chains with dedicated suppliers and centralized procurement and depots. So far, supermarkets have used existing traditional marketing channels for fresh mangoes, but it seems unlikely that these channels will satisfy them.

On the other hand, in the dairy sector, Nestlé has developed a supply chain of small-scale farmers that seems effective and likely to survive and prosper as supermarkets expand.

KEY DATA

	2002	2003	2004
Population (millions)	150	154	157
Per capita GDP (US$)	410	457	492
Urbanization (%)	33		
Agriculture as % GDP			22.6
Per capita total retail food sales (US$)	155	172	183
Per capita modern retail food sales (US$)	32	35	38
Modern retail food sales as % of total			21

Exchange rate (1 January 2006): 1 US Dollar = 59.83 Pakistan rupee (PKR)

TOP CHAINS, 2004

Name of retailer	Ownership	Number of stores	Retail banner sales 2004 (US$ millions)	Market share (%)	Grocery sales 2004 (US$ millions)	Grocery market share (%)
Utility Stores Corporation	Local state-owned	352	21	0.3	19	0.3
Other			7576	99.7	6,672	99.7

Source: PlanetRetail

AGRI-FOOD MARKETING

There are two kinds of markets operating in Pakistan, wholesale markets and retail markets. According to estimates there are 700 wholesale markets in the country, of which 200 are regulated. At the market level, Market Committees are established in a number of regulated markets, comprised of wholesalers, traders, commission agents and farmers' representatives. Contractors (*thekedar*) purchase standing crops or produce at the farm gate either in advance or at the time of harvesting. Contractors use their own capital or get credit from formal sources or credit from the commission agents/wholesalers.

Intermediaries are important in making small-scale sales of perishable and non-perishable commodities at the village level, such as potatoes, onions and grains. They take the produce to the wholesale markets and/or sell it to commission agents. Wholesalers, in the case of cash crops and cereals, often purchase in bulk and supply directly to the processing industries, mills, traders and exporters. They usually work for traders and industry as agents.

Commission agents (*arthi*) are market based, and arrange auctions for the sale of agricultural produce brought into the market and charge a fixed percentage as a fee/commission. Often commission agents own the produce brought to the market, having extended credit to the supplier, which could be either a grower, an intermediary or a contractor.

Purchasers at a market fall into three broad categories: wholesalers, sub-wholesalers (*pheria*), who normally purchase in small bulk from auction lots purchased by the wholesalers and then sell it to retailers, and retailers. These categorizations are generally true for all agricultural commodities such as fruits, vegetables and cereals, but it is entirely different for milk and dairy products.

Pakistan is the world's ninth largest market with an estimated 150 million consumers. Experts believe that the food retail market in Pakistan is in the throes of landmark changes, with the total number of retail outlets expected to have grown by 15 per cent in the 1990s, presently resting at around 290 000 outlets (Farrukh and Dever, 2000). The share of 'food, beverage and tobacco' in household budgets is 48 per cent in Pakistan. But there is a clear division between rural and urban consumption patterns, with residents of urban areas paying considerably more in rent and residents in rural areas spending considerably more on food. Cereals and milk products are the most important components of the daily diet of the Pakistani people, with total expenditure incurred on these two items comprising 42 per cent of the entire food ration consumed in a month.

The development of supermarket outlets is still in its early stages, with the majority of their outlets in the major cities of Karachi, Lahore and increasingly in the capital, Islamabad. Supermarkets account for 10 per cent of retail outlets by market share, compared with 30 per cent for wetmarkets and 60 per cent for traditional markets (Farrukh and Dever, 2000) .

The Utility Stores Corporation is owned by the government and has a nationwide presence. The corporation is seen to be a mechanism for restraining inflationary price increases by being under the direct supervision of the government. However since 1997–98, as part of the company's efforts to improve profitability and efficiency, the most unprofitable stores have been closed. At the end of June 2003, there were 352 stores in all, with net sales of US$ 15 million.

Although in Pakistan there is no presence of international supermarkets such as Wal-Mart or Carrefour, the international brands are easily available to upscale consumers. The Pakistani consumer gives preference to imported goods for quality and class reasons. Although US brands are highly popular, the consumer is not concerned about the exact location of origin. There is a strong demand that the labels on the product give the production and expiration dates, with the language set to Standard English. Since Pakistani consumers are confident in buying foreign brands, there is huge scope for growth in the import of food items.

In 2005, cash and carry operator SHV Makro from the Netherlands announced that it was interested in establishing up to 30 stores in Pakistan, as a joint venture with the House of Habib. The first stores, in Karachi and Lahore, will open towards the end of 2006. Another major global cash and carry player, Metro, plans to open its first outlet in Pakistan by the end of 2005. In the first phase of market entry, two stores apiece will be opened in the cities of Lahore, Rawalpindi and Karachi with a longer term aim of 20 outlets in Pakistan.

Pakistan's retail food sector is evolving and the total number of retail outlets has increased by approximately 15 per cent during the past decade, while the value of processed retail food sales has increased by nearly 12 per cent. Hassan (2002) identifies the following challenges facing retail food marketing in Pakistan:

- The retail distribution chain has a direct link with the consumer, so the chain has become a 'critical area'.
- To date, the retail food marketing sector is still unorganized.

- The quality and retail price of some food items vary from locality to locality, thus making it difficult for the government to monitor and enforce uniformity of prices and quality.
- Supermarkets operate mainly in the major cities, so they do not pose any immediate threat to small-scale farmers and retailers. Any future expansion by the supermarkets is likely to adversely affect the small-scale farmers and retailers, as it is these very agents that are part of a 'small and abused segment in the marketing system'.
- Currently, the commission agents and wholesalers control the marketing channels, thus acting between small farmers and small retailers. The role of these agents is expected to be greatly reduced with the expansion of supermarkets, department stores and fast food organizations.
- At present, the traditional approach is that the products originate from a centralized market place. With the expansion of large retail outlets, a process of decentralization is anticipated, with the majority of products being directly transferred to the market without any public arrangement. This would entail 'proliferation of the pricing points, with the actual price no longer reflecting the cost of product; rather it will depend on 'individual buyer specifications'.
- A positive observation is the use of packaging as an effective merchandizing device.

MILK SUPPLY

Estimates suggest that only 5 to 10 per cent of milk is supplied through formal channels, the rest being supplied by *gawallas* who deliver raw, unprocessed milk from the farmer, or milk collection centre, to the final consumer. Gawallas have an incentive to doctor milk with additives to increase the life of milk, and to increase its volume. Added to this is the inadvertent contamination of milk, given that gawallas transport milk mostly in large metal containers with little regard for hygiene. High-income consumers avoid the gawallas and turn to modern branded products such as those sold by Nestlé.

Small-scale farmers sell their milk to gawallas or other mini-suppliers, while large-scale dairy farmers are directly linked to a company such as Nestlé.

Case study 1: Nestlé's milk procurement scheme

One product that almost all retailers across Pakistan carry is Nestlé's MilkPak brand of UHT (ultra heat treated) milk. The brand Milkpak is perceived as synonymous with quality and nourishment, and has been in the market since the mid-1980s. The price differential, however, between Milkpak and the raw, open milk delivered by the gawalla is huge; on average Milkpak costs twice as much per litre as open milk. The obvious implication of this differential is that Milkpak is consumed exclusively by upper-middle, and upper income groups. The premium paid by consumers for Milkpak is believed to reflect the higher quality of the milk available in the formal sector, which has been processed and packaged, thus extending shelf life up to four weeks (Garcia et al., 2004). Nestlé's market share in the overall market for milk is small, less than 5 per cent.

A joint venture between Milkpak Ltd. and Nestlé S.A. came about in 1988 and the company was renamed as Nestlé Milkpak Ltd. Prior to that, Milkpak Ltd produced UHT milk, butter, cream, desi ghee and fruit drinks at the Sheikhupura factory. Twenty-one branded product lines were added during the period 1990–98.

Nestlé Milkpak operates the largest and most well-reputed milk collection and processing system in the country, which enables it to collect the highest quality milk for production of UHT and powdered milk as well as other milk-based products. It was the first company to start collection from the farmers directly in 1988. It daily collects milk from over 135 000 farmers in 3000 villages. This milk is collected from an area of 71 000 km^2. The company has established its own milk collection centres in the villages called Village Milk Collection Centres (VMCs).

Farmers' organizations have been formed to facilitate each small and large farmer selling milk to the company and getting other benefits. Farmers are organized into different committees according to their share in overall production of milk. On the basis of this arrangement, farmers are divided into five groups. These groups can be broadly categorized in terms of those with direct relationships with the company and others indirectly linked to the collection channel.

Nestlé established an Extension Service in 2002 in order to service small farmers from whom it purchases raw milk. The Extension Service offers technical assistance to farmers on issues of livestock maintenance, identification of disease and remedies, provides high yield seed for fodder and provides vaccination to the farmers' animals at cost. In 2003, Nestlé's Extension Service vaccinated 280 000 animals.

Finally, in the light of the significant share of women involved in producing milk, Nestlé has deployed several teams of Women Milk Promoters, composed of Nestlé employees who work with rural women to encourage increases in the productivity of women milk entrepreneurs at the village level.

OFFICIAL SUPPORT

Despite official lip service to encourage small and medium-sized enterprises (SMEs), there is not much practical help available. One indicator of the severity of negligence towards the small farmer is the fact that all the literature produced by most commercial banks and government organizations is published in English, a language that is spoken essentially by the urban educated elite. Where there are Urdu publications their quality is extremely poor.

The Small and Medium Enterprise Development Authority (SMEDA) was established in 1998 to provide business consulting services to small- and medium-sized entrepreneurs. SMEDA has made significant investments in both the policy formulation of the Government of Pakistan and in conducting wide-ranging, and high-quality research on sectors and sub-sectors that represent avenues of investment for businesses.

While much of SMEDA's research is invaluable to government, businesses and civil society, the organization's name is more of a misnomer than an accurate representation of its line of work. SMEDA advocates a ban on the raw milk that currently is the staple dairy product in 90 per cent of Pakistani households. In addition, SMEDA makes a reasonable case for the large-scale undertaking of modernizing the dairy sector in Pakistan by introducing commercial dairy farms, and mini-dairy plants and has produced detailed documents for both of these.

However, the investment per farm envisaged is beyond the resources available and the programme as a whole is unrealistic. The investment required in the 50 animal commercial dairy farms suggested by one SMEDA report is 2.8 million PKR, of which SMEDA suggests the entrepreneur take on 50 per cent debt and produce 50 per cent equity. SMEDA's suggested mini-dairy goes even further, basing the feasibility on a 10.7 million PKR investment.

Case study 2: Fresh mangoes and citrus

Five store managers were interviewed in Lahore to find out how they procure fresh mangoes. The interviews took place during the mango season. All the stores displayed a large quantity of mangoes in their shops. The prices of mangoes, and in fact all fresh fruits and vegetables (FFV), were higher than corresponding wetmarket prices. The stores only sell Grade A fruit and store managers were not interested in finding new farm-level suppliers unless they could deliver sufficient volume and guarantee it would be Grade A.

The Lahore stores buy mangoes in three ways: (1) from the local auction market (the *mandi*); (2) by contracting out a 'fruit and vegetable counter' in the store for a wholesaler to operate as a tenant; and (3) through direct procurement from farmers. One store in Lahore buys on a daily basis from the mandi. The store has no storage space so this is the best way to buy supplies. Another store manager told us that he would prefer to buy fresh fruit and vegetables from growers directly. The store had a contract with a vegetable grower for the last two years and this grower is responsible for supplying vegetables of agreed quality and quantity to the store every day. The grower himself is responsible for transporting the vegetables at the store.

The second way the stores buy mangoes is to contract with a person who is experienced in selling fruits and vegetables. The contractor is responsible for arranging mango and citrus supplies for the store from the open market. Most of the time there is a written agreement between the contractor and the store management. Under this arrangement, the store management deducts 10 per cent of total sale proceeds of the fruit and vegetables and the rest of the amount is paid to the contractor. In this arrangement, the contractor is responsible for assuring the quality of the products, charging a reasonable price and observing due courtesy to the customers. Either party has the right to dismantle the contract any time in case of a violation of the conditions.

Buying through auction extends the supply chain sometimes because of the practice of buying fruit 'on the tree' in the orchard. To purchase the crop still in the orchard, the potential purchaser usually contacts the commission agent of the local mandi. The commission agent is also in need of a pre-harvest contractor to arrange mango supplies for them during the season.

They formulate an agreement. The commission agent provides a loan to the pre-harvest contractor to purchase the mango orchard. The pre-harvest contractor purchases the orchard through auction. As per agreement, the pre-harvest contractor is obligated to sell the entire produce of the orchard through the lending commission agent. The price of the produce is determined on the basis of daily mandi price during the season.

Usually the pre-harvest contractor brings the orchard produce to the commission agent at the mandi. Transport expenses are born by the pre-harvest contractor. The commission agent auctions the mango and gets a fee in the form of commission on sale proceeds. The commission agent deducts a fee of 6.25 per cent of the total sale proceeds.

Sometimes, commission agents get direct orders from outside markets (mandis). In such a case, they inform the pre-harvest contractor to arrange a vehicle to dispatch mangoes to the buyer of the outer market. On such sales, commission is deducted on the total value of mango earned in the host market. Commission agents prefer to use suppliers who keep to the terms and conditions laid down in the agreement.

Pre-harvest contractors are often said to violate the terms of the agreement. Farmers receive their income in instalments from pre-harvest contractors. A quarter of the sale price is received in advance. At the beginning of the mango harvest season, the pre-harvest contractor pays another 25 per cent to the grower. At the peak of the harvest, a contractor pays 25 per cent and the last instalment is paid at the end of the season.

Having arranged for a supply of mangoes to the mandi, commission agents then look for outlets. In marketing mangoes, commission agents play an essential role. They provide finance to the contractor, arrange the sale of the mango within local and outside markets and get their fee as 'commission'. A trader who buys from the mandi auction is called a *pharia* – a secondary wholesaler who supplies shops and stalls with fruit.

Returning to the situation in Lahore, the third way stores buy mangoes is directly from growers. The growers themselves are responsible for transporting the produce at the time required every day to the store. In this case, two-thirds of the sale value of the supplied products is paid to the grower and one-third is deducted by the store as commission. However, the store management keeps the copies of the agreement and they were not prepared to reveal the terms. Still, both the managers and the growers independently informed that the arrangement gave them better returns than the alternatives. Only a small proportion of mangoes were bought by stores directly.

At the moment there are few modern processors or retailers in Pakistan and little need for preferred suppliers or separate supply chains. The traditional marketing channels (auction, wholesalers and growers) are able to provide the fresh mangoes that shoppers want. Of course, this may not last. Already there are signs that citrus growers want to sell to wholesalers rather than the mandi. Also, it seems inefficient for a store manager to buy supplies in person from a daily auction because of space constraints. As the modern food system expands, either the traditional system must adapt or the new retail chains will create their own dedicated supply chains.

Conclusions

The retail food market in Pakistan has evolved with increased purchasing power in cities, greater access to higher quality products – both imported and those produced domestically – and increased levels of consumer awareness. This in principle should lead to greater margins for small farmers. In reality, small farmers in Pakistan – producers of both milk, and fruits such as mangoes and citrus – continue to suffer from deeply embedded structural challenges.

The likelihood is that the traditional marketing channels in Pakistan for fruits such as mangoes will not be able to provide sufficient quality and volume for an expanding modern food system. On the other hand, the Nestlé business model looks more viable. The challenges to reaching a sustainable solution in agriculture that leads to both a more robust and dynamic retail environment for consumers, and more fulfilling and profitable livelihoods for producers are rooted in four key areas:

* Resources: in relatively crude terms, there are two kinds of farmers in Pakistan, land owners with significant land interests, and landless, or minimal landholding farmers. The playing field for these two kinds of farmers is predictably uneven. Due to the complex interconnectedness of rural wealth, political influence, and bureaucratic sway – the public, the private and arguably even the non-profit sector skew resources and capacities in favour of the wealthy landowning rural elite. In economic terms, this simply crowds the small farmer out of the credit market, the labour market and the market for inputs that are conducive to higher productivity.

- Information: small- and medium-sized farmers also suffer from information asymmetry. At the micro level, this entails dependence on intermediaries for price and demand information at major markets. At the macro level, the cost is even higher to the small farmer, because it negatively affects the farmer's ability to identify new technologies and techniques for enhanced quality and productivity.
- Regulation: public policy is the common gaping hole across all sectors in all spheres in Pakistan. This is not for a lack of will, but rather a lack of capacity. Government is not equipped, and some would argue, not qualified, to produce consistent, far-sighted and compassionate regulatory and legislative measures that serve the interests of the small- and medium-sized entrepreneurs in any sector – agriculture-related or not. Wherever capacities do exist, they work to ensure that the most needy citizens are the ones with least access – to people, resources, information and opportunities. On the demand-side, the public sector again lacks the capacity to enact or enforce meaningful laws, rules, or standards that serve the interests of consumers. The disregard for hygiene by milk gawallas is merely a glimpse of the large-scale lack of recognition of the rights of consumers as equal and important members of the economic value chain.
- Technology: the example of dairy farming is perhaps the most vital among all agricultural pursuits in Pakistan in illustrating the desperate lack of technological resources for small- and medium-sized farmers. Vaccinations of animals – something that should be a given for all animals producing milk commercially – is a novelty to such a large extent that NGOs announce the exact number of vaccinations they have helped facilitate, and Nestlé Milkpak's Annual Report for 2003 carries the exact number of vaccinations it helped conduct – not for free, but at cost (280 000). The notion of advanced dairy technologies that will not only increase yields, but also enhance animal longevity, and help create product and service synergies for farmers is, in such an environment, a distant dream.

The depth of these problems and their generic nature is the most alarming aspect in considering the future prospects for small- and medium-sized farmers. Public sector organizations like SMEDA discuss the importance of the dairy sector, and the need for large-scale commercial dairies with minimum investments that run into millions of rupees. In the meantime, small landless farmers with two buffaloes seek gainful employment as day labourers and turn to dairy farming only as a measure of desperation. While further research needs to be conducted to verify this contention, it is likely that one would find that the very basis for the public sector's encouragement of large-scale commercial dairy farming is the low price at which raw milk can be purchased from the small farmer – much the same way that Nestlé and other milk processing units have leveraged the information and resource gaps that small farmers suffer from.

Generic and simplistic recommendations are easy to formulate. It is in fact much more difficult to formulate strategies that have a chance to survive both red tape enacted by the public sector, and barriers to entry constructed by the private sector, and to ultimately improve the viability of dairy farming by small operators.

In sum, there are several positive endeavours in both the private and public sectors that lend encouragement to the future. These include:

- the government's commitment to livestock and dairy farming as one of the cornerstones of the agricultural section of the five-year development plans

- the success of Nestlé's business model, and its official commitment to supporting the farmers it purchases raw milk from – through for instance technical assistance
- the natural endowment of Pakistan, especially the high quality of its mango and citrus produce, with mangoes in particular among the best in the world
- the best practices of success stories in neighbouring countries, such as that of Amul Dairies in India.

References

Agriculture Census Organization, 2000. *Pakistan Agriculture Census*. Agriculture Census Organisation, Lahore, Pakistan.

Farrukh, A. and Dever, J., 2000. *Pakistan Retail Food Sector Report*. Foreign Agriculture Service, USDA, Islamabad, Pakistan.

Garcia, O., Mahmood, K. and Hemme, T., 2004. *A Review of Milk Production in Pakistan with Particular Emphasis on Small Scale Producers*. PPLPI Working Paper No. 3, Food and Agriculture Organization of the United Nations, Rome.

Hassan, S., 2002. Major issues in retail food marketing. *Daily Dawn*, Karachi, Pakistan. Available: http://www.dawn.com/2002/03/25/ebr11.htm.

Nestlé Milkpak Limited, 2003. *Annual Report 2003*. Nestle Milkpak Lahore, Pakistan.

14 *Bangladesh*

*Khandaker Mainuddin, Moinul I. Sharif, Mozaharul Alam
and Dwijendra lal Mallick*

Introduction

Bangladesh is an agricultural country with a majority of its population (62 per cent) still dependent on agriculture for their livelihoods. Reform measures have been carried out under the structural adjustment programme, in which the monopoly of state-owned enterprises in production, distribution and trade of agricultural inputs has been drastically reduced, and subsidies in agriculture have been curtailed to allow the market forces to govern agribusiness. The South Asian Free Trade Area (SAFTA) aims to reduce the duty among member countries to 0.5 per cent by 2016.

The role of the government has been redefined to provide an environment (policy, institutions and infrastructure) conducive to private sector investments and initiatives, promote fair business practices, perform regulatory functions to facilitate coordination among economic agents and contribute to poverty alleviation. It is also acknowledged that there is a need for assistance to small and marginal farmers so that they can benefit from the reforms and liberalization of the economy.

In Bangladesh, there are a few supermarkets in the main cities of Dhaka and Chittagong and these cater primarily for expatriates and urban elites. At present income levels, it will be some time before supermarkets spread across the country. Therefore, there is still time for traditional marketing chains to adapt and for policymakers to formulate policies to assist small-scale producers to work with the modern sector.

KEY DATA

	2002	2003	2004
Population (millions)			144
Per capita GDP (US$)			362
Urbanization (%)	26		
Agriculture as % GDP			21.2
Per capita total retail food sales (US$)			
Per capita modern retail food sales (US$)			
Modern food retail as % total			

Source: PlanetRetail
Exchange rate (1 January 2006): 1 US$ = 66.25 Bangladeshi taka

THE STRUCTURE OF THE FOOD MARKET

In Bangladesh, the different types of agricultural markets through which agri-products are exchanged are rural primary markets, rural assembly markets, rural secondary markets, urban wholesale markets, urban wholesale-cum-retail markets and urban retail markets. The rural primary markets are scattered over the entire country and are the first link for growers in the six-tier market structure. All types of growers sell their surplus produce in these markets. The rural primary markets mainly attract nearby growers from the surrounding villages, local and visiting traders and small retailers. These markets are held twice a week. There are about 5000 such rural primary markets in the country.

Rural assembly markets are held twice a week but are also open on all other days and are bigger than rural primary markets. Agri-products are carried to the rural assembly markets from the primary markets by the intermediaries (*faria*, *beparies*) and also by the growers themselves. There are permanent structures in these markets used by the commission agents, stockists, wholesalers and others.

Agri-products are transported to rural secondary markets from rural primary and assembly markets by traders and intermediaries. Secondary markets forward the produce to the urban wholesale markets and the urban retail markets. The intermediaries and traders who act in the disposal of agri-products between these markets are the farias, beparies, aratdars, wholesalers and retailers.

The credit market for agribusiness consists of both formal and informal transactions. Various NGOs are offering micro-credit facilities to their members for agribusiness. Credit for agricultural activities, crop loans, and so on, are available from the government-owned commercial banks. However, the loan procedure is complex and the amount of loan is limited.

Output markets are well developed for most commodities although a number of distortions remain and there are high transaction costs for some products. Intermediaries are blamed for making extortionate profits through their monopoly control of output markets

The growth of agribusiness in Bangladesh is retarded due to inadequate infrastructure facilities such as cold chain management of perishable and frozen products, lack of quality control mechanisms, standardization of products and inadequate airfreight for export of perishables. Moreover, irregular power supply, lack of appropriate technology and market-related information, and poor business development services appear as barriers to agribusiness.

Case study 1: Potatoes

This case study covers potato producers, rural and urban wholesalers, cold store owners and processors in both the formal and informal sectors. It is estimated that about 65 per cent of the producers are small, cultivating less than 0.5 acres. Medium producers constitute about 30 per cent of the farmers with between 0.5 and 3.0 acres. Five per cent are large producers cultivating more than 3 acres. There is unequal opportunity and access to facilities including storing, processing and marketing of their produce.

The small scale of Bangladeshi potato producers means that supply chains introduced to provision supermarket chains in the future cannot avoid relying on small-scale producers; there is simply no alternative. The smallest-scale potato growers are especially disadvantaged, as they have little access to the formal channel of storing, processing and marketing. Small, cash-starved, producers do not have the capacity to pay for such facilities. Most often they sell their produce during the harvesting period when the price is very low and cannot reap the benefit from higher prices during the off-peak period. The linkage of the small producers to the other participants in the supply chain, for example, the wholesalers, cold store owners and the potato processors, is rather weak as they do not have the economic and political power to influence the market chain.

This leads us to expect that if and when supermarkets arrive, the main beneficiaries among producers will be the 5 per cent of producers with 3 acres or more. There will be a negative social impact on the very small-scale growers. How much depends upon how far the growers with over 3 acres can satisfy supermarket requirements. Different categories of participants playing their respective roles in the supply chain of potatoes are as follows:

- producers
- rural assemblers
- wholesalers/commission Agents
- cold storage owners
- retailers
- transporters
- processors
- consumers.

Nearly all producers sell the lion's share of the potatoes they harvest. It is estimated that about 90 per cent of the produce is generated as marketable surplus. Most of the growers sell their potatoes from their homes or at the farm gate. Some large growers supply to wholesalers/ commission agents who deduct their commission. Growers in need of cash sell their potatoes at harvest. This is particularly true for the small farmers.

Growers frequently sell their potatoes to rural traders or to local rural consumers. These traders assemble small amounts of potatoes into larger quantities and transport the produce to wholesalers/urban consumption centres. The essential services that these traders provide to the growers include: (1) arranging the transportation and covering the cost for small amounts of potatoes to larger markets; (2) reducing the risks associated with marketing farm produce away from the producers; and (3) providing cash payments to growers as they sell their produce.

Transporters play an important role in the movement of potatoes from one point to another in the supply chain. Different types of transport are used including rickshaws, carts, trucks and boats. Potatoes are also carried short distances by head-load, for example, from boat to cold store, from truck to market, from field to home. Boats are most common in the Dhaka and Comilla regions because of the extensive network of rivers and canals in these districts. By contrast, road transport is widely employed in the northern districts of Bogra, Dinajpur and Rangpur. Road transport is becoming increasingly important in the country compared to river transport as a result of the continued improvement in the road network over the years. Road transport has the comparative advantage in speed and timely delivery of products. However, road transport is expensive compared to river transport.

Wholesalers/commission agents are major intermediaries, as the potatoes shipped to towns and cities pass through their hands. These traders typically have a *godown* or simple un-refrigerated warehouse. They receive, weigh and store the potatoes temporarily in loose form. They also grade and bag potatoes prior to sale. Depending on supply and demand conditions, these traders buy potatoes or receive them on commission basis. During and after harvest, they are supplied by the rural assemblers and large growers. Wholesaler/commission agents sell potatoes to urban wholesalers, retailers and cold store operators.

Cold store owners provide space in a refrigerated store for the preservation of potatoes for a set fee. There are 330 (2003 data) cold stores in the country, most of them privately owned. A small number of cold stores are operated by NGOs such as BRAC and the Bangladesh Agricultural Development Corporation (BADC), a government-owned agency engaged in agricultural development activities. Most of the cold stores are located in the Dhaka and Comilla regions, the principal centres of potato production.

Cold store owners also buy potatoes in order to make profit and to ensure that they maximize the use of their storage facilities. They buy the potatoes from traders, wholesalers/commission agents and from large producers. Cold store owners usually begin storing (and/or buying) potatoes when the main harvest period is at its peak and the price is low. They try to delay releasing potatoes onto the market until the price has risen sufficiently to make maximum profit.

Retailers sell potatoes to consumers throughout the country and especially in the rural markets, towns and cities. They generally own a grocery shop or a small shed in the marketplace or along the roads and lanes in residential areas. These traders generally handle a few hundred kilos of potatoes a week. They buy potatoes from wholesalers/commission agents. The retailers usually buy once or twice a week from wholesalers within the same town. Some rural retailers in the potato growing area buy directly from the growers.

Supermarkets, like other retail stores, also buy from the wholesalers. Some supermarkets in Dhaka city procure local varieties of potatoes grown in specific regions of the country. These local varieties are in short supply and sell at a higher price than the conventional white potato. Supermarkets usually use agents. Most of the supermarkets in Dhaka are independent, single entities, with the exception of AGORA, part of the local Rahimafrooz group, which now has four chain stores located in high-income areas of the city.

The supermarkets generally procure better quality potatoes and vegetables and charge a higher price than other retailers. The prices of agri-products manufactured by large processors are, however, the same between supermarkets and other retail stores. The supermarkets dispose of fresh agri-products before deterioration of quality. The unsold products are withdrawn by the suppliers after a fixed time period.

Procurement directly by retailers is based on cash purchase, whereas wholesalers and cold storage owners often make cash payments equivalent to only 50 to 70 per cent of the procurement value. The rest is paid after they resell their stock. Most procurement is based on mutual trust and relationships, without formal deeds or a written contract between the suppliers and buyers. Cold storage owners, however, do enter into written contracts or deeds with the suppliers for purchase or storage of products. Cold storage owners provide loans to the potato farmers on the condition that potatoes will be stored and preserved or sold to them. The cold storage owners have access to bank loans through the association. It is often difficult for the individual farmers to get loans from the commercial banks. The cost of borrowing is high and the formalities needed to secure a loan are complex. The farmers have to mortgage their land and deposit the ownership documents with the bank to obtain a loan. NGOs provide micro-credit to the farmers for cultivation of crops including potatoes but the amount of credit given by the NGOs is not adequate to meet the cost of seeds, fertilizer and irrigation. Potato farmers often borrow from relatives and money lenders at high interest rates.

Cold storage facilities for the preservation of potatoes are not adequate in all regions of the country. The preservation of potato seeds poses a serious problem, as the existing cold storage facilities do not have the temperature control systems required for potato seeds. Lack of a reliable and stable supply of electricity adversely affects the operation of cold storage and the quality of the potatoes.

The processing of potatoes and the diversification of products constrain the growth of potato markets. Potato products from large processing companies have access to both traditional retail stores and supermarkets. However, potato products such as chips produced by small enterprises and the informal sector have little access to markets, especially to supermarkets because of the lack of quality assurance. Compliance with quality standards by small and medium agri-food enterprises is an imperative for access to supermarkets and export markets. Besides, there is a negative attitude to the quality and standards of food products of SMEs.

Case study 2: Milk supply

Per capita consumption of milk and milk products is 13 kg per year in Bangladesh, and has been increasing since the early 1990s. It is, however, very low compared to other countries in South Asia. The country imports around 0.25 million tons of milk and milk equivalent annually to satisfy national milk demand. It is estimated that only about 3 per cent of the milk produced in Bangladesh flows through the formal channel of processing. The remaining 97 per cent is informally handled as liquid milk through small travelling traders (milkmen, locally called *farias*, and distributing traders).

Dairy production is of three types: (1) rural, (2) pocket, and (3) metro dairies. Rural dairying typically means keeping one or two cows and following traditional practices such as feeding with agricultural residues and weeds. A lot of the cows are also used as draught animals. Pocket dairies have been developed through the encouragement of manufacturers of dairy products. Pocket dairies have emerged in different regions through contractual agreements between the milk producers and the manufacturers of milk products. The milk producers are given a price for their supply of milk to the manufacturers in accordance with the agreement between them. Bangladesh Milk Producers' Cooperative Union Ltd (BMPCUL) and a number of private companies are supporting pocket dairies in selected areas of Bangladesh.

Metro dairies represent the small-scale dairy production system developed in urban and peri-urban areas with the milk marketing support of cities and towns. Milk production responds strongly to marketing facilities. According to the Bangladesh Livestock Research Institute (BLRI), the average herd size, milking cows per farm and daily production per farm were 10.1 animals, 3.82 and 21.5 kg respectively in the market-facilitated areas, and in non-facilitated 5.03 animals, 1.62 and 5.98 kg respectively.

Milk products manufactured by the formal sector occupy an increasing share of the milk market in large cities and other urban areas. The marketing chain is gradually expanding to rural areas with the improvement of the country's road network. Although pasteurized liquid milk, flavoured milk and ice creams produced by the large processing plants are supplied to the cities and selected large towns, other milk products, including powder milk, butter, ghee, condensed milk, are also available in small urban areas as well as rural markets. Expensive and better quality products are targeted at the more wealthy urban consumers, and the market for such products is rapidly expanding in the urban areas. Chain sweetmeat stores are an emerging feature in place of traditional independent shops in the large cities. They collect raw milk from the producers through their agents.

The processing plants buy milk from the farmers/producers through milk collectors. Milk collection centres are located in different regions, especially in the rural areas, depending on the availability of milk at a low price based on field assessment. Each collection centre is equipped with a chilling plant and quality testing equipment. Milk suppliers/farmers are grouped into associations and are given membership certification. Milk Vita, the largest processing plant of the country, has 565 such primary associations of milk producers, each of which comprises 60 to 80 members.

Other processing plants like the PRAN dairy and the BRAC dairy also collect milk from their respective producer associations. The primary association under Milk Vita, a cooperative entity sponsored by the government, is linked to a national federation. But no such national federation exists for primary producer associations under the BRAC or PRAN dairies.

Primary producer associations and members are required to supply an agreed quantity of milk to the chilling centre on a daily basis. However, the milk collectors collect milk from non-members as well. This happens when the association fails to supply the agreed quantity of milk to the processing plants. Members often sell a part of their milk to the market instead of supplying the processing plants. The practice becomes more widespread as and when the market price goes significantly above the price paid by the processing plants. It has been found that the price offered by Milk Vita to its members is quite low compared to the market price in some areas near Dhaka city.

The processing plants make weekly payments to the milk collectors/suppliers. Records of the daily supply of milk are maintained by the collection centre concerned. Sometimes conflicts arise between the processing plants and the suppliers with regard to the quality standard and quantity of milk. Milk production associations and members also receive a warning from the processing plant if they fail to supply the required quantity of milk. Membership of the association is cancelled for continuous failure to supply the agreed quantity of milk. According to field interviews in the Manikganj area, Milk Vita has not adjusted its procurement price over the past few years, although market price has increased significantly during this period. The BRAC dairy adjusts the procurement price twice a year, taking into consideration the changing trend in the market price of milk.

Conclusions

Virtually all farmers in Bangladesh would be regarded as 'small scale' in other countries of the world. There are already policies in place to help higher potential small-scale farmers and processors, as pocket dairies and 'facilitated milk areas' show. Modern processors of potatoes and supply chains for fresh potatoes are also likely to help the top third of growers. The following measures can be recommended to the other two-thirds of producers:

1. Finance is essential in order to modernize both potato and milk supply. Thus SMEs should be provided with low interest credit facilities for production and processing of agri-products, including potatoes and milk. Loan procedures followed by the government-owned banks should be simplified.
2. Both potatoes and milk require careful post-harvest treatment and grading. Therefore, processors should effectively communicate and train the producers/suppliers on the grades and standards of milk required by the processors. Small and medium-scale agri-processors (milk and potato) should be encouraged to adopt and implement national standards. Product testing and certification procedures should be simple and low cost so that there

is no financial burden on the SMEs. Potato farmers should be trained in post-harvest handling, grading, storing and preserving of potatoes to ensure better market access and a fair price.

3. The very small scale of the producers means that cooperative facilities are also essential. Specialized cold storage facilities should be set up for potato seeds, as the existing facilities do not have the temperature control mechanisms required for the preservation of seeds. The pocket dairies should continue to be supported and developed. More milk processing plants under cooperative management would also be beneficial, providing much-needed competition that would serve both producers and consumers well.

4. In order to encourage organization, the formation of associations for potato farmers and milk producers at the local and national level would strengthen and protect their rights. Similar associations might be considered for SMEs engaged in potato and milk processing.

5. For dairy farmers, fodder is critical and often in short supply and of poor quality. Fodder supply should be enhanced through expanding domestic production or making more imports available and ensuring the fodder is distributed to farmers through both processors and farmers' cooperatives at fair prices.

6. In Bangladesh, crop failure is not uncommon. Insurance schemes should be introduced for small- and medium-scale producers/processors (milk and potatoes) to reduce their vulnerability and compensate for the loss of crops and livestock arising from unexpected events such as floods, disease and death.

7. Information is always valuable, particularly in modern food supply systems. In preparation for the arrival of supermarket chains, information systems for agri-marketing should be strengthened to make information easily accessible to different stakeholders, especially the growers, retailers and consumers.

8. Finally, exporting has proved a useful way of introducing modern market discipline and more rigorous standards to small-scale growers in a number of countries. The agri-businesses of Bangladesh might be offered training and information so that they can export agri-products, such as processed potatoes and dairy products.

15 *Kenya*

James K. Nyoro, Joshua Ariga and Isaac K. Ngugi

Introduction

Kenya's economy performed below its potential during the 1990s. Since 1997, growth has averaged only 1.3 per cent, consistently below the rate of population increase estimated at 2.4 per cent per annum. Consequently, per capita income in constant 1992 prices has declined from US$271 in 1990 to US$239 in 2002. In addition, agricultural productivity has been on the decline, competitiveness eroded and international financial support diminished. During this period, poverty and food insecurity have increased.

Supermarkets are emerging in Kenya, but traditional markets will continue to dominate food supply for some time to come. However, especially in the urban areas, there is an expanding modern food system, with over 200 supermarket and hypermarket stores now open. The country's agricultural sector efficiently produces a range of exports including high-value, air-freighted vegetables. This export sector includes small-scale producers as well as large farms and plantations. The country has in many ways led Africa for 50 years in seeking ways to help small-scale farmers.

Therefore, the prospects are good for small-scale producers to gain access to the modern food system as preferred suppliers. There are several successful cooperatives already working in Kenya. In fact, the only ingredient still required seems to be a private sector both willing and able to use small-scale producers as suppliers and cultivate producer organizations as long-term partners in their supply chains. It should be a priority of government to encourage modern food processors and supermarkets to go down this inclusive pathway.

KEY DATA

	2002	*2003*	*2004*
Population (millions)	31.54	32.04	32.54
Per capita GDP (US$)	388	441	458
Urbanization (%)	34		
Agriculture as % GDP	24.4	24.1	23.2
Per capita total retail food sales (US$)	150	174	179
Per capita modern retail food sales (US$)	28	31	32
Modern food retail as % total			18

Exchange rate (1 January 2006): 1 US$ = 72.30 Kenyan shilling (KES)

TOP CHAINS, 2004

Company	Ownership	Number of stores	Retail banner sales 2004 (US$ millions)	Market share (%)	Grocery sales 2004 (US$ millions)	Grocery market share (%)
Nakumatt	Local	14	126	13.9	76	9.7
Uchumi	Local	30	119	13.2	99	12.7
Ukwala	Local privately owned	10	114	12.6	85	11.0
Tusker	Local privately owned	10	113	12.5	68	8.7
Woolworths (RSA)	Franchise	5	19	2.1	0	0.0
Metcash	Foreign (RSA)	19	15			
Other			413	45.7	449	57.8

Source: PlanetRetail (www.planetretail.net)

Case study 1: Fresh fruit and vegetables

Horticulture in Kenya is regarded as a success story. It has undergone dramatic growth over the years with several players getting involved in exports and sales to local markets. Most of the FFV are produced by small-scale farmers. Important FFV crops include French beans, Asian-style vegetables (especially karella, okra), snow peas, baby corn, tomatoes, cabbages, onion, oranges, mangoes, bananas, papaws, pineapples and watermelon.

The sale of FFV in supermarkets is increasing and slowly spreading out of Nairobi's middle- and upper-class areas into poorer areas and rural towns and upcoming cities. In 2004, there were 204 supermarket outlets in Kenya and there were 11 hypermarkets (Neven and Reardon, 2004). Nevertheless, FFV are still mainly (93 per cent) marketed through traditional channels rather than the modern system.

The two dominant chains, Uchumi and Nakumatt have about 70 per cent of the total supermarket market share (Weatherspoon and Reardon, 2003) with smaller supermarkets (Ukwala, and so on) combining to make 25 per cent of the market share. The Nakumatt and Uchumi chains have now opened branches in the major towns of Kenya. Uchumi has been undergoing an ambitious expansion programme locally and into Uganda. The strong strategic positions of Uchumi and Nakumatt have made it difficult for foreign competitors, particularly those from South Africa.

Uchumi has extended its network to Kampala, Uganda, where it is competing with ShopRite of South Africa. Two foreign multinationals (Metro (Metcash) and Woolworths) from South Africa have recently joined the fray. These new chains are currently not yet stocking FFV and are concentrating instead on processed food with a long shelf life. Again, as they are foreign firms, they are less familiar with local suppliers but industry sources indicate that South African firms are bidding for locally owned Uchumi, which has financial problems.

As well as the supermarkets, FFV are purchased by hospitals, schools and prisons, as well as hotels and other tourist facilities and restaurants. Most of these form part of the modern food system and have requirements similar to supermarkets such as standard quality, year-round supply, high volumes delivered directly to institutions and all supplied at low cost.

Five years ago, the supermarkets purchased FFV from open-air markets, traders and farmers directly. But issues of timely deliveries, volatile prices, and quality standards and safety made them restructure their procurement in order to curtail these problems.

Nowadays, supermarkets want supply chains that ensure quality and traceability. Also, supermarkets seek a steady year-round supply and reliable deliveries.

Unless action is taken, we can expect that direct supplies from small producers will dwindle. Small scale producers will not find it always easy to deal with the modern food system since companies change more rapidly than the old market outlets for farmers. At the moment this lies in the future; supermarkets continue to be supplied by various sources that include small producers, preferred suppliers, contracted farmers and intermediaries.

Nakumatt has adopted a centralized procurement system for its Nairobi network. Nakumatt branches deal in FFV supplied by its subsidiary company Fresh 'n' Juici. The company usually sources from medium-to-large farmers and imports, and some (about 10 per cent) from small producers and wholesale markets. It packages and distributes to Nakumatt branches using its own and hired trucks. However, Nakumatt operates a decentralized system of procurement for its Mombassa network because of logistical problems of sourcing everything from Nairobi.

With its dedicated supply chain, Nakumatt has started laying down quality and safety standards for foodstuffs, with some of the produce being labelled with producer identification for traceability purposes. Nakumatt's monthly sales of FFV increased from 10 million KES in 2003 to 19 million in 2004. Nakumatt attributes this increase to high quality standards and competitive prices to consumers (prices 10 per cent lower than other outlets), and improved customer service.

Similar complications and often bewildering changes can be observed at the other supermarket chain. Uchumi is slowly moving towards a distribution centre type of procurement system in Nairobi. Uchumi now applies a dichotomous system, using a centralized Nakumatt-style purchasing system for some stores and decentralized purchases directly from farmers both large and small, intermediaries (who often source from wetmarkets) or traders for other stores.

Smaller and independent stores/supermarkets, which account for 25 per cent of the supermarket market share of FFV, purchase through brokers who get their deliveries from wetmarkets or directly from farms. Direct procurement from rural farms would be more convenient if farmers were organized as groups. Otherwise the brokers would be tempted to give preference to large-scale farmers so that they cut down on transaction costs. The volumes of FFV dealt with in these stores are much lower than those of their bigger competitors. In addition, not all these supermarkets deal in FFV and those that do have less variety to offer in comparison to large chains.

Some of the large farm suppliers to supermarkets also export to Europe. The fee to the retailer for certification to EUREPGAP standard is about US$ 875, excluding air ticket and accommodation expenses for the foreign inspector, which is too high for a small-scale farmer. Although the EUREPGAP requirements target the export market, it is expected that there will be some positive spill-over effects for the local market, especially the supermarkets, hospitals and hotels where producers that export sometimes supply or divert the high-quality products to these institutions. The institutions might procure either directly or through brokers some of the high-quality products produced under EUREPGAP conditions. Some of the quality requirements (for example, emphasis on good hygiene) set by EUREPGAP and those set by the local private sector, including large supermarkets, hotels and hospitals, are the same, an indication that the formally clear distinction between the local and export market is becoming blurred.

This opportunity widens the market for locally produced goods that have been produced in accordance with international requirements. This could yield benefits that trickle down to small-scale farmers, especially those able to access the export market by forming producer groups that could satisfy EUREPGAP. However, if supermarkets get used to export quality and raise their FFV requirements, small-scale producers who have not entered the export market will be excluded.

The Tegemeo Institute is currently conducting a study on why some producer groups have worked and others have failed. Experience from export horticulture reveals that initially some farmers violated contractual arrangements by selling to other exporters. But after a while this became untenable as they became known as risky prospective suppliers for any exporter. But other problems are hindering the establishment of POs, including poor road networks and a non-existent legal framework recognizing POs as entities.

QUALITY ASSURANCE

Through its contractual arrangements with some growers, Uchumi stipulates a list of inputs that suppliers should buy for their crops. This is one way that supermarkets can monitor the quality of inputs used by farmers. The same system is used by Woolworths supermarket of South Africa. This is not very common, though, as it is difficult for the supermarkets to enforce.

Uchumi also specifies the quality of products the farmer is expected to supply in the contract. Further, the supermarket staff make regular visits to the farms to supervise production. The supermarket does not, however, specify who should supply other farm inputs such as herbicides and insecticides. The grower–supermarket arrangements are driven by market demand and recognize consumer sovereignty and therefore decisions are dictated by consumer preferences.

The arrangement promotes consistent supply, quality, food safety standards and availability of wide variety of produce throughout the year. For these arrangements to be successful, the supermarkets need a close relationship with growers. We consider contracts in more detail later in the chapter.

In a move geared to improving quality and standards, the Uchumi supermarket is exploring three options. The first is to set up or hire a laboratory for chemical residual analysis, especially of products sourced from open/wetmarkets and brokers. The second is to partner with Sunripe and HACCP to ensure that suppliers, especially growers, meet the required standards. Thirdly, to establish a central handling and inspection warehouse or facility where adherence to standards and quality will be assessed.

With regard to procurement through brokers, the issues of standards and grades are not of much concern to these small chains. They assume that the producer or the broker supplying the products has observed the expected standards, especially good hygiene. Unlike the big supermarkets, which sometimes use formal contracts, these chains are characterized by verbal agreements with suppliers to set the quantity and price of supplies.

To promote production of quality and hygienic produce, Serena Hotels makes impromptu visits to its suppliers. This is to inspect production and handling procedures as well as assess the producer's capacity to supply as expected.

SUPERMARKET SUPPLIERS

FFV procured from farmers comes from large-, medium- and small-scale farmers who deliver directly to buyers. With this system of direct procurement, it is easier to trace back the product to its source compared with produce channelled through brokers and open markets. East African Growers and Kenya Horticultural Exporters are the main importers for Uchumi and Fresh 'n' Juici (Nakumatt). Supermarkets do not procure directly from open markets. The markets, however, are good sources of the produce that brokers sell to supermarkets and hotels. The respective proportions of suppliers to the retails outlets are shown in Table 5.1.

The selection of suppliers by supermarkets, hotels, greengrocers and hospitals is influenced by factors such as level of trust, traceability, feasibility, and potential for production in terms of quantity and quality, prices, proximity, and reliability. Preferred suppliers differ among supermarkets. For instance, Uchumi prefers procuring directly from growers of all scales though with a bias to those that are large and medium sized. Among these growers, the supermarket prefers those that have irrigation facilities to allow for year round production, with mobile phones to save on transactional costs (85 per cent of orders by Uchumi are placed by phone) and with a bank account to allow for payment through bank transfers. Locally produced FFV are delivered directly to branches. This is due to the perishability of these products and the need to deliver them quickly in order to sell them while still fresh.

For 2003, procurements of FFV under contract by Uchumi were estimated to account for only 5 per cent of purchased volume. This was very small compared with the South African chains, which had more than 90 per cent of procurement under contract. Among all FFV procured directly from farmers, 20 per cent are delivered under contract while 80 per cent are non-contracted.

Nakumatt, on the other hand, prefers to be supplied by its subsidiary company, Fresh 'n' Juici, that procures from various suppliers including brokers, producers and importers. This company has the required facilities, including pack-houses, cold rooms, ample loading and off-loading space, and a warehouse. The company does sorting, washing, packaging, slicing and dicing before delivering the produce to supermarkets. Most of these activities add value to the produce. From Nakumatt's point of view, this arrangement enables one-stop shopping, hence lowering transaction as well as coordination costs.

The medium- and small-sized supermarkets prefer to use brokers, who normally deliver to their doorstep, thus possibly saving on transport costs, especially when there is high competition among brokers who for the purpose of maintaining the client (supermarket) opt to bear the cost rather than recover it by hiking up prices for the products.

Among the hotels and hospitals considered in this study, only Serena has branches in the form of lodges located both in Kenya and Tanzania. Apart from the main branch located in the city centre that procures FFV and milk products independently, procurement for the other lodges in the country is centralized through the headquarters and then distributed on a weekly basis to the lodges located in places such as Maasai Mara, Amboseli and Kilanguni. Serena prefers producers located away from urban centres to minimize the risk of contaminated produce such as that that promoted by the growing use of raw sewage. Safari Park hotel and Kenyatta National Hospital select their suppliers by a monthly and annual tendering system respectively. They normally go for, or prefer, the supplier quoting to deliver at lowest price, though also taking note of other factors such as those described above.

Table 15.1 Retail procurement by source

	Institution		
Suppliers	Uchumi	Nakumatt	Corner shop
Farmers (%)	20	60	80
Brokers (%)	73	32	0
Open market (%)	0	0	20
Importers (%)	7	8	0

Medium-sized supermarkets (not shown in the table) traditionally rely on brokers for their supply of fruit (Weatherspoon and Reardon, 2003). The fact that Safeways supermarkets (medium sized in Kenya) is now engaged in its own production rather than procuring through brokers is an indication that the changing procurement system is not only taking place with large supermarkets. However, small supermarkets are not as quality conscious as medium and large ones. Delivery of supply to the stores by brokers is considered the most traditional channel.

CONTRACTS AND FINANCE AVAILABLE TO SUPPLIERS

Supermarkets offer contracts to large and medium-sized farms with irrigation that allows them to provide a year-round supply. To support contracted farmers, Uchumi negotiates with sellers of seed for better prices on behalf of its farmers.

The supermarket requirement for good quality FFV means suppliers must have access to storage and refrigeration facilities. The supermarkets do not offer finance for this. We found only one trader, Corner Shop, which gave credit to kick-start producers and support them till they accumulated enough working capital, after which the trader withdrew.

Supermarkets do not extend credit to producers or firms. As noted above, however, they sometimes negotiate on behalf of the farmers for lower farm-input prices and better quality inputs, for instance seeds. From the farmer's perspective, this lowers the access costs of the inputs. In addition to these negotiations, some supermarkets act as intermediaries with credit advancing firms for loans. This can enable the financially weak farmers to invest in expensive facilities such as irrigation and delivery trucks.

Micro-finance schemes may be a good source of finance for SMEs. In order to boost investment in the country, the Government of Kenya supports the establishment of micro-finance institutions that in turn lend to small producers. Access to credit through these institutions has of late been very promising. Kenya has 62 micro-finance NGOs whose total client base is 220 000 (Argwings-Kodhek, 2004). Past experience has shown that small entrepreneurs do not default on repayments.

An arrangement boosting SMEs is where the Horticultural Crop Development Association oversees and facilitates contractual arrangements between exporters or NGOs and farmers. Sometimes an NGO or exporter provides the farmer with farm inputs such as fertilizers, seeds and pesticides well before planting. We look at other ways in which SMEs are helped in the conclusions to this chapter.

Sometimes it is the exporter who suggests to a farmer which enterprise to engage in, based on an identified target market, and therefore the decision is market driven as opposed to production driven. Once the inputs are advanced to the farmer and hence a contract signed, the exporter then recovers the cost after the produce is grown, harvested and sold. This provision of credit in the form of farm inputs before or during production considers future harvest as the collateral. Activities ranging from production, marketing and payments are defined in a contract between the two parties. Information contained in such a contract includes expected quantities and prices, time of harvest, person to bear transport and packaging cost of the products, point of rejection, mode and time of payment.

This model of supporting farmers, though applied to export products, might also be a good one to adopt for the local markets. In this case, supermarkets, hotels, hospitals and grocery stores, since they are financially stable, may buy inputs and deliver them to poor small producers, who can then sell their produce to these creditors to first recover the loan and then pay the rest to the farmers.

A growing demand for organically produced commodities is seen in Kenya, especially with some supermarkets and institutions. The Safari Park hotel, Corner Shop and Uchumi have a group of customers who prefer organically produced FFV. This is in line with global trends where sales of organic foods are increasing. To supply this emerging market, farmers would have to increase production of such produce. To distinguish such foodstuffs from those conventionally produced, there is a greater interest in documentation of production practices for FFV.

Import of FFV are common these days and this is expected to continue, especially in the light of the newly created East African trading bloc or East African Union. Kenyan supermarkets are selling agri-foods from other countries, for example bananas and pineapples from Uganda, oranges from South Africa and onions from Tanzania. There is also importation of powdered milk. Kenya also exports to other countries, for example tomatoes to Uganda. This is an indication that what was in the past considered global has become local. The consequence of this scenario is that it makes the distinction between the local and export markets blurred, and local producers must contend with regional and global competitors in their own backyard.

Case study 2: Milk supply

Milk marketing is currently being restructured. Hawkers supply about 80 per cent of raw milk to urban centres, a market hitherto served by Kenya Cooperative Creameries (KCC) before it went bankrupt. There are a number of small-scale producers and small entrepreneurs in the marketing system. This informal market system does not have regulated quality standards or food safety measures. The small formal sector, dominated by large-scale producers, has been lobbying government to regulate or even ban raw milk hawking.

The processing business of KCC continues but currently accounts for less than 14 per cent of the milk market. In addition to KCC, there are 45 registered milk processors with an estimated daily intake of 600 000 litres. Milk processing has been on the decline with about 22 per cent of the installed capacity being used. This is the result of a narrow demand base and also the fact that the bulk of milk produced in Kenya is handled by the informal sector, which targets the poor.

Milk processing is concentrated among a few firms in major towns handling about 80 per cent of the formal market share. Milk processing costs have therefore increased because of the low capacity usage and also because packaging materials account for a significant part of the processing costs. Imports usually consist of processed products, mostly during drier periods of the year but some products, such as yoghurt and ghee, are imported throughout the year.

Results from the Tegemeo urban household survey in October 2003 (Kodhek et al., 2005) indicate that 52 per cent of the households interviewed bought their milk and milk products from shops (*duka*), 12 per cent from kiosks (*kibanda*) and milk bars, 28 per cent from large supermarkets, while 5 per cent purchased from small supermarkets. Hawkers, who have become very prominent since the collapse of KCC, supplied 16 per cent of the sample households with raw milk.

About 50 per cent of the sampled households bought processed milk mainly from shops, kiosks, and supermarkets, 25 per cent bought raw milk from hawkers, shops, milk bars and kiosks, while 25 per cent bought cheese, ghee, and yoghurt mainly from supermarkets. Some of the large institutional consumers (hospitals, hotels) buy their FFV and milk through bids from suppliers who buy from farmers, open-air markets, and supermarkets.

Unlike FFV where there is some grading, with fresh milk there is no grading at all at farm level. This is due to the fact that it is difficult to distinguish bad milk from good milk, because both look the same. Nevertheless, for acceptability at collection points, milk is tested for adulteration. Nairobi hospital, an important milk buyer, goes a step further to test milk and milk products for quality in their microbiology laboratory.

It is too early to say how successful small-scale milk producers and cooperatives will be in supplying the modern food system. The collapse of KCC has left a gap in the supply of milk in Kenya and an opportunity for producers of all sizes.

Conclusions

As the supermarkets in the highest tier, Nakumatt and Uchumi, eventually tighten their demands in terms of consistency in volume and quality, small producers and under-capitalized brokers will face tough competition from larger producers and traders with the financial base to meet these demands. Many bulk-buyers (supermarkets, hotels and hospitals) of FFV and milk products are increasingly looking for supplier channels that ensure quality standards are maintained, provide traceability of produce when needed, provide a steady supply of the expected volume all year round and deliver promptly.

The direct sourcing from small producer farmers may dwindle due to these stringent demands and also because these producers are geographically scattered. It is therefore clear that for small producers to survive in the emerging structure, they have to meet quality standards and also organize themselves into POs that are able to enter into enforceable legal contracts as entities with supermarkets.

Otherwise, if small farmers want to continue selling in the urban market, they will have to target channels such as small shops and wetmarkets. Though the requirements of these non-supermarket channels are less stringent, they are not stagnant and, as may be inferred from experiences from other parts of the world, small shops are likely to aggregate to form procurement clubs while wetmarkets are likely to improve on quality and hygiene.

Already in Kenya, plans are underway to improve operations in wholesale markets. An old project is being revised to modernize wholesale markets in urban areas. This reflects the priority in Kenya; to improve the conditions of the traditional markets where the bulk of the FFV are marketed. Investment in areas such as the following is needed:

- improved infrastructure in markets and improved hygiene
- investment in grade inspection
- help for producer organizations
- more and better market information
- better transport and communications.

Otherwise, small scale-producers will be left behind as change gathers pace in the Kenyan food system.

It is important that skills and knowledge are inculcated to SMEs. This will promote use of new technologies among others. The main parties involved in capacity building of SMEs are the Ministry of Agriculture, universities and colleges. The Horticultural Crops Development Authority (HCDA), the body regulating the horticultural sector, also plays this role to some degree.

Technical assistance to SMEs is also essential. This would enhance adoption of new technologies by relevant stakeholders as well as enlighten them on their use. In connection with the production of FFV, the public bodies playing this role include the Ministry of Agriculture and HCDA. The Horticulture Development Centre (HDC), funded by the United States Agency for International Development (USAID), is involved in a number of areas to support small producer farmers. HDC has a number of agronomists in the country involved with disseminating best agronomic practices and introducing new crops into the market. It has also a component that encourages production for domestic consumption. The Dairy Board of Kenya gives technical assistance related to dairy industry.

Financing is a major constraint to the success of small-scale farmers, particularly due to lack of the collateral required for access to credit. Very few organizations have policies in place that ensure farmers without collateral have access to credit.

With respect to dairy farmers, the Kenya Dairy Board makes loans available and grants subsidies to producers or manufacturers. Otherwise, there are few policies, either private or public, that support SMEs in the production and marketing of FFV and dairy products. Bearing in mind the recent changes in terms of liberalization, rationalization and globalization, these entrepreneurs are now exposed to stronger competitors. These competitors have more resources than an individual small-scale entrepreneur and therefore are likely to dominate the market. Formation of POs would, among other things, increase small-scale farmers' bargaining power and market participation, and improve their access to credit, information, social capital and farm inputs.

References

Argwings-Kodhek, G., 2004. Feast and famine: Financial services for rural Kenya. Draft working paper. Tegemeo Institute of Agricultural Policy and Development, Egerton University, Nairobi.

Kodhek, G.A., Mm'boyi, F., Muyanga, M. and Consumption, G.P., 2005. Patterns of dairy products in Kenya's urban centers. Proceedings of Tegemeo 2005 Conference, Tegemeo Institute, Nairobi Kenya. Available: www.tegemeo.org/documents/conference2005/abstracts/Consumptionofdailyproducts.pdf.

Muendo, K.M., Tschirley, D. and Weber, M.T., 2004. Improving Kenya's domestic horticultural production and marketing system: Current competitiveness, forces of change, and challenges for the future. Tegemeo Institute, Nairobi.

Neven, D. and Reardon, T., 2004. The rise of Kenyan Supermarkets and evolution of their horticulture product procurement systems. *Development Policy Review* 22(6), 669–99.

Weatherspoon, D.D., and Reardon, T.A., 2003. The rise of supermarkets Africa: Implications for agri-food systems and the rural poor. *Development Policy Review* 21(3), 333–55.

16 *Uganda*

Lucy Aliguma and James K. Nyoro

Introduction

The Ugandan economy is dominated by the agricultural sector, which accounts for about 42 per cent of national GDP, 90 per cent of exports and 80 per cent of employment. The soil is generally fertile and the climate favours agricultural production. The country is able to produce all the year round and has a plentiful supply of land and relatively cheap labour.

In Uganda, the dairy industry contributes about 45 per cent of the livestock GDP and about 20 per cent to Uganda's food processing industry. Most of the dairy products processed in Uganda are from cattle and they include UHT milk, cheese, yoghurt, butter, cultured milk, ghee, ice cream and pasteurized milk. The most commonly consumed dairy products in Uganda are ghee, butter, ice cream, cheese, sweet and sour cream and yoghurt as well as indigenous fermented milks. The level of consumption of dairy products is still low in Uganda due to lack of access to these products, poor quality and lack of production skills, coupled with cultural factors.

A variety of fruits and vegetables are grown in Uganda, mainly on a small scale. Passion fruit, citrus, apple bananas (*ndiizi*), avocado, pineapples, mango and papaya are the most common fruits grown. The most commonly grown vegetables are okra, peas, french beans, tomatoes, carrots, onions, sweet potatoes, Irish potatoes, aubergines and capsicum. Fruits and vegetables play an important role in nutritional balance, income generation and food security at farm level and most of them are of high value on the export market. Production of fruits and vegetables has increased over the last few years, resulting in huge marketable surpluses during the peak seasons. Most fruits in Uganda are consumed fresh and fruit processing is limited mainly to extraction of fresh fruit juice, which is sold on the local market.

KEY DATA

	2002	2003	2004
Population (millions)	24.7	25.4	26.3
Per capita GDP (US$)	219	251	251
Urbanization (%)	11.7	12	12

Exchange rate (1 January 2006): 1 US Dollar = 1820.00 Uganda shilling

TOP CHAINS, 2004

Company	Ownership	Number of stores	Retail banner sales 2004 (US$ millions)	Market share (%)	Grocery sales 2004 (US$ millions)	Market share (%)
Metcash (RSA)	Foreign (RSA)	43	30	7.6	25	7.0
Shoprite	Foreign (RSA)	5	11	2.8	8	2.1
Uchumi	Foreign (Kenya)	1	4	1.0	4	1.0
Woolworths (RSA)	Foreign (RSA)	2	4	1.0	0	0.1
Massmart	Foreign (RSA)	1	3	0.8	0	0.1
Other			344	86.9	324	89.7

Source: PlanetRetail (www.planetretail.net)

Case study 1: milk processors

Nationally about 70 per cent of milk consumed is raw, mainly because most people cannot afford processed dairy products. For the minority who have got money, there are many firms involved in the production of dairy products. Eight large-scale milk processing companies are located in the western region, where the supply of raw milk exceeds demand.

A number of micro-processors have come into the market and several are located in Kampala. The Kampala market is increasing because of the higher purchasing power among residents. Substantial quantities of milk and milk products are also imported to supplement local demand and at the same time Uganda exports some dairy products to regional markets.

Production of pasteurized milk is the largest processing activity in the dairy industry and about 80 per cent of processed milk goes into the production of pasteurized milk. All the UHT milk in Uganda was imported mainly from Kenya until 1995. Today, three firms in the country produce UHT milk with a combined capacity of an estimated 45 million litres per year.

All major milk processing plants in the country are operating much below their installed capacities and the biggest plants are making losses. The low capacity utilization is due to poor quality of raw milk, poor plant and processing design which leads to non-cost-effective production and marketing decisions, inadequate management capabilities and lack of marketing studies. Other factors include inadequate advertising to promote milk consumption and the high retail price of processed milk. The latter is attributed to various factors including the high cost of acquiring raw milk, packaging costs and the perishable nature of milk, which requires providing retailers with cold storage facilities to market their milk.

Under-utilization of installed capacities makes operating overheads high in relation to output. This has resulted in increased prices by the milk factories as they try to cover their costs. Market outreach to rural areas and upcountry townships is limited by the additional operating costs. Thus, processors have only concentrated on the Kampala area, which narrows their market outreach.

Strict quality control measures are enforced at the plants to safeguard against such obvious losses due to the poor sanitary conditions commonly associated with farmers and vendors. Milk brought for sale is subjected to tests to ensure that only a good-quality product is paid for. Poor milk is rejected and the sellers are advised to take it back at their own cost.

The preference for raw unprocessed milk is an important factor because it limits the expansion by milk factories, which could potentially buy all the milk produced in the country. The reasons for consumers' preference for raw milk include better taste, cheaper price and accessibility through informal door to door salesmen.

In Uganda, marketing of processed dairy products is done through agents/distributors as well as direct delivery by the processors to the vending outlets, kiosks, supermarkets, groceries and institutional consumers. In the trading of processed milk products, some clients, particularly small buyers such as vendors, groceries and kiosks pay cash for the products supplied while large buyers such as supermarkets and institutions are supplied on credit. In the procurement of raw milk, dairy farmers supply milk to processing companies and some traders on credit.

In the raw milk trade, a number of dairy processing companies have closed down after taking the farmers' milk on credit, and several dairy cooperative societies have lost millions of shillings to almost all the companies that have collapsed. On the other hand, there are many traders that take the farmers' milk on credit almost on a daily basis and pay after the milk is sold. Many farmers complain of being cheated by traders who after selling the milk tell the farmers that the milk went sour and was disposed of. In some cases, this is true because many traders use inappropriate equipment for milk transportation, but in many cases, farmers are just cheated.

The infrastructure for milk collection is still very limited. Out of a total of 239 coolers registered countrywide, only 87 are dedicated to milk collection, while the rest are installed in urban centres for vending milk. The major dairy processing company, Dairy Corporation Limited (DCL), has signed contracts with six dairy farmers' companies/cooperative unions, giving them the responsibility to collect and transport milk from the collection centres in rural areas to the processing plant in Kampala, a journey of about 300 km. The dairy farmers' companies now supervise the procurement process and are responsible for the milk until it is delivered to the processing plant. The other dairy processing companies procure and deliver their own milk but also hire traders to collect and deliver on their behalf.

Most of the dairy products are delivered to small and large supermarkets, hotels and hospitals. Occasionally, small supermarkets procure the products directly from processing factories and sometimes agents of these companies deliver the products. The major dairy companies involved are Alpha Dairy, Jesa and DCL for milk; ice cream is mainly obtained from Showman Industrial; while Paramount Dairies supply cheese and fresh cream. All suppliers of dairy products have formal contracts with their retail customers.

Dairy products are mainly imported from Kenya and/or South Africa. Kenyan import products include cheese, ghee, butter, yoghurt, ice cream and milk, while South African firms supply butter and milk. Butter is also obtained from New Zealand.

Most of the dairy products being sold in the three major multinational supermarkets, Shoprite, Uchumi and Metro, are produced locally. Imports were reported in Shoprite and Uchumi and none in Metcash (RSA) (see Table 16.1).

Table 16.1   Sources of supply of dairy products, Kampala supermarkets

Product	Source		
	Shoprite	Uchumi	Metcasg (RSA)
Milk	Uganda	Uganda	Uganda
Cheese	South Africa, Uganda	Uganda, New Zealand	Uganda
Ice cream	Uganda	Uganda	Uganda
Yoghurt	South Africa	Uganda	Uganda
Butter	South Africa, Uganda	Uganda, New Zealand	Uganda
Ghee	Uganda	Uganda	Uganda
Fresh cream	Uganda	Uganda	Uganda

DAIRY PRODUCER ORGANIZATIONS

Producer organizations are preferred suppliers under contract arrangements with dairy processing companies. The producer groups are responsible for the milk until it is delivered to the processing plant. This saves the processors problems that occur during milk bulking and transportation. POs are preferred suppliers because they relieve the processors of the management of procurement operations. Contracts are signed between the farmers' companies and the processors. Since this arrangement was initiated, the state-owned dairy processing company has started to realize some profits.

In their view, farmers make more profit from contracts. They negotiate the price and sign contracts that are respected by the processing companies. Producers participate in quality testing and put in place measures to improve the quality of their produce. Intermediaries are eliminated or minimized, which also improves the profit earned by farmers. Payment arrangements are negotiated and protected by contract agreements.

The majority of farmers in Uganda do not belong to any form of grouping, and there are no effective grassroots village-based, commercially oriented institutions capable of mobilizing small producers for the production of income-generating commodities. However, the National Agricultural Advisory Services programme (NAADS) has undertaken the task to spearhead the formation of farmer groups in the villages, which will form farmer forums at sub-county level that will eventually be replicated at district and national levels. Existing and new farmer groups are being supported and NAADS is working alongside development agencies and NGOs that are involved with the grassroots demands of farmers. Currently NAADS is operating in 49 districts and is expected to cover the whole country in the near future.

A number of traders and dairy processors are beginning to offer incentives to attract and keep suppliers. These include inputs such as milk cans that are given to farmers and vendors on credit. Farmers who supply milk through cooperative societies may access a number of incentives offered by the society – for example, acquiring inputs such as animal drugs, feeds, chemicals and equipment – on credit. Sometimes they receive advance cash payments, extension advice and veterinary services as well as training and credit facilities. Extension advice and training is usually free, while veterinary services are usually on a cost-recovery basis.

Dairy industry participants offer a number of services, including training and agricultural/ veterinary advisory services through the NAADS programmes, and in areas where NAADS is not operational, private veterinary and animal breeding services.

Input suppliers (animal drugs and chemicals, feeds, equipment, farm implements) also provide some services. Professional consultancy services such as feasibility studies, management, finance and micro-finance services are also offered as well as market information and market surveys sponsored by NGOs.

Dairy farmers who receive credit through their member cooperative societies are expected to sell milk through the society milk collection facility. Daily milk deliveries are maintained at the collection centre and the farmer has to deliver something, even if not all the milk. It is very difficult to completely prevent side selling, but trading partners always monitor the behaviour of their partners.

Case study 2: Fresh fruit and vegetables

The horticulture sector is one of fastest growing sectors in Uganda, averaging 20 per cent growth per annum, and the sector has almost tripled export earnings for Uganda over the last six years. Fresh flowers plus FFV account for about $19 million worth of exports annually. The fruit and vegetables sector is important in the Ugandan economy because it contributes a big share of the non-traditional exports. Recently, close attention has been given to its role in agricultural diversification and foreign earnings in the country.

In Uganda, much FFV is sold by supermarkets such as Uchumi, Metro and Shoprite. Many of these are sourced from outside the country (see Table 16.2). In Shoprite, most fruits are imported from South Africa while the vegetables are mainly obtained locally. In Uchumi, most of the FFV are obtained locally. In the Metcash supermarket only imported apples are sold with no vegetables, but the company indicated that in the near future, they would be selling FFV. Other important outlets for FFV are the upcoming locally owned medium to small supermarkets spread out in all the suburbs and petrol stations run by supermarkets alongside their business.

Some of the marketed FFV are imported because the country's agronomic conditions do not favour their production or because it is cheaper to import the required quantities and qualities. Most of the imported fruits marketed in Kampala are obtained from Kenya and South Africa.

Large supermarkets prefer direct procurement from farmers in order to meet customers' needs, including consistent supply and quality, food safety standards, and provision of a good variety of produce throughout the year. They inform their suppliers of their volume requirements, private standards and quality requirements regarding size and colour. Because of the insignificant number of commercial producers in Uganda, Uchumi buys approximately 51 per cent of its vegetables and 53 per cent of its fruits from small producers and uses brokers to supply the rest (Weatherspoon et al., 2003). The other half is shared evenly between traders who in turn buy from small growers and sometimes import from Kenya and South Africa. Large supermarkets procure from open markets mainly in case of shortages. Small supermarkets procure mainly from open markets and sometimes from farmers and brokers.

Table 16.2   Sources of FFV, Kampala supermarkets

	Shoprite		Uchumi	
Fresh fruits	Granny Smith apples, Top Red apples, pears, nectarines, white grape	South Africa	Royal Gala apples, green apples, Top Red apples, Outspan oranges, green African pears, green seedless grapes, tangerines	South Africa
	Minneolas (*mangada*), oranges, grapefruit, sweet melon	South Africa and Local	Black globe grapes	South Africa and Israel
	Mangoes, mango apples, coconut	Kenya	Washington navel oranges	Kenya
			Sweet melon	Kenya and local
	Sweet bananas, pineapples, passion fruits, avocados	Local	Avocado, fresh ginger, sweet banana, bogoya, gonja, round water melon, passion fruit, papaw	Local
Fresh vegetables	Garlic	China	Garlic	China
	Butter nut	Kenya	English cucumber, butter nut	Kenya
	Potatoes	Kenya and Local	Turnips	Kenya & Local
	Tomatoes, pumpkins, nakati, ginger, coriander (*dania*), fennel, parsley, cauliflower, leeks, turnip, broccoli, French beans, beetroot, green pepper, brinjals, oyster mushrooms, carrots, cucumber, cabbage, lettuce, bugga, onions	Local	Courgettes, baby courgette, French beans, bullet chillies, hot red pepper, white onions, onions, Irish potatoes, plantain garlic, dudi, cabbage, Uganda yellow capsicum, tindora, okra, cauliflower, tomatoes, brinjal small size, cucumber, green pepper, spinach, carrots	Local

Farmers or agents deliver high volumes of FFV to large supermarkets every morning. From these the purchasing officer in charge of FFV sorts and purchases the required volumes. Sometimes farmers who supply large supermarkets obtain the FFV from other farmers to raise the required quantities. In most cases, agents/traders obtain supplies from produce markets and occasionally from small farmers to supply the large supermarkets. Supplies are obtained either daily or every other day and virtually each day products are thrown away due to perishability. FFV are sorted by the supplier before delivery.

Big hotels and hospitals have agents who purchase the FFV from the produce markets of Owino and Nakasero and deliver to these institutions, rarely purchasing direct from farmers. Wholesalers of FFV in produce markets mainly have agents who supply them with FFV and rarely obtain them from farmers directly, and grading is mainly based on quality, size, appearance, variety, level of maturity and ripeness.

In most cases, small supermarkets purchase their fruits and vegetables directly, that is, not through agents, from the produce markets of Owino, Nakasero and Nakawa. A few small supermarkets source their FFV directly from small farmers. Most of the fruits and vegetables are obtained from nearby places because of their perishable nature with the exception of a few such as apples, which are obtained from Kabale. Fruits with high demand include avocado, sweet banana, bogoya, and gonja while vegetables with high demand include courgettes, baby courgettes, cabbages, tomatoes, onions, pepper, spinach and carrots.

Most of the imported fruits marketed in supermarkets, produce markets and at the roadside are obtained from South Africa and Kenya. Apples are the most widely sold and are estimated to account for over 50 per cent of the total value of fruit imports. The varieties of applies marketed include green, Top Red, Royal Gala, Fuji, Pink Lady and Golden Delicious. The main outlets for apples are both the small and large supermarkets and service stations. Significant volumes are also traded at the roadside. Some apples are sold loose, while others are pre-packed to cater for various categories of customers.

Other fruits are grapefruits, tangerine, Israel minneola, Outspan oranges, black plums, green plums, kiwi fruits, peaches and nectarines. Grapes are imported from either South Africa or Egypt and vegetables such as red pepper capsicum are also imported from South Africa, while button mushrooms are imported from Kenya. Peaches, pears, nectarines and plums are not well known among consumers and are sold mostly by large supermarkets. Shoprite imports directly from South Africa while Uchumi depends on importers who deliver to the market. Most of the small supermarkets and service station shops have suppliers/distributors who pick apples from Nakasero importers and deliver to them.

Supermarkets, hotels and hospitals have reliable preferred suppliers who provide quality products on time at agreed prices and give bonuses. The preferred suppliers are mainly traders (agents/brokers) and rarely farmers. These are selected based on working relationships, experience, trust, reliability and ability to meet contractual obligations.

In Uganda, the current procurement systems for FFV do not seem to discriminate against the small-scale producers as yet. Currently small-scale farmers who produce high grades and standards of FFV with low wastage are finding markets in the supermarkets.

Similarly, the traditional markets in Uganda are an important source of FFV for low-income urban consumers. Consumer demand in these markets is high because of the low prices offered. The traditional produce markets will survive in spite of issues of quality, hygiene and disorganization because they serve the majority of poor consumers. Poor producers, who do not have the transportation to regularly deliver to various supermarkets, will continue to find wetmarkets as their only option to sell their produce.

Since these markets are important centres for the sale of many FFV from small producers, improving quality, cleanliness and other hygienic conditions, and assuring traceability of FFV can attract supermarkets to procure from markets.

As the marketing of FFV evolves, brokers/agents are the clear losers in the modern supply chain as supermarket chains seek to contract directly with producers to ensure traceability, food safety and production methods. Small producers are also at high risk of becoming marginalized in the new supply chain if they are not able to meet the stringent quality and safety requirements and offer the product in a 'shelf-ready' format all the year round.

However, supermarkets will raise standards for marketing of FFV. Production of high-quality and more hygienic FFV could stimulate the domestic consumption. These institutions are also influencing the organization of small-scale farmers to form groups that are focused on quality, quantity and consistency of delivery, and which will participate in the more profitable supermarket supply chain through contractual and partnership arrangements in the future.

SUPPLY CONTRACTS

There are no written contracts in either the small or big supermarkets to supply FFV. Whereas supermarket owners prefer having them, farmers fear written contracts because of seasonality in supply; because most farming is rain fed, farmers may fail to meet the required volumes and hence face legal action for breach of contract. However, some big hotels and hospitals have contracts with suppliers of FFV. In case of failure to meet contractual obligations, management would immediately terminate payments. Risks in supply contracts are distributed according to the responsibilities of the concerned parties.

FINANCE FOR SMALL-SCALE PRODUCERS

Financial resources are not available for the direct actors in the market chain of most agricultural produce. Loans are available but attract very high interest rates of 24 per cent or more. The commercial financial sector has minimal involvement with small holders due to the perceived high risks of rain-fed agriculture, and the inability of small producers to meet banking requirements including the provision of collateral. For these reasons, there is a very low banking presence in rural areas. Other sources of credit and financial services, such as NGOs, have not reached small producers to any significant extent. However, some NGOs have been active in offering small amounts of credit to small producer farmers and entrepreneurs.

SMALL BUSINESS ENTERPRISE DEVELOPMENT

In Uganda, the micro and small enterprise (MSE) sector makes a very significant contribution to both the household and the national economy. MSEs provide alternative sources of income for people from other activities such as agriculture. A recent study by USAID estimates that the MSE sector employs about 20 per cent of the population of working age, and that more than 60 per cent of the entrepreneurs depend upon their business for at least one half of their household income. The sector also provides a graduation process especially from agricultural production to processing and marketing and provides local inputs to the manufacturing sector.

Conclusions

A modern food system is still emerging in Uganda and that gives the government time to help small-scale producers gear up to become preferred suppliers. They are helped in this because there is no large farm sector to capture the opportunities and imports, even from other African countries, are too expensive.

As we see above, dairy processors and supermarkets court small-scale farmers because they offer the only supply option for the modern food sector.

The following are recommendations to the dairy sector:

- The Dairy Development Authority (DDA) should regulate the dairy market for quality and health safety and government should provide financial support to this initiative until the system becomes financially self-sustaining through revenue collections.
- Initiatives to promote consumption of high quality milk and dairy products should be supported by the government, the private sector and the donor group.
- The formal milk processing sector should work with the informal milk wholesaling and distribution sectors to improve efficiencies in milk distribution.
- Government should develop supportive viable infrastructure like transportation facilities (cold storage and refrigeration facilities) for milk and milk products and adequate storage facilities to minimize post-harvesting losses.
- The DDA, National Agricultural Advisory Services, the Uganda National Dairy Farmers Association and interested donors should support farmers to form efficient POs and where they exist, assistance in improving their commercial skills is recommended.
- Government should ensure that sufficient credit facilities are made available and accessible to small-scale farmers to increase production, and to processors to purchase equipment. Integrated quality assurance across the entire production chain from the farm to the consumer should be supported by the government, through the Uganda National Bureau of Standards.
- Government, with donor support, should launch campaigns to educate people on the benefits of consuming milk and other dairy products.

Recommendations to the fruits and vegetable sector:

- Government should develop supportive viable infrastructure such as transportation facilities (cold storage and refrigeration facilities) for FFV, simple irrigation and adequate storage facilities to minimize post-harvesting losses.
- Government should ensure that farmer-friendly credit facilities are made available and accessible to small farmers to increase and diversify production of fruits and vegetables.
- Both government and the private sector should ensure that capacity is developed within the farmer community and control measures instituted to meet the accepted health standards for fruits and vegetables.
- Group production and marketing should be promoted by both the private sector and the government to meet the required volumes of fruits and vegetables at the right time because the low output of highly heterogeneous qualities released to the supermarkets limits the capacity for small producers to retain market share.
- Government should provide the Uganda National Bureau of Standards with whatever additional legislative authority is required to strengthen its capability to ensure market quality production.
- Both government and the private sector should support the training of producers to ensure the quality of fruits and vegetables. This can be achieved through training of management

personnel, product design and packaging and encouraging exchange visits between the local producers among others.
- Both government and the private sector should support the production of organically produced fruits and vegetables since their demand is increasing in most supermarkets.
- Government, with donor support, should launch campaigns to educate people about the benefits of consuming fruits and vegetables.

Reference

Weatherspoon D.D., Neven, D., Katjiuongua, H.B., Fotsin, R. and Reardon, T.A., 2003. *Distributional impacts of supermarkets in South Africa, Kenya, Zambia and Uganda*. World Bank Report, Washington DC.

17 *Zambia*

Rosemary A. Emongor, André Louw and Johann F. Kirsten

Introduction

Small-scale producers dominate agriculture in Zambia, and have a measure of protection from imports because of high transport costs in this landlocked country. There is a large farm sector that has developed to supply local processors and retailers with food. Therefore these farms, often in organizations, are preferred suppliers for commodities such as milk, meat, sugar and grain. Small-scale producers have to compete against these and have most potential in FFV. However, even here there is competition from large farms that export FFV by air.

Policies to encourage foreign investors have been in place since 1991 when the Zambia Investment Centre (ZIC) was created as part of the government's strategy for economic reform. As an autonomous organization, it promotes local and foreign investment in Zambia.

Much of the new investment, especially into the food system, has come from South Africa. Until 1993, sanctions against the apartheid regime prevented this. From 1993–98, South African companies made investments in Zambia of US$240 million, about 20 per cent of total investment in Zambia. This has made South Africa the second largest investor in Zambia after the UK (Haantuba, 2003). The South African supermarket chain Shoprite is one of the leading investors in food retailing in Zambia.

KEY DATA

	2002	2003	2004
Population (millions)	10.0	9.7	11.2
Per capita GDP (US$)	251	255	
Urbanization (%)	40		
Agriculture as % GDP	6.9	7.2	21.7

Exchange rate (1 January 2006): 1 US Dollar = 3540 Zambian kwacha (K)

TOP GROCERY CHAINS

Company	Ownership	Number of stores	Retail banner sales 2004 (US$ millions)	Market share (%)	Grocery sales 2004 (US$ millions)	Grocery market share (%)
Shoprite	Foreign (RSA)	19	39	10.5	35	10.4
Massmart	Foreign (RSA)	1	2	0.5	0	0.1
Woolworths (RSA)	Foreign (RSA)	2	2	0.5	0	0.0
Melissa	Zambian	3				
Other			330	88.5	298	89.5

Source: PlanetRetail

FOOD RETAILING

Shoprite is the largest supermarket retailer in Zambia. The government withdrew from the retailing sector by selling its loss-making retail chains to Shoprite. The deal included a five-year tax holiday and other incentives and this gave the company the edge over other local chains. Shoprite owns 19 stores (18 supermarkets and one wholesale) in Zambia, each with floor space of about 2,000m², and has total retail sales of nearly US$ 40 million. The stores have fresh food counters and an in-store bakery.

In 1999, neighbourhood stores and supermarkets accounted for 70 per cent of food retail sales, cash and carry 4 per cent and other retailers 27 per cent. By 2003, the share of cash and carry type stores had increased to 28 per cent.

A survey carried out in Zambia on urban agriculture in 1992–93, showed that about 80 to 90 per cent of the respondents in the urban areas of Lusaka, Ndola and Kabwe obtained their vegetables from the council markets. These markets include the well-known 'Soweto' market in Lusaka (Drecher, 1997).

During our survey in Lusaka in June 2004, key informants estimated that about 75 per cent of tomatoes and other agricultural products are still sold through the Soweto market, the adjacent city market and other local markets.

Soweto market caters to all segments of society and it is estimated that about 70 per cent or more of the farmers' fresh produce is sold through the Soweto market. The large exporting farms also sell the non-exportable produce, such as snap beans, through this market. Even those who have contracts with supermarkets also end up selling at this market if they fail to sell to Freshmark or the independent supermarkets. Soweto market therefore acts as the market of last resort for many of these farmers. Very rudimentary standards are considered in this market such as 'good quality', size and shape of the produce.

Shoprite uses its subsidiary Freshmark in Zambia to buy fresh fruits and vegetables from local producers, mainly large-scale farmers and processors. The buying is done through verbal contracts. Some independent supermarkets source their fresh produce directly from farmers and also use verbal contracts.

At the moment Freshmark sources about 80–95 per cent of fresh vegetables from local farmers, both small scale and large scale. However, the issues of consistency of both quality and quantity prevail with the small-scale farmers.

Given the large volumes required by the Shoprite stores throughout the year, Freshmark tends to source mainly from large-scale farmers. According to Freshmark, 90 per cent of fresh produce in their Zambian operation is sourced from large-scale farms. Small-scale farmers lack the necessary infrastructure such as irrigation systems to be able to meet the volumes required by Freshmark. However, small-scale farmers are supplying vegetables such as rape, tomato, impwa (local egg plant), sweet potatoes, onions and brinjals to Freshmark.

Freshmark have signed a memorandum of understanding (MOU) with the Chamba Valley Growers cooperative, negotiated through an NGO – the Partnership Forum, based at the University of Zambia – to supply rape, sweet potato, and impwa. This MOU gives farmers easy access to Freshmark and enables them to sell the fresh vegetables specified. This means that supermarkets and their subsidiaries deal with farmers with whom they have formed relationships of trust. There are 150 farmers in the Chamba Valley cooperative but at the time of this survey, only 15 farmers were supplying to Freshmark. The major constraints are the lack of irrigation and capital.

For the Shoprite stores in the other parts of Zambia, arrangements are made for local farmers to supply fresh vegetables directly to the stores. This happens, for example, at the Shoprite stores in Chipata (550 km from Lusaka) and Solwezi, and is necessary because consumers need fresh produce and transporting it from the Freshmark facility in Lusaka to these stores would take a day or two. There has also been the situation where local farmers started selling their vegetables directly in front of Shoprite stores. To stop this practice, Shoprite changed its sourcing policy to accommodate local producers.

Freshmark sets its own standards with which the tomato supplier, whether small or large farmers, must comply. These specifications include size of tomato, colour ('champagne' colour is sought by buyers), barcode and taste (that is, no foreign taints, odours or flavour). Most of the small-scale farmers interviewed said that champagne red was confusing as their 'tomatoes may be rejected by Freshmark and yet similar tomatoes supplied by a large farmer or a farmer friendly with the manager are accepted'. If the specifications are not met farmers' produce can be rejected. However, the rejection rate is rather low thanks to prior training of farmers in these aspects by the Zambia Agribusiness Technical Assistance Centre (ZATAC) and other organizations. Freshmark has a policy of not getting involved in farming practices and farm management (apart from providing the specifications for the product), and relying on partnerships with other organizations to ensure that a good product is produced. The large-scale farms are usually independent and have their in-house experts to assist the farm to meet the supermarket specifications.

There is only one Spar store in Zambia, located at Arcades in Lusaka. It is operated as a franchise and wholly owned by local people. It started its operation in December 2003. Farmers supply their produce to the Spar distribution centre. Spar buys directly from the farmer to cut out intermediaries, which means that its fresh produce is much cheaper. Quality and price are important when buying from the farmers. Spar buys whatever the farmer can grow and whatever they can pack for the consumer. Farmers deliver vegetables such as rape, spinach, cauliflower, broccoli, cabbage, lettuce, tomatoes and onions to Spar. The large dairy processors are the only source of supply of dairy products to Spar. Canned milk powders and condensed milk are imported from South Africa.

Melissa is a chain of smaller supermarket stores owned by Zambians. Generally, farmers supply fresh vegetables directly to the individual Melissa stores. They are paid cash on delivery. Dairy products are sourced from local processors in a similar way to Shoprite.

Clearly, it is difficult to set up a PO for small-scale producers and supply to strict supermarket standards. Nor are large-scale farmers likely to use small producers as FFV out-growers, as they do in the air freight export of vegetables. As the group of large farmers who are preferred suppliers of potatoes told us: 'We do not buy from out-growers who own less than 20 ha because the time spent managing a 1.5 ha farm is the same as the time spent managing 20 ha.'

Case study 1: Fresh fruit and vegetable agreements

The supply agreements between small-scale farmers and Freshmark to supply fresh produce are largely only verbal agreements. Written contracts only apply in the case of processed products and for large-scale farmers. The preference for verbal contracts largely lies in the increased flexibility provided to the supermarket buyers or their agents. It allows them to vary purchase prices according to trends in market prices. By having these verbal contracts, the buyer avoids paying a very high price when the market price of the product is low. The verbal contract also provides more flexibility for small-scale producers, since they are often in a situation where they would not be able to meet the volumes and terms specified in written contracts. Production volumes from small-scale farms tend to be very erratic, mainly because of limited investment in irrigation. Thus, for both parties, a verbal agreement allows flexibility that reduces the risk considerably.

However, the danger with verbal agreements is that they are not always honoured – creating some mistrust between small-scale farmers and Freshmark. It quite often happens that there is excess supply to the Freshmark depot resulting in them not being able to purchase the produce. This forces the farmers to make alternative marketing arrangements at short notice, such as selling at the Soweto market where the produce may fetch much lower prices.

Farmers interviewed said they would generally prefer written contracts because they provide a guaranteed market and price. Large-scale farmers secure more binding contracts (even though also verbal) largely because the buyers would like to be sure of continuous supply and large farmers have formed relationships of trust and credibility based on historic performance. Some small-scale farmers, especially the more affluent ones, make their own arrangements with Freshmark. Other small farmers, such as the farmers in Chamba Valley, negotiate through cooperatives.

There is a spill-over from the airfreight vegetable business. For products that are exported, such as baby corn, mange tout and snap beans, high quality (colour, shape, and so on) and standards (EUREPGAP) are adhered to. Companies such as Agriflora and York Farm ensure that they and other small- and medium-scale out-grower farmers meet these standards. On the other hand, products ('rejects') that fail to meet the European supermarket standards are sold to local consumers through Soweto and supermarkets (Shoprite, Spar and Melissa). The managers argue that these products are still safe and nutritionally sound but may have failed in their appearance, shape or length and size of product required for the export market.

Case study 2: Milk supply

In Zambia, fresh milk is produced by three distinct groups of producers, namely small-scale farmers, large-scale farmers (called 'commercial' in Southern Africa), and 'emergent' farmers (emergent farmers are, as in South Africa, identified as having the potential to become more like 'commercial farmers'). The contribution of small-scale farmers is about 40 per cent of all marketed milk. In total, all these farmers produce approximately 190 million litres of milk per year compared to the country's total milk requirement of 253 million litres of milk, a 25 per cent deficit. Out of the 190 million litres of raw milk produced, approximately 22 per cent (41 million litres) is processed by the dairy processing industry. The balance is marketed through informal channels directly to consumers.

Some farmers, especially large-scale producers, market directly to processors while small-scale farmers supply to cooperatives (collection points) where processors collect the milk. Cooling tanks have been provided at the collection points that are located on cooperative sites. These cold storage tanks are provided on loan by ZATAC, or in some cases by the dairy processors to which farmers supply milk. Other farmers, mainly in the traditional sector, sell raw milk directly to consumers.

The small-scale, traditional dairy producers account for the largest number of dairy cattle but milk production per cow is very low – about 2 litres per cow per day. These producers do not actively work to improve the milk yield or quality of their milk, as this aspect of their livelihood is not considered paramount. The milk produced in this system is mainly for subsistence and the surplus is marketed to neighbours. Only 40 per cent of their output is marketed through formal channels. They usually market their excess milk to the community as and when they have it and, accordingly, they sell their milk at low prices, usually around US$ 0.20 per litre.

The breeds of animals are generally local breeds with low milk production. However, these animals are more adapted to local conditions and are kept and fed on natural pastures with little supplementation. This therefore means lower maintenance costs and reduced risk. Small-scale producers sell their milk directly to the consumers and in some instances, to vendors.

Few small-scale dairy farmers meet standards set by the government with regards to disease control, such as in the case of ticks and foot and mouth. As a result, the milk they produce often does not meet the processors' standards. This milk is sold in local markets. The majority of commercial dairy farmers are forced by the milk processors to meet the standards with regard to food safety and disease control in their herd. They manage to do this with varying levels of success.

The bulk of milk supplied to the dairy processing industry is produced on large-scale commercial farms. These farmers use dairy feeds and improved breeds, and most of them have formed strong relationships with milk processing firms. Milk is normally supplied directly to the processors. The farms are well capitalized and have the necessary equipment to be able to supply the large amounts of milk required by the processors. Farmers in this group supply milk directly to the processors such as Parmalat and Finta. Some of the large farms process milk at the farm into pasteurized milk, yoghurt, cheese and butter. Farms that are involved in on-farm milk processing include Momba farms, Cedrics and Northern Dairies.

There are 19 milk processors in Zambia according to the Directory of Processors. They produce a range of products with the notable exception of powdered milk; this is imported. With the increasing involvement of milk processors in the supply chain, especially making long-life milk, milk has become more available to consumers and there has been an increase in per capita milk consumption, especially in urban areas such as Lusaka. Milk processing and long-life milk production has enabled milk exportation from Zambia to other countries such as the Democratic Republic of Congo. Finta, a dairy processing company located in Livingstone, is the main exporter.

Due to the inadequate supply of liquid raw milk, some dairy processing companies make up the deficit by recombining powdered milk for further processing into UHT milk, yoghurt and other products that would otherwise not be produced in the desired quantities. The processors will switch to liquid raw milk as more becomes available on the market.

Dairy farmers receive technical assistance from processors such as Parmalat and Finta. These processors collect milk in bulk from collection centres. They have also provided equipment to the milk cooperatives to test for the quality of milk at the point of purchase. Organizations such as Land O' Lakes (1999, information updated to 2004 as a result of an interview with the Land O' Lakes Zambia coordinator) are helping dairy farmers to manage their farms better and increase production by assisting them to form and run cooperatives. The organization also trains dairy farmers on management of their cooperatives. As a result of the efforts made in integrating small-scale dairy producers into the supply chain, more farmers are in groups and the processors collect milk from these cooperatives with which they have formed working relationships.

Through the implementation of the Zambia dairy enterprises initiative project by Land O' Lakes, a total of 557 small-scale farmers are producing and supplying milk to both small- and large-scale processors through 11 milk collection centres (Land O' Lakes, 2004). This has resulted in the increased involvement of small-scale dairy farmers into the dairy supply chain since 2002. Farmers are supported to form dairy farmers' groups/cooperatives. Through these groupings, basic facilities such as cooling storage tanks are provided under loan to farmers. Other facilities provided include testing equipment such as lactometers to test for milk freshness and other quality standards. These cooperatives and milk collection centres are mainly in urban areas and surrounding peri-urban areas mainly on the railway lines, such as Choma, Monze, Kalomo and Kazungula in Southern Province and Palabana and Buteko in Lusaka Province. The viability of these cooperatives as a model for including farmers in the dairy supply chain will be tested when the project comes to an end and farmers have to continue producing and supplying to the collecting centres that have been established.

Land O' Lakes links small farmers to the formal market through processors; for example, Dairy King buys milk from Buteko cooperative. Small-scale farmers supply between 2.5 litres and 80 litres per day. This means that some of these farmers produce a lot of milk and their production can be greatly improved if markets are assured. Of the total amount of milk collected by large-scale processors such as Parmalat, 80 per cent is from large-scale producers and 20 per cent from small-scale producers. ZATAC provides technical assistance by training organized dairy farmers in book keeping and record keeping and simple accounts. Buteko cooperative farmers have received this training. Raw milk is sold to consumers directly by farmers and fetches higher prices than milk supplied to cooperatives.

ZAMBIA DAIRY PROCESSORS COMMITTEE (ZDPC)

ZDPC is an association of dairy processors that consists of both small-scale and large-scale processors in Zambia. Each member pays a membership fee of 500 000 K (about US$ 100). Through membership of this organization, processors receive technical assistance to improve processing, quality and food safety, and also advertising for their products on TV, in the print media and through education campaigns. This is particularly important for the small-scale processors such as Dairy King, who cannot meet the cost of advertising their products on their own.

Conclusions

The agri-food system in Zambia is changing in response to a number of factors both internal and external to Zambia. Domestic policies such as market liberalization, regional integration and FDI have gradually brought private companies and corporations into the supply chain of most agricultural products. The entrance of large firms, especially in food retail and processing, has been accompanied by increasing concentration of the processing and retail sectors of the food chain and hence the problems related to chain governance issues. The new food systems evolving from this will affect the small-scale farmers and micro enterprises.

The major issue of concern is that in a country with high levels of poverty many small-scale producers will be excluded from the mainstream economy. The majority of rural people depend on agriculture and related agro-industries for their livelihood and therefore their inclusion into supply chains is important if rural poverty is to be addressed effectively. However, doing business with many small-scale farmers increases the transaction costs for large retailers and processors.

Can small-scale farmers in Zambia access the modern food system? The answer is a qualified 'Yes'. We found a number of encouraging moves made by the government and private companies to help small-scale producers, for example Agriflora and, to a limited extent, Spar and Land O' Lakes. The standards small-scale farmers currently meet are generally well below those required by processors and supermarkets. The 'spill-over' effect from air freighted exports of vegetables will probably help raise FFV standards among small-scale producers. The big advantage of small-scale producers is that in the future, supermarket and processor requirements will out-run what large farms can provide and imports of FFV and dairy products will remain expensive.

Currently, some farmers who are organized in groups have been able to acquire the inputs and skills required to produce products of high quality to supply to supermarkets and processors. The formation of collective and intermediary organizations has shown that if small-scale farmers are organized in groups they can be linked to agribusinesses through contracting and forms of partnerships.

The recommendations below are made for the increased inclusion of small-scale farmers and SMEs in the supply chain of the selected products.

Policy recommendations for the private sector:

- POs such as cooperatives, farmer associations and community-based groups should be strengthened. Through these organizations it will be possible to reduce transaction costs by bringing many small farmers to operate as one unit and increase their market power to negotiate better trading terms with agribusiness. This will make it easier to provide inputs and services such as extension and information delivery.
- Currently these producer groups are mainly in peri-urban areas and rural towns. It is important to extend the formation of new producer groups at the village level. Most of the cooperatives have been formed through partnerships with NGOs through projects and most groups are still young and cash strapped. Technical and financial support for such cooperatives is required if they are to become sources of increased agricultural production and gain access to markets.
- Other markets should be developed, for example wholesale markets and traditional retailers which can easily be accessed by small-scale farmers.
- There is also a need to upgrade market information to small producers and SMEs (price information, technology information, extension information) to improve market accessibility.

- More small-scale producers can be helped to enter into contract farming but structures for enforcement of these contracts need to be improved.

Policy recommendations for the public sector:

- Provision of credit to farmers, especially small-scale farmers, has been difficult because of the high transaction costs and risks involved. Formal credit organizations (such as banks) should be able to grant credit to emerging farmers who have been organized in groups. The current support of farmers through organizations should be extended to offer support to farmers producing crops such as tomato and potatoes for the domestic markets. Mechanisms for recovery of loans can be organized with the agribusiness firms where the farmers sell their produce, especially if contract farming is used, as in the case of Agriflora.
- Market access should be looked at in a wider context of how the participation of farmers in the supply chain is affected by Zambia's participation and integration in the regional markets.
- Policies to facilitate the provision of services to small-scale farmers and processors in the country need to be reviewed. Services such as extension are urgently needed if farmers and SMEs are to improve the quality of their products and be able to compete on a global scale.
- Grades and standards are becoming very important in the local as well as the export market. Various NGOs have been training farmers to increase their knowledge of the application of quality and standards. More could be done, especially for those who intend to access and supply to supermarkets. This can be achieved through partnerships between producers, the government and the private sector.

References

Drecher, A.W., 1997. *Urban agriculture in the seasonal tropics of Central Southern Africa: A case study of Lusaka Zambia*. Urban Agriculture notes. Available: www.cityfarmer.org/axe1B.html.

Haantuba, H., 2003. *Linkages between smallholder farm producers and supermarkets in Zambia*. Consultancy report for Food and Agriculture Organization.

Land O' Lakes, 1999. *Market channel development for the Zambia Dairy Industry*. A consultancy report submitted to USAID/Zambia.

5 *Conclusions*

In this final part of the book, we seek to draw out the key findings from the Regoverning Markets project and highlight the areas in which we believe policy-makers and corporate managers should focus their efforts to give small-scale producers a better chance to engage in the process of restructuring, which threatens to engulf them.

18 Restructuring of Agri-food Systems and Prospects for Small Producers

Bill Vorley, Andrew Fearne and Derek Ray

The main focus of this book is the position of smaller-scale agricultural producers in emerging modern food supply chains. Most of the country studies point to one central fact, that supermarkets and multinational food companies are accelerators of structural change in agriculture and food. They are not the only drivers of change, but are clearly the most poorly understood by policy-makers, producer organizations (POs) and the 'development' community.

Supermarkets and food companies, in turn, appear all too frequently to lack either an understanding of the impact they are having on local markets or a clear, proactive strategy for the wider inclusion of small-scale producers therein. As a result, they are often accused of not caring about 'development' and growing their margins at the expense of local food producers. In some instances this is doubtless the case, but in the majority of cases supermarkets have a vested interest in working with local producers, large and small.

With a view to bridging the gap in knowledge and understanding within and between different stakeholder groups, this chapter summarizes the key insights from the Regoverning Markets country studies, and points to policy options for producers and their organizations, governments and donors, the private sector, and civil society. We emphasize policies to anticipate and adapt to the changes associated with the restructuring of agri-food systems in mid- and low-income countries. We attempt to spotlight interventions that could increase the likelihood of supermarket expansion benefiting the many rather than the few. We also point to priorities for further research.

The relative importance of supermarkets

The first point we would highlight is that the traditional retail sector is quite resilient – supermarkets are not the dominant players in every country/region and are unlikely to become dominant for some time. For example, in India, where the sector is still dominated by traditional retailers with single outlet businesses mainly using family labour, only three companies have a turnover higher than US$100 million – about the average sales generated by a single Carrefour hypermarket in France. Traditional markets are resilient, especially in Africa, where populations are less dense than Latin America or East Asia, where incomes are lower, and where there is an important informal sector. In a few countries such as the Philippines, the traditional sector is actually expanding (ACNielsen, 2005).

Existing traditional trading and retail structures have a number of competitive strengths that mean that they are able to maintain their markets in the face of competition from supermarkets by offering benefits to consumers or to producers.

These include low operating costs and overheads, low margins, proximity to customers, long opening hours and additional services to customers such as home delivery. On the consumer side, small, local retailers sometimes offer credit and sell products in small units, in line with the needs of low-income consumers, who provide an important market for farmers who are unable to adapt to the demands of agri-food restructuring. Moreover, long-term relationships between producers and market intermediaries, and the trust that this engenders, may provide a brake on change, as producers prefer to transact with their existing trading partners, even in the presence of numerous alternatives.

There is evidence from Latin America and the Philippines that producers continue to sell to traditional traders for a number of reasons, including the additional services provided (including transport, sorting, market information, loans, advances), immediate payment in cash, and social ties that create trust. Nevertheless, there is widespread evidence from most study countries of a rapid shift towards modern retailing formats.

The phases of restructuring

The country chapters show that 'supermarkets' are a highly variable and adaptable phenomenon, with the different phases of supermarket growth having very different implications for small-scale producers and small and medium scale enterprises (SMEs). As well as multinationals, there are locally owned domestic chains (such as Lianhua in China, La Favourita in Ecuador, Shoprite and Pick 'n' Pay in South Africa), and buying and marketing groups (such as CBA in Hungary) that are very successful thanks to their knowledge of local consumer preferences and access to key policy-makers.

Supermarkets build differentiation around price for the staples that would normally come from the 'mom and pop' retailers, and around food safety for the products – fresh fruit and vegetables (FFV), meat, dairy — which would normally come from wetmarket traders. Food quality has emerged as a critical driver of vertical coordination. The assurance of food integrity and food safety (pesticide residues or pathogens), as well as of the reliability of supply, are emerging as key drivers for the growth of supermarkets yet are widely regarded as constraints that often preclude farmers from participating in modern supply chains. What is evident from many of the country studies is that the supermarket revolution is viewed very positively by consumers, especially in former centrally planned economies, where consumers have been denied choice and service for generations, and South-east Asia, where an emerging middle class can afford to care much more about the provenance and safety of their food.

Supermarkets may start with a wealthier customer base, but expand across the socio-economic spectrum through a diversity of formats. There is also the expansion from staples, packaged and processed goods and non-food, to meat and dairy, and eventually FFV. The situation described in Ecuador seemed to mark the point when supermarket FFV moves from being considered by most customers to be of inferior quality and availability and higher price, to one where supermarkets are seen as sources of higher-quality and lower-price produce – a triumph for consumers but often a 'bridge too far' for small-scale producers. This means that small-scale producers need to adapt quickly to the changing needs of their customers and the final consumer and that supermarkets need to work harder to help them in the process of adaptation, with much clearer signposting of the hurdles (quality, cost, scale, service) that lie ahead and provision of (or at least support for) investment in training and infrastructure to 'train' small-scale producers in the ways of modern food supply chains.

Other changes are taking place, such as the consolidation of wholesale cash-and-carry by global and regional companies (such as Metro, Makro, Metcash,[1] PriceSmart, and Wal-Mart's Sam's Club) that can influence procurement patterns without discernable changes in the structure of retail. The studies in Thailand and Poland show the impact of this consolidation in the middle of the chain, with many 'mom and pop' stores reporting that they procure some of their stock from cash-and-carry stores or even from the supermarkets. The effect of the rise in cash-and-carry on the structure of agricultural production is yet to be properly understood.

However, consolidation in any market or supply chain generally results in cost reduction and in increases in the scale of operations upstream and downstream, to the benefit of the final consumer but invariably to the detriment of other stakeholders and most of all to the smallest ones. Thus, the trend towards consolidation can only increase the need for much more (and better) horizontal coordination among small-scale producers, a message that is repeatedly made in the country chapters.

The trade dimension

Lack of domestic supply that meets the demands of modern supermarkets and food processors may pull in imports to fill the gap. There is a very interesting and under-researched link between restructuring, trade and liberalization. The Uganda study shows that a considerable portion of supermarket FFV in the country, especially fruit, is imported, and this trend is certainly much more pronounced for packaged and processed goods.

Later in the restructuring process, the organization of production and distribution on a regional rather than national level also increases cross-border trade. An example is the trade in manzano (salad) tomatoes from Guatemala to Nicaragua through the auspices of Hortifruti. Throughout Central and Eastern Europe (CEE), imports of foods into newly established foreign supermarkets has been a feature of transition, until a local supply base is built. In Romania, local milk supplies are gradually being restored and in Hungary, new investment by local and foreign processors means there is less reliance on imports.

Supermarkets establish procurement hubs for global sourcing in some countries, such as Wal-Mart Global Procurement, Carrefour Global Sourcing, Tesco International Sourcing, and Metro Group Buying operations in India, China and/or Poland. Such two-way flow of goods – mostly non-food but increasingly also food products – is also an important political demonstration of commitment to local development.

The trade dimension in the restructuring of modern food systems is a double-edged sword. Centralized procurement encourages international trade and provides opportunities for small-scale producers and their collective organizations to grow and achieve the kind of scale economies that are essential for their long-term survival. However, success for one group of small-scale producers – the 'exporters' – represents a significant threat to another: those in neighbouring countries and regions who see their market share decline and with it their prospects for survival. This is the reality of increasingly competitive global markets in

---

1   Metro Cash & Carry Ltd, also known as Metcash, is listed on the Johannesburg Stock Exchange. It has no links with the German Metro group.

which country boundaries are swept aside in the interests of efficiency. While supermarkets' understandable focus is on incremental growth and development of *their* markets, much greater consideration needs to be given to the 'bigger picture'.

The impacts on suppliers and producers: The four pillars

The country chapters provide fascinating and often salutary insights into the realities of dealing with rapid and continuous change in modern food supply chains. Small is seldom beautiful when it comes to supplying supermarkets. Small-scale producers have problems relating to volume, consistency, quality and perhaps food integrity and safety. Even more significantly, they often face problems of logistics, risk, services, and compliance.

The 'Four Pillars' of change identified by Reardon et al. (2004) – the rise of centralized procurement, the emergence of specialist wholesalers and logistics firms, the use of preferred suppliers and the development of private standards – are evident throughout the county chapters. We now look at each of these in turn and their impact on small-scale producers.

PILLAR 1: CENTRALIZED PROCUREMENT

One change that takes place during the course of development in supermarket supply chains is that they change from purchasing products at a store level to purchasing them centrally, and at some point in their development they build regional depots to which suppliers are required to organize their deliveries. This change is part of the structural adjustment that supermarkets make to capture economies of scale and improve service levels for consumers. Central purchasing provides leverage to negotiate better prices and volume discounts, and regional distribution centres facilitate the development of integrated logistics and transportation systems that reduce the supermarkets' costs of servicing stores, while reducing stock levels, improving availability and extending shelf-life. However, it often makes it more difficult for small-scale suppliers to begin to supply, as they struggle with the (im)balance of bargaining power and the scale of operation (volume of sales and logistics services) that this requires.

This was an issue that emerged in most of the country cases, but in some instances suppliers had learned to live with it and adapted their organizational structure, through horizontal co-operation. In Ecuador, for example, central procurement for one retailer has been in place for many years, but this brought advantages to those suppliers located near the depots, who experienced a reduction in their transport costs, while penalizing those located further away from the depot but nearer the individual stores, who saw their transport costs rise.

Supermarkets could clearly help here, by taking a segmented approach to their suppliers just as they do to their customers – one size clearly does not fit all and there would seem to be merit in considering the option of central procurement and regional depots for the bulk of the products, but with some deliveries permitted direct to stores when the net impact on the supply chain as a whole is positive. These direct deliveries will tend to be small volumes so will have little impact on the economics of central procurement as a whole but could mean the difference between profit and loss for a small-scale producer.

It is also worth remembering the small-scale example from South Africa, of a single store that contracted FFV from a local association of growers and paid in cash. Such a particular, local arrangement would not survive if supplies were routed through a central depot. The case study illustrates both the positive aspects (community development and freshness of vegetables) and the negative ones (high transaction costs, fluctuations in volumes and quality) of direct procurement by stores.

PILLAR 2: SPECIALIZED WHOLESALERS AND LOGISTICS COMPANIES

Early phases in supermarket growth may be characterized by external companies operating produce concessions within each store. This is still a feature of supermarkets in the Philippines, China and Pakistan, as well as the new up-country formats in Thailand.

There is also a transition to the use of dedicated wholesalers. Writers on Central America and Ecuador distinguish two types of intermediary: (1) dedicated suppliers or specialized wholesalers who supply one or two advanced supermarket chains, and are in charge of supplying an entire category to the supermarket's grades and standards; and (2) traditional wholesalers serving a wide variety of clients, one of which may be a supermarket chain.

A number of examples of dedicated FFV wholesalers emerged from the country cases, of which Shanghai Xingcheng foods in China and Hortifruti in Central America stand out as examples of good practice. In these operations, the wholesaler takes on the procurement function on behalf of the supermarkets, reducing transaction costs and removing the pain of procurement from a diverse supply base. In the case of Hortifruti, they contract to buy FFV in several neighbouring countries and suppliers agree to transport to Hortifruti depots, which in turn service a range of supermarket customers. This regional trading system has meant that many small-scale producers and their associations have gained access to supermarkets and is an excellent example of how upstream stakeholders embrace change and adapt. This model offers a 'win–win–win' for supermarkets, wholesalers and primary producers and is one that warrants significant support, not least because it will stand the test of time – this is the structure of procurement for fresh meat, FFV and many dairy products that is used in mature supermarket supply chains the world over.

Dedicated wholesalers often work with preferred suppliers, a position usually closed to small farmers unless intensive technical, financial and managerial assistance is available (potentially an important role for extension services, the banks and government agencies). In emerging economies, the most common approach is for a supermarket chain to source from a wholesaler who is specialized in a given category, such as fruit, and who deals with a certain type of client, for example, supermarkets and exports. Specialist wholesalers are the firms in charge of managing standards for supermarkets, and sub-standard supplies are rejected by them. In order to make up a shortfall, the specialist may buy on wholesale markets or, as in China, have a 'production base', in other words, farm on their own account.

The role of a specialist 'go-between' in other sectors is played by processors. Meat and milk are often assembled, products differentiated and branded and delivered to depots by large-scale processors. This is the system for milk in nearly all the countries we looked at. Collection centres are established with coolers that can accept small amounts of milk on a daily basis. The milk is then kept cool through to the milk factory and on to the storage and distribution of final products.

Processors may prefer to use a few large-scale milk producers, but when supplies are insufficient, they are obliged to turn to small-scale producers. This has been the case in Romania where small-scale milk producers have grown in importance during the transitional period. Other examples of using small-scale producers for milk supply include India and Vietnam. In Pakistan, a multinational milk processor has developed a supply chain based upon small-scale producers.

The evidence suggests that there is a shift from traditional wholesalers to specialized wholesalers and preferred suppliers as supermarkets evolve. This is a cause for concern for many, as it invariably results in exclusion and a reduction in the supply base when what is often needed, from a development perspective, is an expansion of the supply base in line with the growth of supermarket sales. One possible solution to this problem, again, is for much greater collaboration between wholesalers, to provide an 'integrated solution' that combines the benefits of scale and flexibility while allowing specialist operators to focus on their core areas of competence. There is little evidence of this anywhere in the world, as in most cases wholesalers regard each other as direct competitors – a fruit wholesaler can very easily expand its operation to include vegetables and will see supermarket growth as an opportunity to grow its business. What is missing here is a depth of strategic vision – competing locally – which in the short term prevents organizations from seeing the 'bigger picture'. The coordination of multiple wholesale businesses (leaving ownership and operation largely independent), offers potential benefits to everyone, but requires a strategic perspective on competitive advantage that is the exception rather than the rule in this part of the supply chain.

One such exception is the 'Dragon Head' companies found in China. These organizations encompass both supply and trade functions in a supermarket supply chain. The functions performed can be both at the grower side (such as providing finance) and at the retail end (such as delivering to depots or stores agreed volumes per week).

PILLAR 3: PREFERRED SUPPLIERS

These are preferred (that is, 'listed') suppliers who are large-scale farmers, groups of farmers, processors and specialist wholesalers. The supplier joins a list of firms that are offered contracts by a supermarket chain. Such relationships are often called 'partnerships', though one partner (the supermarket chain) is much more powerful than the other.

The idea behind a preferred supplier relationship is that the link is long term and brings the two businesses close together. The supermarket chain may provide services such as advice and training. The supermarket may also help its supplier-partner pay for investment, particularly in information technology (IT) services to improve communications in the partnership. Even if it is unwilling to foot the bill, the supermarket is in a good position to act as a loan guarantor so that the supplier can get credit elsewhere. In some cases, the simple fact that the farmer has a supermarket contract can help get a loan (for example, in Guatemala, where a contract with Hortifruti helped growers obtain finance).

In Poland, pig producers switched from state procurement contracts to a free-for-all at the beginning of transition. However, the new private processors soon moved to a contract system, but one now negotiated with pig producers. The farmers were clear that independent producers have less power to influence the contract price than pig producing groups – the latter have much more to offer in terms of volume, quality and consistency of supply. Thus, the move towards preferred suppliers and direct contracting prompted the development of producer groups. Indeed, it is often the case that the restructuring of supermarket operations is a catalyst for change upstream. Most change is painful, but is often necessary if scarce resources are to be used as efficiently as possible. However, when change occurs as a by-product of supermarket behaviour rather than as a planned outcome, the implications can be negative. For example, when producers form cooperatives to combat aggressive direct contracting between supermarkets and producers, an important structural adjustment is made, from which most producers should benefit, but the adversarial tone is set for trading relationships to continue at arms-length, when the real benefits of having preferred suppliers come from working closely, exchanging sensitive information and developing a culture of trust and mutual dependence.

PILLAR 4: PRIVATE STANDARDS

Probably every country has a system of public grades for farm products that may or may not be enforced. However, supermarkets invariably set up their own standards and enforce them. Naturally, enforcement is stricter when supplies are abundant than when they are scarce. However, overall, it is commonly accepted that supermarket standards for food are higher in most cases than public standards. In some instances, this is a positive development, particularly when public sector food safety systems are inadequate and supermarkets reduce the food safety risk to which consumers are exposed. However, private standards are often regarded as major hurdles for small-scale producers, who struggle to reach these higher standards and, when they do, discover that they are now competing at a national or regional level, rather than at the local level, as the establishment of standards permits supermarkets to source from a wider geographic region. As Reardon et al. (2004) put it,

> ... evidence is mounting that the changes in standards and the implied investments have driven small firms and farms out of business in developing countries over the past 5–10 years, and accelerated industry concentration.

The question here is not whether or not higher standards of food safety are a good thing. Rather, it is a question of the level of standards, the rate of change and the means by which they are introduced. In many cases, decisions relating to quality and food safety are made without any consideration of the supply chain impacts, as supermarkets understandably give top priority to the needs of their customers. In these circumstances, what is needed is greater awareness of the supply chain implications and some consideration of how suppliers might be assisted in the adjustment process – a clear role for public/private partnership in the provision of training and investment in infrastructure to support the achievement of higher quality and higher levels of food safety upstream. However, in other cases, the ratcheting up of standards is used as a mechanism for rationalizing the supply base – weeding out the smaller, weaker suppliers and paving the way for large-scale producers to take a greater share. The incentive for horizontal cooperation is evident once again, as is the by-product of adversarial relationships, as producers feel compelled to collaborate just to survive. Clarity of purpose, awareness and consideration of the implications upstream and a strategy for managing change are essential here, but, once again, these are the exceptions rather than the rule in the race for market share.

Interventions at different stages of restructuring

The purpose of the Regoverning Markets programme is not merely to identify barriers to (and explain the reasons for) the inclusion of small-scale producers in modern food supply chains, but also to identify potential interventions – by policy-makers, government agencies and the private sector – to remove the barriers and facilitate the wider inclusion of small-scale producers in what should be an opportunity for development, not a threat.

What is evident from the country studies is that different kinds of intervention are necessary from different stakeholders at different stages in the process of market restructuring.

We identify three key stages in agri-food restructuring (see Figure 18.1). Each stage is different in terms of the choice of intervention to influence developments in ways which are more inclusive of smaller scale producers and SMEs.

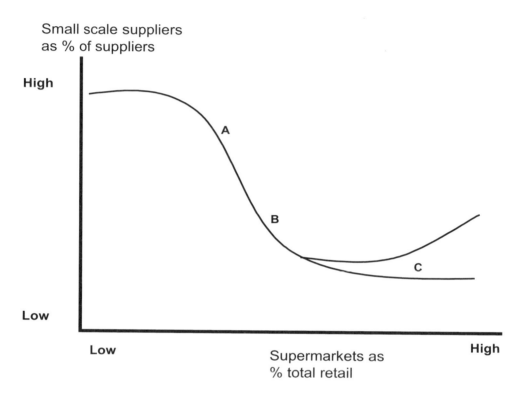

Figure 18.1   The growth of supermarkets and the involvement of small-scale producers over time

Stage A occurs when the importance of small-scale farms and processors starts to decline. As we have already noted, there are economies of scale associated with off-farm operations such as logistics and compliance with private standards. As a result, even where small-scale producers have a comparative advantage (for example, horticulture), the non-production-related factors swing the advantage to large-scale farms.

In China and Romania, where small farms predominate and there is insufficient production on large-scale farms and plantations, supermarkets and processors have developed ways of relating to small producers during this early phase. In Stage A, neither farm groups nor policy-makers are usually aware of changes that are starting to take place in the structure and governance of agri-food supply.

In Stage B, there is a more rapid decline in the share of small-scale producers in the provision of food supplies. This reflects the accelerating pace of supermarket expansion. Producer lobbies react and anti-supermarket sentiment grows.

Stage C usually comes much later and is a characteristic of industrialized countries in which high income consumers have created 'niche markets' for specialist (artisanal, local, and so on) food and drink products. Some of these products are marketed through supermarkets, others are marketed through Farmers' Markets, home delivery schemes and the internet. As a result there may be a gradual and partial resurgence in small-scale producers and suppliers.

The fundamental perspective of the Regoverning Markets programme is that policy priorities and appropriate stakeholder interventions change at each stage of the restructuring process.

At Stage A, before there are dramatic changes, policy can be more anticipatory. The emphasis here should be on raising awareness of the drivers of change, the provision of information, the communication of what has been learned from other countries that have had similar experiences, investment in traditional markets (the demand for which is still strong in the early stages of growth), and support for the development of POs – fundamental to the longer term inclusion of small-scale producers, but a significant challenge that therefore needs to be tackled as soon as possible.

Supermarkets and food manufacturers can do much more to prepare the ground for their arrival, investment and growth with the support and involvement of small-scale producers. Why wouldn't Carrefour or Tesco, Metro or Makro seek to partner with extension providers and government agencies in training potential suppliers in the systems that they use, the practices they adopt and the processes upon which they depend for delivering what consumers want – more choice, better quality, lower cost? Why shouldn't small-scale producers be able to respond to these demands and share in the benefits of growth and restructuring, given the appropriate support, from stakeholders working in cooperation rather than at loggerheads? Policy-makers and CEOs need to wake up to the reality – of business and politics – and combine their efforts to deliver a sustainable model of growth and restructuring for the benefit of the many rather than the few.

At Stage B, once restructuring is advanced, intervention must be adaptive in order to help ensure that restructuring is as inclusive of small producers as possible. It is at this stage that the private sector needs to take greater responsibility for improving pro-poor incentives and removing or diminishing anti-poor biases, or run the risk of regulation – another by-product of the failure of re-structured markets to make a positive contribution to development. Seeking to delay the penetration of supermarkets can be a short-sighted strategy, but one that it is inevitable if large corporations fail to take adequate consideration of the bigger picture and wake up to the longer-term benefits of an inclusive strategy in developing and transitional economies.

At Stage C, when changes are quite advanced (even to the extent of the UK, where three-quarters of the market is in the hands of major supermarkets), there are still lessons to learn for producers, policy-makers, for civil society, and for business. Appropriate competition law and fair trade regulation, zoning laws, and so on, can reduce abuse of market power.

Recommendations for stakeholder intervention

We now look in more detail at the priorities for stakeholder intervention, focusing on the six key stakeholder groups – national governments, producers and their organizations, companies, donors, civil society, and researchers.

PRIORITIES FOR NATIONAL GOVERNMENTS

In many countries, supermarkets are viewed by governments as positive economic actors, delivering on the economic ambitions of governments (low inflation and high employment) and consumers (more choice, higher quality and lower cost). As a result, the political scrutiny of the sector is relatively light and the drive to a more competitive regulatory environment in many countries has handed regulatory responsibility for important areas of the food system, most notably food safety and quality standards, to supermarkets themselves. Moreover, where there are strong government investments in retail, as in China, supermarkets can work in a very favourable policy environment with access to cheaper credit and preferential rents. Thus, they can ensure that there is a policy 'push' (as well as consumer 'pull') towards their establishment and growth.

In some emerging economies, governments have to deal with strong lobbies from producer alliances or small retailer interests against the growing might of supermarkets. Where there are large rural populations and a diverse small-scale retail sector, powerful agrarian and independent retail lobbies have emerged that oppose the liberalization (and inevitable concentration) of the retail trade, as it introduces competition on an unprecedented scale. For example, in India, the Agriculture Produce Marketing Committee (APMC) complained bitterly about the entry of Metro and the end of APMC's monopoly role in the marketing of agricultural produce.

Supermarkets thus present governments with a serious policy dilemma – to facilitate or regulate? The answer depends largely on the phase of supermarket development and restructuring of the retail food market, as discussed above. However, there are three policy areas that all governments need to focus on – investment in traditional markets, control of supermarket power and support for producer organizations.

Investment in traditional markets

Improving traditional markets may offer the best prospects of increased sales for the smaller-scale and less capitalized producers, many of whom find the pace and scale of structural change that comes with supermarket growth difficult to cope with. Indeed, the South African experience revealed the importance of the traditional wholesale markets as a training ground and an intermediate step for farmers who eventually wish to become supermarket suppliers. However, traditional markets have a history of reproducing rural poverty through low prices. Both the India and Bangladesh cases speak of traditional markets as havens of manipulation and exploitation – supermarkets do not have a monopoly in the abuse of market power.

The rate of growth of supermarkets around the world makes it easy for policy-makers to downplay the importance and developmental impact of efficient traditional markets. This results in a diversion of scarce development funds from the development and upgrading of traditional wholesale and wetmarkets, which continue to serve the majority of consumers in developing countries, to niche markets, which is exactly what supermarkets are in the early stages of restructuring.

There are numerous benefits from upgrading the small-scale, open-air and wholesale markets. Most notably, it helps them to:

- compete with supermarket chains, which in turn gives suppliers more options
- make the transition to be able to serve both supermarkets and non-supermarket players
- ensure basic levels of food safety and quality, preventing the development of multiple standards in consumer protection.

The message is here is that national governments and international donors should not ignore what is already in place – serving the masses but invariably inefficiently – but invest in traditional markets and support their development in parallel with supermarkets. They should not leave these markets to wither and decline, dragging swathes of small-scale producers with them.

Controlling the power of supermarkets

One of the biggest problems that results from the abandonment of traditional markets in favour of supermarkets is that one source of market power is replaced by another, altogether more extensive and sophisticated, which if left unchecked can result in the economic goals of government and consumers being pursued in isolation from the broader goals of sustainable growth and agrarian development. Supermarkets are successful because they are focused, almost exclusively, on the needs and wants of consumers. It is the role of government to balance consumer interests with those of other stakeholders, which is why careful consideration must be given to the regulation of supermarket development, right from the early stages.

A range of regulatory instruments is available and has been used in different countries at different stages of restructuring. It may be desirable to design interventions that help to delay or shape the restructuring process, allowing breathing space to introduce other policies that help producers and small retailers to prepare for change. These might relate to investment policy, competition law, limits on store size, location or business hours, minimum local content requirements (as in the Philippines), or recognition of purchasing agreements among small retailers to match the buyer power of large competitors.

Emerging economies, such as Thailand, have responded to the supermarket challenge with quite tough regulations, in an effort to protect the interests of producers and small retailers. The danger to be avoided is that punitive regulations at an early stage can have the effect of reinforcing the dominance of the first entrants into these markets, or simply favouring one form of supermarket business over another, rather than managing the growth of the supermarket sector as a whole. The message here is that regulations to control the emergence and early growth of retailers should be flexible and adaptive to the changing market circumstances, not cast in stone.

Market power (and the abuse thereof) is an issue that overshadows the many positive aspects of supermarket growth and restructuring of food markets all over the world. It has been difficult, if not impossible, to constrain supermarkets' abuse of suppliers in mature economies, which implies that it will be even more difficult in emerging markets, where legal systems are less well developed and where producers and suppliers may have little political influence.

The first step in regulating the abuse of buyer power in developing countries is to reform as many as possible of the trading practices that hit small producers particularly hard. For example, there are regulations in Argentina that govern the credit period within supermarket–supplier relations. In Thailand, the internal trade department is in the process of setting fair trade guidelines to restrict retailers' use of bargaining power with suppliers and their demands for heavy price reductions, and to protect small- and medium-sized businesses.[2] The guidelines will also prohibit retailers from producing private label brands using the know-how of branded manufacturers or similar packaging.

---

2   Contribution submitted by Thailand under Session IV of the OECD Global Forum on Competition held on 12 and 13 February 2004, available: www.oecd.org/dataoecd/24/55/26370337.pdf.

The Thai government has also set up Allied Retail Trade Co. (ART) – in effect a state-owned operator of franchised shops – to help grocery stores and family-run stores compete with modern trade retailers. ART consolidates volume from small retailers to achieve the same level of bargaining power as modern trade (Deloitte, 2004), and expands the range of goods offered to small grocers beyond basic consumer goods.

New zoning regulations drafted by the Town and Country Planning Department in Thailand, which came into effect from August 2003, will curb the expansion of large chains by imposing zoning ordinances in provinces outside of Bangkok. Large (at least 1000 m² of retail space) retail stores have to be located at least 15 km from the commercial centres of provincial towns. The effect will be to limit hypermarket and superstore expansion in the future. Tesco, Casino and Carrefour have rushed into all areas of Thailand, especially the north, in order to secure sites before the draft regulations become reality. The Malaysian government has been limiting the expansion of hypermarkets in major cities such as Kuala Lumpur, Johor Bahru and Penang and in towns with less than 350 000 population, in part to help regional players.

In the enforcement of competition law in Korea relating to unfair trading practices, the Korean Fair Trade Commission has sanctioned Wal-Mart Korea for unfair refusals to receive goods, unfair return of products, coercive demands for suppliers to buy its goods, reduction of prices after purchase of products, and imputing of advertising fees to suppliers. Korea Carrefour has also been sanctioned for unreasonably reducing prices for products bought from suppliers (Jhong, 2003). The Mexican competition authorities have accused the local Wal-Mart company WalMex of abuse of power by forcing suppliers to sell below cost. The evidence of abuse of market power is there for all to see, but not all national governments are as proactive as the Korean and Mexican governments in regulating supermarket behaviour. The food retailing environment is fiercely competitive and the entrance of supermarkets into new territory will always bring threats as well as opportunities. It is the role of government to suppress the former and maximize the latter.

The UN Conference on Trade and Development (UNCTAD) concludes: 'In practice, competition laws in OECD countries have been used to discipline abusive buyer power relatively infrequently, largely because suppliers are reluctant to complain for fear of reprisals' (UNCTAD, 2003).

Support for POs

A national policy priority should be catalyzing and fostering the types of institutional and organizational change that increase the benefits of restructured agri-food systems to small-scale producers and rural entrepreneurs. The fundamental issue is building the capacity of producers to provide sufficient quality, in terms of product specifications, capacity and ability to deliver, and service. This is highlighted in the case of China and is central to the AMUL story in India. However, strengthening the level of organization of rural producers cannot be left to governments or the private sector alone. This critical enabler of the inclusion of small-scale producers in modern food supply chains requires a public–private–civil society partnership (van de Kop et al., 2004).

The evidence from Zambia highlights the need for policy support in the areas of credit provision, creation of cooperatives, standard setting and implementation. In the Philippines, vegetables and mangoes are produced mostly by small farmers (unlike bananas and pineapples) and therefore consolidation is a key factor of achieving consistency in quality, volume and variety, and payment terms demanded by supermarkets. But none of this works without investments in infrastructure such as roads, post-harvest facilities and grading systems. The lessons from the South African case are that creating a viable group of small-scale suppliers to supermarkets requires a number of complementary inputs such as mentoring, credit, market information and infrastructure, which could resolve problems of discontinuity of supply.

A country where many policies have been implemented to help small-scale producers in both traditional and supermarkets is Costa Rica, where there have been improvements to market facilities, transport, information services and extension services for farmers by government. Such measures complement private initiatives, such as the number of independent shops who, with government backing, have organized their own wholesale assembly points to create supply depots.

Development interventions have traditionally focused on building POs that can deal directly with supermarkets, to consolidate the required volume of product and improve supply, distribution and management, and in effect to bypass traditional intermediaries ('cutting out the middle man') in the name of improved market access and equity. However, in many instances there is more to be gained from strengthening relationships between producers and intermediaries than from trying to forge links between stakeholders who, at least in the early stages of restructuring, speak distinctly different languages.

Intermediaries can absorb marketing risks between smaller producers and supermarkets and perform many of the services that supermarkets seek – such as grading for quality, packaging, and delivery – which allow producers to remain active in supermarket supply chains. An example of this is the emergence of new intermediaries who are contracting with growers for chemical-free products for supermarkets in Vietnam.

In summary, the policy options for governments are many and varied, but the research carried out for the Regoverning Markets programme clearly indicates that a flexible and customized approach is essential – one size does not fit all and it changes over time. However, a three-pronged attack that provides support for traditional market channels, controls the abuse of power by established supermarkets and promotes the development of POs is most likely to deliver benefits for small-scale producers wherever and whenever it is implemented.

PRIORITIES FOR PRODUCERS AND THEIR ORGANIZATIONS

Strengthening horizontal and vertical market linkages is of utmost importance to mediate the relationship between small-scale producers and formal market structures. Many of the scale issues that exclude small-scale producers from restructured markets can only be addressed through cooperation with other producers.

Horizontal coordination comes in different guises – cooperatives, producer groups, associations, partnerships, 'new generation' coops, or 'peasant economic organizations', but the crucial ingredient for success is the ability to impose discipline on members in order to deliver consistently on the promises that are made in contracts or agreements to supply different market channels, including supermarkets. History is littered with failed producer cooperatives, and supermarket buyers are understandably sceptical about the ability of such organizations to comply with their quality and service requirements.

POs can suffer from bureaucracy, a lack of coordination, political pressures or dependence on external support. Organizations can be imposed, lack skills, or pay their managers so poorly that there is no incentive to invest in improvements. As noted in Bangladesh, discipline is required to prevent members from chasing higher spot prices and 'side selling'. All too often, they are created purely to create countervailing bargaining power, with little consideration of customer value and customer service. Such organizations are doomed to fail, with or without the growth of supermarkets and the restructuring of food markets.

The kind of collective action that *is* likely to work in the interests of small-scale producers is rarely spontaneous. Capacity building programmes in support of small producers' collective action can enable small-scale farmers to: (1) organize themselves to improve product quality, reduce production costs and participate in supply chain management; and (2) build a market intelligence capacity and design marketing strategies including strategic alliances with market entrepreneurs and/or consumer groups.

The positive side of supermarket engagement with these organizations is that they encourage the process of 'professionalization' and the adoption of good management practices. Much attention has been paid to capacities within POs to implement systems of supply chain management and meet required market standards, including the capacity to design and finance investments, administration, technical support and strong organizational structure. The key priority for these organizations is to establish the strategic vision – with customer value and service at the core – and then demonstrate their ability to deliver. The former requires an awareness of market developments and the identification of the role for POs. The latter requires substantial investment in training and management systems, which should be provided collectively by government agencies and the private sector, including supermarkets, in order to ensure that resources are targeted at what the market requires.

The evidence from Guatemala shows that supermarket buyers prefer to work with organized cooperative structures rather than with dispersed farmers, and that POs allow farmers to minimize marketing costs, specialize on quality production and plan around pre-agreed prices. Links between POs and supermarkets work best when there is an effective combination of the right product, output capacity and intermediary/sales contact with the leadership to help them improve supply, distribution and management aspects.

Trust is an essential ingredient for success, yet this is often a scarce commodity, both within POs and between the POs and their customers, particularly supermarkets, who have earned a reputation for abusing their power once they gain a significant share of the market. Interdependency is often seen as a weakness by organizational buyers and sellers, yet without it we will be stuck in an adversarial trading environment. Thus, there needs to be a significant shift in the strategy and culture of POs and supermarkets if we are to see significant improvement in relationships between the two, and if the benefits of horizontal coordination are to be fully captured.

Supermarkets can and should be more proactive in encouraging POs to invest in services and infrastructure, offering their own resources and expertise. In many instances, this will give small-scale producers the incentive they need to join a PO. For example, evidence from Nicaragua suggests that net income for growers from supplying supermarkets is the same as from traditional marketing. What makes the supermarket supply business attractive is the services and investments the supermarket has made in the PO, and the services and investments that the POs are willing and able to offer their members.

The involvement of intermediaries in the process of vertical coordination between small-scale producers (and their organizations) and supermarket buyers, drawing in hitherto under-served small-scale producers, was highlighted in relation to fruit in Colombia and beef in Central America. The shift to specialized/dedicated wholesalers means that the farmer's relationship with the buyer is formalized and more secure, and can bring technical assistance, sometimes credit, often transport. But it also means a greater capacity from the buyer's side for monitoring volumes and consistency.

In some instances, the vertical coordination role is being undertaken by large-scale producers. For example, in Zambia the export sector has a long tradition of large farms working with small-scale out-growers to high standards through the provision of inputs and training, and these companies are now supplying domestic supermarkets. The Vietnam case also describes how interaction between large farmers and small-scale farmers can manage trade and deal with official requirements, in effect bridging the informal and formal economies. This out-grower model is another potential way ahead for small-scale producers and their organizations.

Thus, an important message to emerge is the need for POs to search for partners if small-scale producers are to benefit from working with the new breed of dedicated wholesaler distributors or large-scale producers that are fast becoming the gatekeepers in developed supermarket supply chains.

PRIORITIES FOR COMPANIES: BUSINESS AND SUSTAINABLE DEVELOPMENT

The preceding discussion has established the very interesting context in which international supermarkets need to conduct themselves if they are to implement the principles of corporate accountability, play a constructive role in development and reap the commercial rewards from a thriving supply base. The picture that emerges from our study of supermarket and food industry growth around the world is of an economic sector with wide consumer appeal operating in increasingly competitive and price-sensitive markets, with relatively low levels of state interference, but with some emerging voices of dissent from small-scale farming and independent retailing – two sectors of declining political influence.

While some producers will gain substantially and see accelerated growth in their businesses, many producers, processors and service companies will be damaged as supermarkets expand their commercial influence using buying power to squeeze their suppliers (through low prices and long payment terms), with very few legal constraints.

As regards processors, the example of tomato paste and canned tomatoes, which are standardized global products, is typical. The demands of retailers, processors and food service companies for scale and consistent quality has meant that countries with tomato production based around small producers have seen their industries decline, whereas industries based around large monocultures have survived (Pritchard and Burch, 2003).

From a policy perspective, the goal of international retailers is to be able to trade freely across borders, and set up their preferred retail formats without restrictive national legislation. Of particular relevance in this respect is the WTO Agreement on Trade in Services (GATS), because it both opens up markets for 'distribution services', including wholesale, franchising and retailing, and curtails national governments' ability to inhibit the expansion of distribution services through restrictions on zoning, advertising, opening hours, foreign ownership and competition policy.

The leaked requests of the EU to the GATS negotiations reveal that the EU requested 60 countries to open up their markets for distribution services according to GATS rules. The EU's position is based on arguments that opening up supermarkets to foreign ownership has positive effects of improved efficiency, better knowledge about sector-specific marketing and management, cheaper prices for customers and more consumer choice. However, there is a suspicion that the main reason for the EU's request is that it would allow the European global supermarket chains, such as Carrefour, Ahold and Metro to be able to operate without any restrictions (Stichele, 2004).

Industry responses to accusations of extractive business practices – by-passing small producers and killing off small retailers – have so far been a mix of counter-lobbying and pilot initiatives, mixed with presenting parts of existing corporate strategies as 'social responsibility'. For instance, the current expansion into convenience and discount formats can be advertised as 'support for the local community', and a business decision to use in-store concessions can be advertised as 'support for the local economy'.[3]

In South Africa, Shoprite's use of franchising is presented as support for the Black Economic Empowerment (BEE) programme, a government initiative devised in 1994 to encourage the redistribution of wealth and to provide opportunities in the economy to communities and individuals that were disadvantaged under the Apartheid regime. The BEE programme supplies the funds for the franchise rights for Shoprite's OK convenience and neighbourhood stores, while Shoprite provides the stock, supply and know-how.

Shoprite has been an active partner in the Luangeni project in Zambia, a project now famous in corporate social responsibility (CSR) circles, in which the International Business Leaders' Forum convened a partnership to build capacity among rural communities to produce high-quality vegetables that could be marketed to Shoprite (IBLF, 2002). Shoprite has also pledged to aid farmers in Tanzania, helping them to achieve higher quality crops and improve logistics so that the company does not have to import food. These initiatives help to counter criticism of economic imperialism and 'southafricanization' during Shoprite's expansion through Africa.

Metro, which has encountered fierce opposition in India (Indo-Asian News Service, 2004), has responded with statements and commitments to fairness and opportunity in trading practices. In Vietnam, Metro has launched an effort with German support to provide local suppliers with the skills and techniques to meet high standards in agriculture and aquaculture.

But within the sustainable development debate, should governments and communities be expecting more from international supermarkets, especially in building more inclusive trading relationships? Should supermarkets be a means to connect the rural poor to the pockets of urban wealth? Should there be lessons transferred from the Fairtrade movement – such as procurement from small producers and their organizations and advance payments – to ensure a greater developmental impact from supermarket-driven restructuring?

Supermarkets must come to terms with this debate, but international retailers feel that their financial flexibility to implement CSR is increasingly constrained now that quality is a customer expectation rather than a distinguishing characteristic, price is ascendant in the battle for consumers, and deep discount chains are aggressively expanding. Intensive price competition and deeper CSR are poor bedfellows.

So far, there are few indications that commitment to fairness and equity in trading will extend beyond the focus of creating customer value, which has underpinned the business strategies of the most successful players. Within the logic of exclusive customer accountability and consumer value, ethics is marketed as a consumer choice – such as for Fairtrade-labelled speciality products – rather than a corporate standard. The conflation of 'customer' and 'citizen', 'stakeholder accountability' and 'customer accountability', and 'public good' and 'customer value' has to be addressed for CSR in food retailing to progress.

---

3   In 2002, Tesco deputy chairman David Reid was quoted as saying that the company's Value Store concept in Thailand could improve links with local communities and support the local economy by retaining consumer spending within the community - money that would otherwise be spent elsewhere. 'This support of the local economy is also reflected in the decision to sublet the fresh-market section of the Value Stores to local suppliers' (PlanetRetail, www. planetretail.net).

Fairtrade and CSR philosophies are a weak counter-weight to favouring large-scale producers. With the powerful trends towards a consolidated supplier base, Fairtrade and CSR will have limited impacts on improving supplier welfare.

In addition to the rationale of corporate citizenship, there are two more explicitly self-serving reasons why supermarket companies – as well as cash and carry companies, and food manufacturers – must take the issue of small producer inclusion seriously when they invest in middle- and low-income countries. The first is assured supply, and the second is domestic politics.

Supermarkets that rely extensively on importing fresh foods from neighbouring countries when they enter new markets are exposing themselves to risks that are necessary in the short term – a lack of local market knowledge can make it even riskier to enter a new market and procure from within – but unnecessary and potentially uncompetitive in the longer term. Once established, investment in the supply base creates an alternative source of supply, thereby spreading risk, and potentially reducing the cost and improving the quality of fresh food due to the shorter supply chains that are associated with procurement from within as opposed to outside the country/region.

In terms of domestic politics, expanding into countries where small-scale agriculture and 'mom and pop' retailing provides livelihoods for a significant proportion of the population requires a very different approach. Supermarket companies have been able to follow close behind the liberalization of trade and investment regimes without much attention to public policy, based on models from their home markets, built around quality, availability, price and consumer focus. But the regulatory backlash in Thailand has shown that this *laissez-faire* approach carries significant risks. Consider that one-third of the population in Romania is engaged in agriculture; one-half in China; and 60 per cent in Vietnam and India. And in India, there are over 12 million retail enterprises, mostly small family businesses using only household labour. Just railroading liberalization of retail services through the GATS is not the way to develop political support in these new markets. Retailers will have to implement policies that provide economic and market opportunities for more than a token few smaller-scale producers and SMEs.

PRIORITIES FOR DONORS

External assistance can provide analysis of supply opportunity, facilitate the exchange of information between buyer and supplier, and support the farmers' process of integrating into the supply chain.

The traditional donor interventions have been in the form of private sector development, capacity building and infrastructure, often aimed at the export market. Examples include pesticide testing laboratories and cold stores. But there are also examples of explicit donor support to bring small farmers into supermarket chains and to pull the private sector into a more explicit development role. For example, in Vietnam, German Technical Cooperation (GTZ) is working with the Metro Cash & Carry group and the Trade Ministry to strengthen domestic distribution networks, including training programmes for producers.

But the first priority for the donor community is to get informed on the changes that are underway and look beyond public policy in engagement in agriculture and food. The donor community must work much more closely with business, POs and national governments to develop and deliver a sustainable response to the challenge of including small-scale producers in modern, restructuring supply chains.

Fundamentally, donor funding can provide the essential lubricant in increasingly complex food marketing systems that are in various stages of development around the world, but they cannot deliver sustainable solutions in isolation. Bringing key stakeholders to the table is no easy task and a little lubrication can go a long way – therein lies the priority for donors.

PRIORITIES FOR CIVIL SOCIETY

Supermarkets have a high level of public acceptance in comparison with most public institutions, for the very reason that supermarkets are such customer-driven institutions. The majority of consumers have been willing players in the relocation of retail from street markets and specialist shops such as bakers, butchers and greengrocers or doorstep deliveries, to one-stop shopping in supermarkets. The same trend at greater speed is noticeable in CEE and China, where the massive changes in the structure and governance of the food system that supermarkets have ushered in are compared extremely favourably with the quality and choice associated with centrally planned regimes.

In comparison to consumers, civil society organizations have been deeply critical of the perceived hegemony of supermarkets over the agricultural and food system. Supermarkets are accused of driving a 'race to the bottom' by procuring food 'grown anywhere, anyhow' without care for standards of labour, the conservation of wildlife and landscapes, the livelihoods (or even survival) of family farms, the congestion of roads, the demise of the high street, the management of waste, the welfare of farm animals, or the health and food security of neighbourhoods. They are accused of running huge centralized distribution systems along extractive 'food-in, profits-out' lines. One month alone (May 2004) saw the publication of three books in the UK critical of supermarkets and the associated politics of food (Blythman, 2004; Lawrence, 2004; Young, 2004).

It is clear that supermarkets are drawing an increasing amount of attention and concern from a wide range of civil society interests about their growing dominance of the food system. Friends of the Earth UK and some farming groups have been particularly critical of supermarkets' supposed lack of commitment to fair trading and local produce.[4]

The challenge that faces civil society organizations is translating the evidence of the negative impacts of supermarkets into action – in the headquarters of multinational corporations and in consumers' shopping baskets. If there is a criticism of these organizations, it is that they struggle to communicate very powerful insights into the way modern food systems are threatening our environment, our rural communities, our culture and our health to those that are causing the problems and those that, arguably, have the greatest power and incentive to change – the general public. Thus, the priorities for civil society organizations must be to (1) continue the scrutiny of and research into supermarket supply chains and the longer-term implications of the restructuring of modern food markets; and (2) to work much harder at engagement with corporations and consumers.

PRIORITIES FOR RESEARCHERS

We have seen that there is an urgent requirement for anticipatory policy responses to agri-food restructuring, which focus on inclusion of small-scale producers in dynamic markets. The capacity for public policy response is currently severely limited, because these changes are invisible to the majority of policy-makers. The debate around pro-poor growth and rural livelihoods is still proceeding as if national public policy is still the key determinant of rural livelihoods.

---

4   See FoE Real Food Campaign at www.foe.co.uk/campaigns/real_food/resource/retailers.html.

There is a lack of strategic analysis and advice in the public domain, and a weak framework for information and lesson sharing within and between stakeholder groups and across countries and regions. The capacity for the private sector to respond to the particular challenges of small-scale producers is also limited, in particular where there is a lack of incentives to change business activities in ways that deliver development benefits.

In recognition of these development challenges, the research community needs to understand the keys to inclusion into these agri-food systems under different degrees of restructuring. It needs to deepen the research on implications and opportunities for small-scale producers and SMEs. It needs to understand what is best practice in connecting small-scale producers with dynamic markets. And it needs to bring these findings into the wider policy arena.

The focus should be on dynamic restructured national and regional markets that are displacing existing chains and their interface with small-scale farmers and local rural economies. The objective should be to inform public sector policy and private sector strategies with practical approaches, and engage with policy processes, taking advantage of comparisons across countries and regions and thereby the range of degrees of market restructuring and the differing policy environments. Research needs to support learning platforms and activities at international, regional and national levels, with the aim of sharing lessons learned and contributing to policy dialogue and policy influence.

It is with this challenge in mind, that research on 'regoverning markets' can assist business leaders, policy-makers, donors, producers and advisers to anticipate changes and make them work better for more sustainable and equitable development.

References

Nielsen, A.C., 2005. ShopperTrends 2005. Available: uk.acnielsen.com/reports/2005_Shopper_Trends. shtml

Blythman, Joanna, 2004. *Shopped: The Shocking Power of British Supermarkets*. London: Fourth Estate.

Deloitte, 2004. Global powers of retailing. Deloitte Touche Tohmatsu.

IBLF, 2002. Risks, values and business reputation: Addressing societies' expectations. Annual Review 2002. The Prince of Wales International Business Leaders Forum, London.

Indo-Asian News Service, 2004. German MNC upsets Bangalore's grocers, wholesalers. 11 September 2004. Available: www.eians.com.

Jhong, Kim Shun, 2003. Anti-competitive practices in the distribution sector in developing countries. Paper presented at the APEC Training Program on Competition Policy, 5–7 August, Hanoi, Vietnam. East Asia Competition Policy Forum.

Lawrence, Felicity, 2004. *Not on the Label: What Really Goes into the Food on Your Plate*. London: Penguin.

Pritchard, B. and Burch, D., 2003. *Agri-food Globalization in Perspective: International Restructuring in the Processing Tomato Industry*. Aldershot: Ashgate.

Reardon, T., Timmer, P. and Berdegué, J., 2004. The rapid rise of supermarkets in developing countries: Induced organizational, institutional, and technological change in agri-food systems. *Electronic Journal of Agricultural And Development Economics*. 1(2), 168–83.

Stichele, M.V. (2004) Expanding buying power of supermarkets through GATS negotiations: Impact on agriculture. SOMO, Netherlands.

UNCTAD, 2003. Market entry conditions affecting competitiveness and exports of goods and services of developing countries: Large distribution networks, taking into account the special needs of LDCs. Note by the UNCTAD secretariat for Commission on Trade in Goods and Services, and Commodities.

Van de Kop, P., Alam, G. and De Steenhuijsen Piters, B., 2004. Developing a sustainable medicinal plant chain in India: Linking people, markets and values. Paper presented at International Conference on Agro-food Chains and Networks as Instruments for Development, Wageningen, 6–7 September.

Young, William, 2004. *Sold Out: The true Cost of Supermarket Shopping*. London: Vision Paperbacks.

Index